ERNESTINE SHUSWAP GETS HER TROUT

ERNESTINE SHUSWAP GETS HER TROUT

a "string quartet" for four female actors

Tomson Highway

Talonbooks
Vancouver

Talonbooks
P.O. Box 2076, Vancouver, British Columbia, Canada V6B 3S3
www.talonbooks.com

Typeset in New Baskerville and printed and bound in Canada.

First Printing: 2005

Library and Archives Canada Cataloguing in Publication

Highway, Tomson
    Ernestine Shuswap gets her trout / Tomson Highway.

A play.
ISBN 0-88922-525-7

    1. Indians of North America—British Columbia—Government relations—Drama. I. Title.

PS8565.I433E75 2005   C812'.54   C2005-902462-3

The publisher gratefully acknowledges the financial support of the Canada Council for the Arts; the Government of Canada through the Book Publishing Industry Development Program; and the Province of British Columbia through the British Columbia Arts Council for our publishing activities.

*The author dedicates this story and this play
to the Shuswap Nation from whom it came.*

Ernestine Shuswap Gets Her Trout was commissioned by the Secwepemc Cultural Education Society (of the Kamloops Indian Reserve) together with the Western Canada Theatre (of Kamloops, British Columbia). It had its world premiere at the Sagebrush Theatre, Western Canada Theatre, Kamloops, British Columbia on Saturday, January 24, 2004, with the following cast and production personnel, everyone of whom the author thanks from the bottom of his heart:

ISABEL THOMPSON	Lisa Dahling
DELILAH ROSE JOHNSON	Cheri Maracle
ERNESTINE SHUSWAP	Janet Michael
ANNABELLE OKANAGAN	Lisa C. Ravensbergen

Director: David Ross
Scenic & Costume Design: Kim Nielsen
Lighting Design: Gerald King
Movement Coach: Mary Ellen MacLean
Stage Manager: Kelly Manson
Apprentice Stage Manager: Trent Scherer

READINGS AND WORKSHOP ARTISTS:
Western Canada Theatre would like to acknowledge the contributions of the following artists who participated in developmental workshops and/or public readings of the script in process: Layla Alizada, Marie Clements, Lisa Dahling, Margo Kane, Lanni McInnes, Cheri Maracle, Lori Marchand, Jody-Kay Marklew, Janet Michael, Renae Morriseau, Lisa C. Ravensbergen, Lori Ravensborg, Yvonne Wallace, Val Pearson, Jennie Young, Gay Hauser, Budge Schacte and Del Surjik.

Author's Note

On August 25, 1910, then-Prime Minister of Canada, Sir Wilfrid Laurier, came to Kamloops, British Columbia to meet with the Chiefs of the Thompson River Valley. The list of grievances these chiefs presented to him at that historic meeting has since come to be known as "The Laurier Memorial."

CAST OF CHARACTERS

ERNESTINE SHUSWAP, *53 years old, strong-faced and handsome, one of those women who has weathered much in life but has weathered it with grace, with wise intelligence,* and *with humour.*

ISABEL THOMPSON, *43 years old, one of those people with a huge axe to grind and that axe, in her case, is religion. She is, that is to say, the world's most "generous," most saintly, most perfect woman ... in her mind.*

ANNABELLE OKANAGAN, *32 years old, moody to a fault, either, a) she is one of those people born with a dark cloud hanging over her, b) something unresolved is chafing at her conscience and/or, c) that "something" is costing her her sleep which, of course, is what makes her so darn grouchy.*

DELILAH ROSE JOHNSON, *21 years old, beautiful, and three months pregnant. A high-strung girl to begin with, something about her bird-like physicality suggests a split personality, or something just as unsettling.*

TIME: *Thursday, August 25, 1910*

THE SET: *There is none. Rather, at centre-stage-middle and six feet in the air "hangs" a cowboy hat, seemingly suspended from the middle of the sky, as if a ghost were wearing it. Four styrofoam cubes—to be used as chairs, rocks, other "objects" as the need will arise—sit scattered at random. An ancient gramophone (ca. 1900) sits open on the floor by one of these "chairs." Last, a plain white backdrop hangs slashed by a line, curved, horizontal: the land in silhouette. The rest is lights, sound, music.*

NOTE: *The language spoken by the women in this play, it must be stressed, is not English. Simply put, the Native people of the Thompson River Valley at the time here depicted (the early twentieth century) did not know the tongue. Rather, they spoke Shuswap, Okanagan, Thompson (or Couteau, as the latter "Nation" is otherwise known), and other Native languages. In this play, they speak Shuswap, a tongue that works according to principles, and impulses, different entirely from those that underlie, that "motor," the English language. For instance, because the principle that "motors" the Shuswap language is, in essence, a "laughing deity" (i.e. the Trickster), it is hysterical, comic to the point where its "spill-over" into horrifying tragedy is a thing quite normal, utterly organic. That is to say, as in most languages of Native North America (that I know of anyway), the "laughing god" becomes a "crying god" becomes a "laughing god," all in one swift impulse.*

PROLOGUE

*First, from the darkness, the gurgle of a river—rich,
evocative, the voice of a land. It rises, fades. Out of it
"bleeds" a very low note, on a cello, bowed. And sustained,
all the way through the opening trio of monologues, with
sporadic, jarring little "grace notes," changes of key, that sort
of thing, the whole point being: though the monologues are
comic more than anything, what has to be established, right
off the top, is, a) an atmosphere of ominous foreboding and,
b) the counterpoint of comedy and tragedy.*

*Next: three women will appear, each in turn, under icy
pools of light, as from a silvery moon, one woman stage left,
the second stage right, the third stage centre. The pools of
light should be limited to their faces, however, so that these
faces look like masks in a Greek tragedy. In fact, that is what
their voices should sound like as well, like those in a play by
Euripides, that is, a mesmerizing weave of chant and prayer.
The point here being: though, at first glance, this may
appear to be a very funny play, right from the start, there are
undercurrents of darkness, of horrifying tragedy. (Last, this
being 1910, the women are wearing long-sleeved, high-
collared white cotton blouses, floor-length black skirts, and
moccasins.)*

*ONE: fade-in on ERNESTINE SHUSWAP as she stands
looking out her window at the "moon," or so it seems for, in
fact, what she is looking at is her conscience. For these are
the words—and thoughts—that will resonate inside her*

mind, her heart, her body through the course of this day we are about to see her live through.

ERNESTINE

(*long silence, then:*) "Ernestine Shuswap, I'm gonna get you," he says to me, first thing this morning. "Get me?" I says back to him, from my side of the bed, "Get me for what?" And the sun's not even up yet, okay? It's still pitch dark and he's already got me going. "A fish," Joe Shuswap says to me from right there on his pillow next to mine, like he's talking to the ceiling, "A fish. I'm getting you a fish." "Oh," I says to him, relieved, kind of, cuz you see, I guess I heard him wrong. Hey! It was only 5 A.M., okay? I'm not even awake yet, okay? Not really. "Oh," I says to him—my husband—from right there on my pillow next to his, "What kind of fish, Joe Shuswap, what kind of fish you gonna get me?" I says to him, as if I didn't know what kind of fish, what am I, born yesterday? Anyway. He's sitting up in bed now, yawning, stretching, trying real hard to come back from the dead. "A trout," he says to me, his wife of thirty-seven years, "A rainbow trout, biggest, hugest rainbow trout ever seen in this part of the world, that's what I'm getting you," is what he says to me, Ernestine Shuswap of Kamloops, B.C. "Down by the river," he says, yawning real wide. And now he's walking to the kitchen, looking like a ghost cuz his long-johns are all white. Me? Lying there still looking like a corpse, feeling like one, too. "I'm going to the river and I'm sitting right there until the biggest, hugest, most gigantic rainbow trout in the history of the world lands right here in my hands," my husband Joe, that's what he says to me, first thing in the morning. And now he's in the kitchen, lighting up the woodstove, priming up the pump, pouring water in the kettle, getting coffee ready, and he says ... (*Big voice.*) "Ernestine Shuswap, I'm getting you a trout." (*Freeze. Pool of light stays on her face as ...)*

TWO: fade-in on ISABEL THOMPSON as she stands looking out her window at the "moon," or so it seems for, in fact, what she is looking at is her conscience. For these are the words—and thoughts—that will resonate inside her mind, her heart, her body through the course of this day we are about to see her live through.

ISABEL

(*long silence, then:*) "Now how's he gonna do *that,* Ernestine Shuswap," I says to my dear friend and neighbour, Ernestine Shuswap of Kamloops, B.C., "How's Joe Shuswap supposed to go down to the river and capture you a trout, rainbow or otherwise, when fishing's not allowed?" We're sitting in her kitchen having coffee, talking shop, taking pleasure in the simple act of living, Joe's out fishing, the youngest of her twelve, the teens Alfreda, Elias, and Mary Josephine, they're still sound asleep, so it's just her and me across the table from each other. "When fishing's not allowed?" Ernestine Shuswap turns to me and says, "What do you mean, Isabel Thompson of Kamloops, B.C., what do you mean just sitting there contented with my coffee, smiling like a mink while trying to upset me by telling me that fishing's not allowed? Why, ever since the day he popped like a pickle from the belly of a woman name of Minny—and that wasn't yesterday, Isabel Thompson of Kamloops, B.C., that wasn't yesterday—ever since that day, old Joe Shuswap's been fishing in that river, so what exactly do you mean when you announce to my person that fishing's not allowed in the Thompson River, hmm?" (*Freeze. Pool of light stays on her face as ... *)

THREE: fade-in on ANNABELLE OKANAGAN as she stands looking out her window at the "moon," or so it seems for, in fact, what she is looking at is her conscience. For these are the words— and thoughts—that will resonate inside her mind, her heart, her body through the course of this day we are about to see her live through.

ANNABELLE

(*long silence, then:*) It's true what my dear friend and neighbour, Ernestine Shuswap, is saying when she explains to the people that her husband has been fishing in that river since the morning his mama Minny first let him breathe. We been fishing there, too, my folks and me—and by folks, I mean family, of course, *my* family, *my* kin, my own flesh and blood—we been fishing in that river for a very long time. Me, Annabelle Okanagan of Kamloops, B.C., my dear, late husband Johnny Okanagan of Kamloops, B.C., my father Jeremiah Jerome of Kamloops, B.C., my dear grandfather Benjamin Jerome of Kamloops, B.C., my great-grandfather, my great-great-grandfather, my great-great-great-grandfather, my great-great-great-great-grandfather, my great-great-great-great-great-grandfather, my great-great-great-great-great-great (*pause*) grandfather, and on and on and on, and on and on and on, *and* on and on and on, ever since the cave days, ever since the age of the dinosaurs, ever since the day God said, "Let there be light," yes, ever since that day, we been fishing in that river, my folks and me, the river you can see there in the distance away over yonder? That winding, greenish-bluish river that's so busy just a-weaving its way through the mountains over yonder, down, down, and down, down, down, and down, right through our hunting grounds, right through our pastures, right through our fields and fields and fields *and* fields of wild saskatoons, right through our houses, through our windows, through our doors, through our children, through our lives, through our dreams, our hearts, our flesh, our veins, our blood. So we been fishing in that river, my folks and me, for a very, *very* long time. Fishing's not allowed? Why, that would be like me, Annabelle

16

Okanagan of Kamloops, B.C., that would be like me coming right into your homes, opening my mouth, and telling you, yes, you. And you and you and you, and you and you and you, and you and you and you, and you there in the tight red sweater—that would be like me telling you, "No more breathing. Stop right now."

Freeze. Stop cello music. Beat. Then fade-out on all three women's faces, into black, then ...

Act One

*Fade-in on ANNABELLE OKANAGAN and ISABEL
THOMPSON walking up the "road" toward the "house"
where lives DELILAH ROSE JOHNSON. Bag for berry-picking
hanging by a shoulder strap and down by her waist, ISABEL
looks all bushy-tailed and bright-eyed, while ANNABELLE is
moody. As their dialogue progresses, the two keep stopping,
their promenade increasingly resembling a syncopated dance,
a fractured tango.*

   *As their scene progresses, moreover, the "statue" of a girl
aged twenty-one or so "bleeds" slowly into view. Sitting on a
"chair" (i.e. a styrofoam cube) at centre-stage-middle, she is
hemming a tablecloth of pure white muslin, the material
strewn over her knees and falling to the floor all around her
… like a waterfall or chute. Scissors in her right hand,
"needle" in her left, she is just about to snip off the length of
"thread" at its knot by the hem. For ISABEL and
ANNABELLE, of course, there is no "statue," they see nothing.*

ISABEL
   She can always bring her to our house, is what I said to
   Barnabas first thing this morning. We like Daisy-May,
   Barnabas and I. She has such a gentle, giving
   disposition, don't you think, Annabelle Okanagan of
   Kamloops, B.C.? …

ANNABELLE
   Yes, but …

ISABEL

(*charging right through*) Apparently, however, she doesn't
eat just anything. In fact, Chicheelia herself was telling me
that her precious little gem, as she calls her, eats only
certain kinds of ... of vegetation, Chicheelia Kaboom was
saying at the store just yesterday ...

ANNABELLE

Yes, but ...

ISABEL

Anyway, the point I was getting at, Annabelle Okanagan
of Kamloops, B.C., is this: Daisy-May Kaboom can eat in
our yard ...

ANNABELLE

Daisy-May Kaboom ca ... ?

ISABEL

She can eat there all she wants. Not only do we have acres
upon acres upon acres upon acres of God's green grass,
we also have the best—bunch grass, Annabelle Okanagan,
bunch grass, not that other ... ordinary, everyday variety!
And that's all thanks to the ingenious irrigation system
Barnabas designed for me twenty-one years ago ...

ANNABELLE

But Daisy-May should ...

ISABEL

... the very day we got married.

ANNABELLE

... But Daisy-May should be able to graze anywhere she
wants, Isabel Thompson of Kamloops, B.C. That's her
right. That's always been her right. What Johnny would
have said ...

ISABEL

Cows have rights? Oh, for the love of George and the
dragon! Next thing you know, Annabelle Okanagan of

Kamloops, B.C., you'll be telling me a log has rights, or that a bump on that log has rights, or that a frog sitting on that bump on that log has rights ...

ANNABELLE

But that's just it. They do. In a way, they do. What Johnny used to say ...

ISABEL

Oh, for the love of George and the dragon! Don't be ridiculous.

ANNABELLE

(*anger rising*) What Johnny Okanagan used to say ...

ISABEL

All I am saying, Annabelle Okanagan of Kamloops, B.C., is that Daisy-May Kaboom can come and live with us, *if* she wants. Now that right she has. It's *my* house, *my* yard, *my* pasture, *my* grass, *my* irrigation system. No one can take it away from me *or* from Barnabas.

ANNABELLE

But that's just it, Isabel Thompson of Kamloops, B.C., don't you see? My point, and what Johnny Okanagan would have said, is: if they can take Chicheelia Kaboom's pasture away from her ...

ISABEL

She'll get it back. Chicheelia Kaboom has the spirit of a cougar.

ANNABELLE

... they can take anything. They can take your house. They can take your yard. They can take your pasture. They can take *your* grass right out from underneath Daisy-May Kaboom's pendulous, large-nippled, milk-heavy udder.

ISABEL

They will not!

ANNABELLE
They took the river.

ISABEL
How, Annabelle Okanagan of Kamloops, B.C., just *how*
did they take the river? Who took the river? Why ...

ANNABELLE
(*flabbergasted*) Who took the river?! *Who* took the river?!

ISABEL
How in the name of George and the dragon can someone
come along, bend over, pick up a river, and carry it off
into the distance away over yonder as if it were a sack
jam-packed with potatoes? Hmm? Can you tell me that,
Annabelle Okanagan of Kamloops, B.C.?

> *Finally, and with great force, ANNABELLE steps in ISABEL's
> path and stands there impregnable as rock. And ISABEL, of
> course, is left no choice—she has to stop.*

ANNABELLE
We are not allowed to fish the waters of that river
anymore, are we now, Isabel Thompson of Kamloops,
B.C.? (*Pause. Finally, ISABEL is listening.*) Not as of
yesterday, Wednesday, the twenty-fourth of August, 1910 at
ten past eleven. (*shouts right in ISABEL's face, her spit flying*)
P.M.! (*back to normal voice*) And if that's not taking the river
away from us, then tell me, Isabel Thompson of
Kamloops, B.C., please, tell me: *what* is?

> *For ISABEL, finally, it begins to jell. She, after all, can not
> go anywhere. And what's more, she can't think of an answer.
> The two stand eyeing each other with even more venom.*

ISABEL
Hmmm ...

ANNABELLE
Egg-zactly.

Silence. They eye each other even harder. Beat. Then, just as quickly as they stopped, they snap back to life. Pop! And resume their journey. For a good ten beats, they walk in silence—pensive, brooding, and as restless as the natives of Papua New Guinea—ANNABELLE simmering away like an old black kettle. Up the "road" they go, down the "road" they go, up, down, up, down, up, etc. Suddenly, missing not a step, ANNABELLE spits out her next words hard as nails.

ANNABELLE

So why did you say Benjamin Jerome used to be so short he had to stand on top of a little wooden box in order to *schlu-um* women?

ISABEL

Beg your pardon?

ANNABELLE

I said: *why did you say Benjamin Jerome, my grandfather, used to be so short he had to stand on top of a little wooden box in order to schlu-um women?*

ISABEL

I said that?!

ANNABELLE

Yes! *You* said that.

ISABEL

Where? Where did I say that?

ANNABELLE

At the store.

ISABEL

At the store?

ANNABELLE

Yes, at the store, just yesterday.

ISABEL

At the store, just yesterday?

ANNABELLE

Yes, Isabel Thompson of Kamloops, B.C. Wednesday, the
twenty-fourth of August, 1910 at five past ten. (*shouts in
her face, spit flying*) A.M.! (*back to normal voice*) Peter K.
Mitten's General Store, Main and Third, in Kamloops
village. Delilah Rose Johnson? *She* was there.

ISABEL

(*flustered to the max*) She ... she ... (*gulps*) ... was ... ?

ANNABELLE

Yes, she was, standing right there five feet behind you.
Watching. *You. And* listening. As you stood there inches
from the lard, the salt, the flour, and the Burns' Baking
Powder hissing and whispering and flickering your
tongue at Chicheelia Kaboom. She saw you ... she heard
you! I'm on my way to Delilah Rose Johnson's, *as we speak*,
Isabel Thompson of Kamloops, B.C., as it just so happens.
So you might as well come on in with me. Why waste a
perfectly divine opportunity to verify the saintly, kind-
hearted Isabel Thompson's fabulous description of the
dear, late Benjamin Jerome's contortionist proclivities, is
what I think, now that I think of it.

ISABEL

(*waves her shoulder bag at ANNABELLE*) I have berries to
pick!

ANNABELLE

The berries can wait.

ISABEL

I have 624 saskatoon pies to bake, Annabelle Okanagan of
Kamloops, B.C.! By nine o'clock. Tonight! *I have no choice!*

ANNABELLE

(*pulls her by the sleeve*) Oh yes, you do.

ISABEL

(*pulls sleeve back. A tug-of-war/tango begins.*) Oh no, I don't!

ANNABELLE
Yes, you do.

ISABEL
No, I don't!

ANNABELLE
Yes, you do.

ISABEL
No, I don't!

ANNABELLE
Yes.

ISABEL
No.

ANNABELLE
Yes.

ISABEL
No.

ANNABELLE
Yes! (*rips the sleeve a little*)

ISABEL
NO!!!

> *Rips the sleeve (i.e. her own) right off so that, for the remainder of the first act, she has one hell of a time just trying to keep it hanging from her shoulder (for it keeps slipping back off).*

ANNABELLE
(*grabs ISABEL by the shoulders*) Yes. (*lifts her*) You. (*whips her around*) Do. (*bangs her down like a fencepost*)

> *Light change. And, boom, we are at DELILAH ROSE JOHNSON's where ... the "statue" of the girl sitting centre-stage-middle snaps suddenly to life. Snip. With her scissors, she snips in two the thread off the hem of the tablecloth of fine white muslin that she has been stitching, the scissors*

*giving off a blinding, terrifying flash of light. Cello music
starts: Bach, unaccompanied.*

*DELILAH ROSE JOHNSON sits in her "living room" sewing
with a fury. Styrofoam cube for a chair, white tablecloth of
muslin strewn across her knees and cascading to the floor all
around her like a waterfall or chute, she puts down the
scissors to resume with her stitching at the hem of the
material. Obviously, however, she is frantic, running very
late, a high-strung girl to begin with ...*

*Gradually as well, it becomes apparent that not far
behind her and off to the side hangs a cowboy hat, seemingly
suspended in empty space six feet in the air, as if a ghost
were wearing it though, in reality, it is hanging on a "coat
tree," the latter, of course, invisible to the audience. On the
floor by DELILAH ROSE JOHNSON, moreover, sits a
gramophone which, for some reason quite bizarre, is playing
unaccompanied Bach for solo cello, the source, in a sense, of
the low, held note we heard underscoring the trio of
monologues at play's opening.*

*Like a moose gone mental, ISABEL THOMPSON charges in
to the "living room" and up to DELILAH ROSE. Though
furious with the girl for having "snitched" on her, she knows
she can't do much about it at the moment, except, perhaps,
pinch, scratch, or insult her when, if, and where she can.
Pressed for time as she is, for her part, DELILAH ROSE
JOHNSON has very little choice but to keep on sewing, come
what may, all the way through this scene (barring, of course,
at that point where ISABEL will commandeer her needle and
material).*

ISABEL

Why in the name of George and the dragon I had to run
into a woman named Annabelle Okanagan of Kamloops,
B.C. on this dusty old road first thing this morning, is
what I'd like to know, Delilah Rose Johnson of Kamloops,

B.C. All I was doing was heading for the trail that winds its way up the slope of the mountain we call Mount Paul where ...

DELILAH ROSE

Oh yes, of course. To talk to God. As usual. (*laughs a gorgeous, silvery, unforgettable laugh, then addresses both women*) Tea?

ISABEL

No. Not this time. This time, it was to pick saskatoons. Then I was going to come back down, go home, take a nap, then bake those 624 saskatoon pies in a matter of hours for tonight's big banquet when, of all the people in the world, I had to run into Annabelle Okanagan of Kamloops, B.C. Now look at what she's done. To *moi*.

DELILAH ROSE

What, sister dear, what has the horrible, terrifying creature done to you now?

ISABEL

She's plunged me. Plunged me deep—*and hard*—into an agitated ... an agitated ... condition. My pies will be wretched. Just bloody awful wretched! The Great Big Kahoona of Canada will be so unimpressed with the baking abilities of the Shuswap Indians he'll never listen to a word they say.

ANNABELLE

There are many other roads on this reserve, Isabel Thompson of Kamloops, B.C., you didn't have to go and stink up the one I was walking on. (*turns to DELILAH ROSE*) So, Delilah Rose Johnson, you were at the store.

ISABEL

Reserve? What in the name of George and the dragon are you talking about now? *Reserve?!* Let me guess. It's a game park for wild, savage animals. No. A summer camp for lunatics.

ANNABELLE
Egg-zactly. A small piece of land for people like you is
what *that* means.

ISABEL
Honestly, the things that come oozing like a jism from the
mouth of this dreadful woman, even on a day like today/

ANNABELLE
(*dismissing her*) /Pfff! (*turns to DELILAH ROSE*) So tell us,
Delilah Rose Johnson, you were at the/

ISABEL
/even on this beautiful, clear-skied, not-a-cloud-in-sight,
we-are-all-happy-children-of-God-kind-of-day, Thursday,
the twenty-fifth of August, 1910 ...

ANNABELLE
(*to DELILAH ROSE*) Yesterday morning, at Peter K. Mitten's
General Sto ...

ISABEL
For today will surely be the most historic day in the
history of our village, the history of our valley, of our lives,
our province, our country, the world, I can feel it. I can
feel it deep inside my hot Shuswap Indian capillaries
coursing up and down like the great Thompson River as it
comes cascading from the Lollipop Mountains away over
yonder. Imagine, Delilah Rose Johnson of Kamloops,
B.C., just imagine. Today. Thursday, the twenty-fifth of
August , 1910. The Great Big Kahoona of Canada is
coming to our village!

ANNABELLE
(*bitingly sarcastic*) Well, whoop-dee-doo. Let's throw a
party. (*turns once more to DELILAH ROSE*) Come, Delilah
Rose Johnson, tell us. Tell us what you heard at Peter K.
Mitten's General Store just yesterday morning at five
past ...

ISABEL

The banquet, Delilah Rose Johnson of Kamloops, B.C.,
our banquet? It will be so monstrously, disgustingly,
mouth-wateringly, taste-bud-titillatingly spectacular, don't
you think? Imagine, just imagine, steaming, juice-
effulgent sweet potatoes, wild onions, wild asparagus, wild
beans, wild this, wild that, the trout, the stuffing, *your*
beaver spread across the table like a carpet for the devil,
my saskatoon pies, your tablecloths, the squeals of delight,
the moans of pleasure, the ambiance, the feeling, the
rhythm, the cat, oh yesssssss, Delilah Rose Johnson of
Kamloops, B.C., yesssssssssss ... (*pinches DELILAH ROSE,
viciously, in a place [her bum?] where ANNABELLE can't see her
hand*)

DELILAH ROSE

Ow!

ISABEL

(*sweetly innocent*) ... How are you doing with those
tablecloths, little sister dear? Will they be ready in time
for the big jambalaya? Oh, I hope for your sake, for my
sake, *and* for the sake of the Shuswap, Okanagan, and
Thompson Indian Nations that they are.

ANNABELLE

Isabel Thompson of Kamloops, B.C.? If I had a mouth
like yours, I'd shove it in that big, hot, deep, dark, steamy
oven of yours! The one you're so damn proud of.

DELILAH ROSE

Tea, anyone?

ANNABELLE

And what's more ...

ISABEL

This big, hot, deep, dark, steamy oven of mine ...
(*DELILAH ROSE bursts out laughing, quite in spite of herself*) ...
I'll have you know, Annabelle Okanagan of Kamloops,

28

B.C., has done many, *many* incredible things for the people of this village, the people of this valley, as it will yet again, tonight. You should talk. You don't even know how to bake a …

DELILAH ROSE
(*screaming*) *Tea?! Anyone?!*

ISABEL
… a tart. All you know is how to eat them. If I were you, Annabelle Okanagan, I'd consider going on a very, *very* serious diet. *Or* joining the circus. (*DELILAH ROSE laughs*)

ANNABELLE grabs a "chair" and is about to smash it over ISABEL's skull when, as diversionary tactic, DELILAH ROSE suddenly stops laughing and, instead, flies into a girlish flap.

DELILAH ROSE
Oh, I can't, I can't, I can't get this miserable, wretched, horrible seam the way I want it to go! I can't, I can't, I can't and it's driving me insane!

ISABEL
Oh here, let me help you dear.

Rushing to DELILAH ROSE's side, she snatches the needle and material from her hands and sews with a vengeance. And quite viciously, for her real agenda is to hurt DELILAH ROSE, as quickly as possible, as secretly as possible, as effectively as possible.

ISABEL
I've done that kind of stitching before. Why, when Barnabas and I first got married, the very night we got married? He was in such a rush to fulfill his … his manly duties that he tore his underwear on the bedpost. So I had to root around like a rodent for my sewing kit, which happened to be there on the dresser not far from the bed, thank George and the dragon, rush back to

Barnabas, bend him over. Whereupon, with a hurried exclamation and a prayer in my heart, I plunged my instrument deep into the crack of his hot, brown kispiox.

DELILAH ROSE

Ow! You're hurting me!

ISABEL

The problem ... the problem was, it was pitch black in there, I mean in the bedroom, not the kispiox. Fortunately, fortunately I, Isabel Thompson of Kamloops, B.C., was born with the eyes of a large, brown owl, see? (*shows a terrifying eyeball right up at DELILAH ROSE who recoils with a shudder*) Here you try it.

Viciously, she thrusts the needle and material at DELILAH ROSE so that the latter has no choice but to take them.

DELILAH ROSE

(*distraught*) Oh, I'm sorry, Annabelle, really I am. But I am so, so late with these tablecloths I don't even know if ... if I'm gonna have the time to talk to you the way I promised you I would. (*She is, in fact, on the verge of tears.*)

ISABEL

(*manhandling DELILAH ROSE's hand mercilessly*) Thrust. Twitch. Thrust. Twitch.

DELILAH ROSE

Got it.

ISABEL

Faster! Harder! Deeper!

DELILAH ROSE

(*genuinely angry*) I said I got it!

ANNABELLE

I understand, Delilah Rose Johnson of Kamloops, B.C. ...

ISABEL

You keep doing that and by four this afternoon, you'll be done. Four this afternoon! ... Oh my God, my pies! My wild saskatoons! I have to go to the washroom, quick, where is it? (*rushes around for a bit*) And then I really, *really* have to go.

DELILAH ROSE

It's outside. You've been here, what now? Twice? Thrice?

ISABEL

Just once. Oh how I wish, I wish, I wish, for the love of George and the dragon, that you and that ... that ... that Billy Boy of yours would just get yourselves a nice, decent toilet. Barnabas and I? *We* have a toilet *inside* the house. The very first one in this whole valley! Thanks to the ingenious irrigation system Barnabas designed for me ...

> *Realizing they just can't "get" her, DELILAH ROSE and ANNABELLE simply deflate.*

ISABEL/ANNABELLE/DELILAH ROSE

... all those years ago ...

ANNABELLE/DELILAH ROSE

... the very day we got married.

> *Pause. ISABEL looks daggers at them—how dare they make fun of her; worse, how dare they make fun of Barnabas!— but they simply sit there blinking back at her. Unable to scare them with her monster glare, ISABEL hiccups one tiny hiccup, turns, and zooms out the "door."*

> *Silence. At first, DELILAH ROSE and ANNABELLE sit there drained, stunned. Beat. Little by little, however, they start laughing, at ISABEL, yes, but also from sheer nervous energy. Their laughter builds. And builds and builds and builds until they are laughing so hard they almost die. Then long silence, stillness, except, of course, for the cello which goes on "weeping." Complete change of mood—anxiety, intrigue,*

31

darkness. DELILAH ROSE goes back to her stitching, the pressure of her work playing havoc with her dialogue.

DELILAH ROSE

So what were you trying to squeeze in between that ... that monologue from hell?

ANNABELLE

Oh, what's it matter? I'll get her back, some other time, some other way.

DELILAH ROSE

Tell me when ... (*mimicking ISABEL, sarcastically*) ... Annabelle Okanagan of Kamloops, B.C. ... (*normal voiced again, but nastily, the last word genuinely evil, scary*) ... I want to ... Watch.

ANNABELLE

It's not as if she's gonna die tomorrow, though I can't think of a better thing to happen to a village so boring the gurgle of a stomach sounds like a music festival, as Johnny would have put it.

DELILAH ROSE pauses for, instinctively, she knows: one difficult discussion is on its way. She breathes deeply, then goes back to her sewing, her voice back completely to its gentle, genuinely kind, gorgeous tone.

DELILAH ROSE

(*to self, under breath*) Thrust, twitch, thrust ...

Pensively, ANNABELLE goes to look out a "window." A rush of "river-sound" balloons and fades—rich, evocative, the voice of a land.

ANNABELLE

So?

Silence.

DELILAH ROSE

So what?

ANNABELLE

How do you think this whole ... fishing/river thing is going to affect you and ... well, you know.

DELILAH ROSE

How do I think this whole ... fishing/river thing is going to affect me? You mean other than kill myself with these tablecloths I was fool enough to volunteer to hem? Why on Earth do we have to serve this man a dinner in the first place? I mean, isn't he the world's richest man or, at the very least, the country's? Isn't he the Great Big Kahoona of Canada? Can't he bring his own food, own chefs, own stoves, pots, pans, dishes, waiters, dishwashers, own godforsaken tablecloths? And if he has to eat here, then why on Earth does he need one hundred white tablecloths to eat on? Would bare wooden tables just not do? Would the ground not do? We've eaten on the ground, for what now, sixty thousand years? It's like, all of a sudden, God himself is coming to the house for dinner.

ANNABELLE

(*beat*) Not. Quite. Not yet anyway. (*beat*) Where's your cauldron? I need it. For my beaver. And fast. I ain't got all day.

DELILAH ROSE

It's in the shed. Just ... just look under the beam.

ANNABELLE

What beam?

DELILAH ROSE

The one where Billy Boy's old chaps are hanging. Right beside the Shuswap Indian Jesus ... (*chuckles, just a little sarcastically*) You'll see it.

ANNABELLE

Why I had to volunteer to boil half a ton of beaver for this dinner, I'll never know. Stuff the buggers, too. Stuffed beaver for two thousand people *and* the Great Big

33

Kahoona of Canada, holy! I'm sitting there tryna figure it out and tryna figure it out and tryna figure it out when, ka-choing, it all flashed before me. I know, I says to myself, I can borrow Delilah Rose Johnson's great, big pot, the one they call "the cauldron," the one where Isabel Thompson used to boil her babies until they looked like scrow-tie (*note: plural of "scrotum"*), as Johnny used to put it when he was feeling rather chipper. Anyway, that's the idea that hit me like a bong. (*DELILAH ROSE starts to correct her, when ANNABELLE stops her*) I know, I know, it's "*gong*" not "*bong*" but Johnny? Johnny Okanagan? You're a little young to remember but ... (*wistful, aching*) ... he used to like, well ... he used to like these ... these dumb little jokes, the dumber the better, jokes like ... well like ... (*chuckles sadly*) ... word play, puns, that sort of thing. "If I'd a been a white man," he would say to me as he's sitting at the table practicing his signature, "I'd a been a writer, not a goddamn ranch hand who ... who traps on the side." Where'd you say that pot was again? All I can think of is that goddamn Great Big Kahoona of Canada. Even in my dreams, for god's sake, he's sitting there gorging himself on beaver and tits.

DELILAH ROSE

Tits?!

ANNABELLE

The common ordinary bush tit, the golden-throated bush tit, the yellow-bellied bush tit, the rarely spotted southern Okanagan tomtit? You name it, he eats it. (*DELILAH ROSE bursts out laughing*) Tit's true!

DELILAH ROSE

(*laughing even harder*) "Tit's true." Oh! That's funny! That is funny! Oh! Oh! "Tit's true!" (*laughs and laughs*)

ANNABELLE

Johnny Okanagan humour. Listen. I really gotta go. If my
beaver isn't ready in time for his dinner, the Great Big
Kahoona of Canada will get mad and then we're in a
pickle. (*starts to go, but then stops, turns*) Which reminds
me, what if he doesn't even like beaver in the first place?

DELILAH ROSE

The English. *They* don't like beaver, Billy Boy was telling
me. But the Great Big Kahoona of Canada is French,
Annabelle Okanagan, French, not English, so Billy Boy
was telling me. And the French *love* beaver—did you know
that, Annabelle Okanagan of Kamloops, B.C.?—*especially*
young beaver, so Billy Boy has read? This Frenchman for
example, the Great Big Kahoona of Canada? What's his
name again? Sir Willpaletch Lolly-something-or-other?

ANNABELLE

Lolly-yay. Sir Wilfrid Lolly-Yay. Prime Minister of Canada,
is what they call him, in English, as if …

DELILAH ROSE

Anyway, he finds old beaver tough and rubbery,
impossible to chew on, and not much juice, Billy Boy read
in the *Kamloops Sentinel* just the other day. It's the Great
Big Kahoona of Canada's teeth, apparently, they ain't
what they used to be. Anyway, the point I was getting at is:
the Great Big Kahoona of Canada, at age sixty-five, can
partake only of the juice-filled, soft-fleshed, sweet and
tender succulence of very young beaver. I hope that
doesn't mean too much extra work for you.

ANNABELLE

Oh, I'll just boil the shit right out of it. Until it's all
puckered up, as Johnny would have put it. The Great Big
Kahoona of Canada won't know the difference. The last
thing Annabelle Okanagan of Kamloops, B.C. plans on
doing is waste her time and energy standing in her

kitchen the live long day separating the young from the old, the French from the English, Anglican from Catholic, the good from the bad, the white from the Indian, the Shuswap from the Okanagan, the Thompson, and the Kickapoo. That is *not* what I volunteered to do.

Pause. Again, she looks wistfully out the "window." And, again, a rush of "river-sound." At this point, the cello music stops; the "record" on the gramophone has run its course.

DELILAH ROSE

(*to self, under breath*) Thrust, twitch, thrust, twitch ...

ANNABELLE

So what do you think they're gonna do to you? (*pause*) And Billy Boy? (*pause*) And ... your ... child? (*pause*) After this whole fishing thing is over and done with? (*silence*)

DELILAH ROSE

What are *who* gonna do to me? Nothing, Annabelle Okanagan. No one's gonna do anything to me. Or Billy Boy. Or our child. (*Frightened nonetheless, she touches her belly which protrudes just a little.*)

ANNABELLE

What Johnny would have said ...

DELILAH ROSE

(*suddenly enraged*) Johnny is dead, Annabelle Okanagan. Johnny Okanagan has been dead for six long years. What's he gonna do? Climb out of his grave, walk to this house, open that door, and shoot Billy Boy? (*Pause. ANNABELLE is cornered, not to mention alarmed.*) The pot's in the shed. You've got work to do. I've got work to do. (*silence*)

ANNABELLE

Okay? If you don't wanna talk, like you promised me you would, then it's your funeral, Delilah Rose Johnson. Just remember. You *know* who made that law.

DELILAH ROSE
(*sarcastic*) Which one?

ANNABELLE
You know the one. The one about the fishing.

DELILAH ROSE
(*laughs, sarcastically*) Oh. That. My father-in-law is only a, what do they call them again? In English? A "servant"? Of some sort?

ANNABELLE
A *civil* servant. A servant with an awful lot of power. Come on, admit it.

DELILAH ROSE
He's *still* just a servant. To the Great Big Kahoona of Canada, ultimately. Now *that* is the man with the power, don't you think, Annabelle Okanagan? (*jabs her finger by accident*) Ow! Now look what you've done.

ANNABELLE walks over to peer at DELILAH ROSE's finger.

ANNABELLE
And the people of this village? The people of this valley? They're going to believe that Delilah Rose Johnson's father-in-law was *not* the man who took away their right to fish in the Thompson River, their cherished, much-loved, fish-teeming Thompson River?

DELILAH ROSE
Look, there's blood.

ANNABELLE
Oh, just rub some cow shit on it. It'll heal in a day. Speaking of which, know what happened to Daisy-May today? Crack of Don ... Jenkins Jr., as Johnny would ... (*stops herself*)

Fleetingly, the two lock eyes, as if they've just seen a ghost walk past them. Billy Boy's cowboy hat jerks ever so slightly. The women snap their heads to look. What was that? Billy

37

Boy's ghost? Or Johnny Okanagan's, giving them some "warning"? Pause. From which rises, then fades, a rush of "river-sound."

DELILAH ROSE

(*spooked*) What?

ANNABELLE

(*spooked*) What what?

DELILAH ROSE

Daisy-May Kaboom? You were saying?

ANNABELLE

Oh. Evicted from her pasture, pfft.

DELILAH ROSE

A cow? Gets evicted from her pasture? *They* can do that?

ANNABELLE

Look. It's a long story, okay? My boys Ron, John, and Tom will be getting home from Johnny's old tra ... I mean ... from *their* trap ... line ... other side of Lac Dubois and they promised me, their ever-loving mama, more beaver than anyone has seen around here since the day Muskoosees Chimasoo went and had her triplets. I'll get the pot. (*Starts to go. Then, at the "door," turns*) Billy Boy's back from Cache Creek when?

DELILAH ROSE

Tonight? Tomorrow? Depends. He's ... (*indicates the hat, shrugs*) ... a cowboy.

ANNABELLE

(*gravely*) Lock your door. (*exits*)

> *DELILAH ROSE returns to her sewing, when ANNABELLE pokes her head back in.*

ANNABELLE

Especially tonight. (*exits*)

DELILAH ROSE sits for a bit, pondering this last comment, then jumps to her feet, runs to the "door," and yells.

DELILAH ROSE
Who kicked her out?

ANNABELLE
(*offstage, yelling back*) Daisy-May the cow?

DELILAH ROSE
Yes.

ANNABELLE
(*offstage*) Same guy who said, "no more fishing."

Troubled profoundly, DELILAH ROSE stands there thinking, then goes back to her sewing.

DELILAH ROSE
(*to self*) Same guy who said ... So would that mean ... No, it couldn't ... Oh yes, it could ... On the other hand ... (*back to her flap*) Oh, I don't have time to worry about these things, like ... like ... today. What's that expression again? We'll cross that bridge when we ... ? (*thinks, then resumes her sewing*) Thrust. Twitch. Thrust. Twitch. Thrust ...

She laughs one final time, her gorgeous, unforgettable laugh, like a loon at sunset, and exits.

A ways up "Mount Paul," ERNESTINE SHUSWAP stands before some saskatoon "bushes" picking saskatoons, the "bushes" are, of course, invisible to us. All we see of them, in fact, is the dance of light—the shimmer of leaf, branch, and stalk doing shadow-play across ERNESTINE SHUSWAP's handsome face, her body. With the movements of her arms as she picks the berries, she gives the impression of doing some ritual dance. First she hums, sings, then talks to herself (i.e. the audience) in fits and starts ... in fits and starts, because, at the same time, she's picking saskatoons and pitching them into a bag that hangs from her side by a shoulder strap.

ERNESTINE

(*sings*) Tara Raboom-deeyay, Sir Wilfrid Lolly-yay, will he love you today, or will he boom-deeyay. Da-da-da-da-da-da, da-da-da-da-da-da ... (*groans, then speaks*) Oh, why in the name of Jesus and his crucifix I had to go and volunteer to cook that trout for the Great Big Kahoona of Canada, I'll never know. And why, of all the fish in the world, a trout? Why can't the Great Big Kahoona of Canada eat salmon like everyone else around here? "He doesn't eat salmon because he's not from the west," Joe says to me. "In the east, people eat different from us westerners. For instance, they don't eat bear ... "

Way behind ERNESTINE, and therefore unseen by her, ISABEL THOMPSON appears in the "distance" trudging her way up the "mountain trail" in very, very slow motion for, a) the climb is steep and therefore quite arduous, and b) it is so hot she has to keep stopping to pat dry her forehead, ever so delicately, with a handkerchief. As well, she puffs and pants like an old steam engine.

ERNESTINE

" ... Never, *never* serve an easterner bear," is one of my husband's more enchanting little ... philosophies. And what's more, Joe says to me as we're lying there in bed looking at the ceiling examining our lives from one end to the other, what's more, Joe says to me, the Great Big Kahoona of Canada is French. French, not English. Very, very important distinction. You think all white people are the same, Joe says to me? You think they all look alike? Perhaps, but scratch their skin just a little and what you uncover is a totally, totally different animal, Joe says to me. The French, for one thing, are Catholic, Catholic as a rosary. The English? Protestant, Protestant as ... a bank, yes, that's it, a bank. When Catholics die, Joe says to me,

they go straight to heaven. Protestants? When they die?
First they go for coffee, then they go to hell. At least that's
what that old priest used to tell us was the truth God the
Father gave the Pope. Thank God the Great Big Kahoona
of Canada is French *and* Catholic, I says to Joe, and then I
kissed him on the lips. And squeezed his crucifix.

*Like a great tall ghost, ISABEL looms ever closer, behind
ERNESTINE. Catching sight of a ponderosa pine bough lying
on the ground, she bends over to pick it up, and, taking a
break, stands there fanning her face and panting as
discreetly as she can.*

ERNESTINE
The French, moreover, are extremely particular about
what they eat, Joe says to me, the English? Not particularly
particular. That is to say, the French won't eat just
anything, just like Daisy-May the cow won't eat just any
kind of vegetation, right? Right.

*Unable, for one second, to keep her panting under control,
ISABEL snorts a great big snort.*

ISABEL
Skbmnyzxx! (*slaps hand over mouth*)

*Startled, ERNESTINE whips herself around. Like a cougar,
ISABEL leaps behind a "ponderosa pine" (invisible to us, of
course), thus evading ERNESTINE's terrified glare. Seeing
nothing, ERNESTINE breathes a huge sigh of relief, then
resumes berry-picking and talking, as, inch by inch, ISABEL
ventures back out of her hiding place to resume her
"journey."*

ERNESTINE
Jesus and his crucifix, for one flashing moment, I was sure
it was a cougar pouncing on my person to chew it to a spit
ball, hooo! (*makes a sign of the cross, then resumes her story*)

ISABEL now standing mere inches behind ERNESTINE, the latter remains oblivious to the presence at her back. And ISABEL, of course, is eating up every juicy word ERNESTINE is saying.

ERNESTINE

What's more, the French won't go nowhere near a dead animal belly with nothing inside it, which is why I, Ernestine Shuswap of Kamloops, B.C., am standing on the slope of old Mount Paul at ten o'clock on a scorching Thursday morning picking wild onions, wapas'chagoos, and chamook—a herb that titillates the tongue to the point of madness—*and* wild saskatoons of the very best kind, size, and texture for the stuffing for the trout that the Great Big Kahoona of Canada, who's as French as a cheese and Catholic as a rosary, will be eating at that big banquet, right beside our humble little Indian chief, tonight, Thursday, the twenty-fifth of August, 1910 at nine P.M. So you see, it all makes a disgustingly delightful, monstrously delicious, juicy-Lucy kind of sense, don't you think?

ISABEL

(*like a fog horn*) It most certainly does.

ERNESTINE

(*startled half to death*) JESUS AND HIS CRUCIFIX!!!!!!!

She whips around. And as her "berries" go flying, she reels like a top, for she's lost her foothold on loose, very sandy soil.

ISABEL

Ernestine Shuswap of Kamloops, B.C.? I saw you stealing *my* saskatoons. Now put them back.

ERNESTINE

Oh for the love of Chicheelia Kaboom and her old brown cow, Isabel Thompson of Kamloops, B.C., these saskatoon bushes belong to the people, not just to you or to Barnabas. What are you? God?

ISABEL

Yes. I mean no. I mean … oh, for the love of George and the dragon. Now look what you've done. You've plunged me. Plunged me deep—*and hard*—into an agitated … an agitated … condition. And you know, you *know*, Ernestine Shuswap, what that name …

ERNESTINE

What name?

ISABEL

… God, the mere sound of it, does to people with pronounced, extra-sensitive, overly-developed spiritual proclivities! Hup! (*Suddenly, she notices something in the distance [i.e. hovering invisible over the audience].*) Now what in the name of George and the dragon might that be?

ERNESTINE

Now what?

ISABEL

That. That sign over there. On the far side of that gully in the distance. Just past that great clump of sagebrush?

ERNESTINE

There's a sign?

ISABEL

Yes.

ERNESTINE

A sign of what?

ISABEL

A sign of the devil, I'm sure of it. There's never been a sign there before.

ERNESTINE

(*finally noticing it too*) Well, by the name of Chicheelia Kaboom and her old brown cow, I guess I just never noticed it before, my eyes, after all, being nowhere near as powerful as yours.

ISABEL

True. And there's a fence in front of it, too, see? So we can only get so far across this slope of mountain, or so it would appear. Who put up that sign? When did he put it up? And what was his purpose? Come, Ernestine Shuswap, come. Let's go and tear it down right this minute.

ERNESTINE

Oh, it's probably just another one of those ridiculous, meaningless, whitemanish things that says, "time is money, money is time" or "people who need people are the luckiest people in the world." If I were you, Isabel Thompson, I would pay it not one stitch of attention. Come. Let's pick saskatoons together, like the friends we used to be in the days of our youth on the banks of the Thompson. We don't have much time. They say the Great Big Kahoona of Canada is only fifty miles away.

ERNESTINE goes back to berry-picking. But ISABEL will not stop scrutinizing the sign, even from a distance that strains to the limit her legendary vision.

ISABEL

I, unfortunately for you, Ernestine Shuswap, am going to try reading that sign, even from this great, daunting distance, as it seems to be on the other side of a fence *and* a gully we're not meant to cross. Remember. I was born with the eyes of a large, brown owl, see? (*shows ERNESTINE a huge, bulging eyeball*)

ERNESTINE

(*feigning melodrama*) Oh, my gawd!!!

ISABEL

Unfortunately, however, Ernestine Shuswap, my English is as weak as pee. In fact, I can't speak a word of it, never mind read it, as neither can you.

ERNESTINE

As neither can Barnabas.

ISABEL

As neither can Joe. Which is not to say that I, Isabel
Thompson of Kamloops, B.C., am not going to give it one
robust, enthusiastic try.

ERNESTINE

So? Read it. Read the sign.

ISABEL

Well, let's see, now. (*she aims a powerful eye, like a telescope*)
From this great, daunting distance, it's difficult to read,
but I can almost be dead certain that that very first letter
says … "N." There. I've read it.

ERNESTINE

That's it? Just … "N"?

ISABEL

Of course not. What do you take me for? Some kind of
wild savage animal?

ERNESTINE

Just … just tell me what the next letter says?

ISABEL

The second letter? Hmmm, let's see now. (*aims a powerful
eye, like a telescope*) Well, by the love of George and the
dragon, I do believe that second letter says, "O." There.
I've read it.

ERNESTINE

"O." Hmmm. "N" plus "O." Well, by the love of Chicheelia
Kaboom and her old brown cow, I do believe that adds up
to "no." N. O. No. Joe practices it all the time, late at
night, when we're lying there in bed just looking at the
ceiling, for that's exactly what he intends to say to the
Great Big Kahoona of Canada when he gets here.

ISABEL

Oh, I give up. It's just too far away. But whatever the rest
of that sign says, Ernestine Shuswap, we can almost be

dead certain that it means one thing and one thing only: we've been cut off, just like that. (*snaps fingers*) We've been forbidden from going anywhere near our own saskatoons, saskatoons we've been picking, free of charge, ever since the day the great prophet Moses descended from his mountain bearing on his bosoms the tablets of love, truth, and justice.

ERNESTINE
Oh, why do you always have to be so ... so damn theatrical?

ISABEL
Theatrical? *Moi?* Theatrical?

ERNESTINE
Yes.

ISABEL
Ha!

ERNESTINE
"Ha!" yourself.

Silence. They look each other in the eye—sense of foreboding. Light change. Now, ISABEL's body and face, too, are splashed with the shadows of saskatoon-bush leaves and stalks and branches, a shimmering, gorgeous effect. And, as in a pact of defiance, the two start "plucking" berries off their respective bushes—in effect, it is a dance of ritual.

Fade-out. Cello music starts.

Cross fade-in on DELILAH ROSE JOHNSON sitting on her chair, still sewing feverishly away (only this time, her tablecloth of muslin is twice as long as before). Beside her, of course, sits her Billy Boy's gramophone, behind her his hat, hanging on its invisible "coat tree." And the gramophone, again, plays a Bach cello suite, unaccompanied.

DELILAH ROSE

    (*to self, in an undertone*) Thrust, twitch, thrust, twitch, thrust ...

        Suddenly, she stops, looks up, gulps (i.e. swallows a terror that haunts her), closes her eyes, then re-opens them. Lights snap to one silvery, metallic pool of light that isolates her face so that, for a while at least, it looks like a mask. And she begins talking to her "conscience" (i.e. the audience) like the other women did in the prologue. Only in her case, there is just the slightest edge of madness (schizophrenia?) to her delivery. For, instance, nervous laughter punctuates it with increasing regularity.

DELILAH ROSE

    (*long silence, then:*) Delilah Rose Johnson of Kamloops, B.C., twenty-one years old, though you can't really tell. Cuz up close, I look thirty-five, bet you a dollar. Why? Because today, I'm in trouble. You see, two years ago come end of August, which is only six days away, come to think of it, I made the mistake, so they tell me, of falling in love with ... well, a white boy, a cowboy, in fact—this being ranch country, ya know?—this real cute cowboy with hair like straw and eyes like emeralds named Billy Boy Johnson. Why? Because he was different, because he was special, because he liked ... classical music, yes, that's what he called this curious music I still don't understand. And wouldn't you know it but he brings along this gramophone just to prove it, to me ... (*indicates the gramophone*) ... isn't that bizarre? Said he had a cousin away over in England who played this thing called a cello. Somehow, says Billy Boy to me, that music—that's the only thing that could assuage the pain, the unbearable pain of feeling ... out of place, of not belonging. Isn't that bizarre?

        Laughs, beautifully, then talks directly to the "ghost cowboy" as the hat appears to turn to face her. On the backdrop, meanwhile, gradually appears the shadow of a cello-playing cowboy, the actual, "real-life" source of all the unaccompanied Bach (on cello) that we've heard so far. (All additional music is pre-recorded string quartet music, on the theatre sound system that, for all intents and purposes, will appear to be coming from the "gramophone" on stage. NOTE: from now on, moreover, we can "play" with the image of this cello-playing cowboy; at certain points, that is, he will be invisible, at others, visible, or just a shadow ... a portent of DELILAH ROSE JOHNSON's incipient insanity.)

DELILAH ROSE

That's what made me fall in love with you, Billy Boy Johnson—don't matter how hard they talk, don't matter how hard they laugh, but there is only one like you in the whole wide world, far as I'm concerned. (*laughs*) So that night among the rushes on the banks of the Thompson River, when you asked me if you could kiss me on ... the ... well ... (*to audience [i.e. again the Greek mask effect]*). But you see, around here, in *my* family? An Indian girl does *not* fall in love with, much less marry, a white boy. And neither does an Indian boy dare marry or love or even think of a girl who is white. And, forbidden above all else? A Roman Catholic does *not* marry, or love, a Protestant. *That's* a no-no. My eldest sister, Isabel Thompson of Kamloops, B.C., the one with the mouth like a trumpet? (*A light comes up on ISABEL, at far stage left, frozen like a statue, picking saskatoons in her saskatoon patch.*) She's the one who's most insistent on this point. And she's the one who raised me, God knows cuz, you see, our mama, Madeline, died when I was six years of age, she twenty-eight—there's twelve of us, five brothers, seven sisters, Isabel the oldest, me the youngest—so she raised me as her own, raised me together with the twelve other kids that come a-popping from her womb like peas from a pod. And to this day, Isabel Thompson of Kamloops, B.C.,

is *still* my mother, which can be a pain but anyway, ...
(*light on ISABEL fades into dark*) ... There's a new law on
land, Indian land, land used for grazing. And the man in
charge of making this new law a reality? In these parts,
meaning Kamloops, B.C. and environs? The father of the
man I love, for the love of George and the dragon, the
father of the man I married just this spring, the father of
the father of the child right here. (*pats her little round belly*)
My father-in-law? His name? Charles Peter Johnson
formerly of Manchester, England but now from here. His
son? My husband? My lover? My Man? The father of my
child ... The white man—the *Protestant!*—named—ta-
da!—William August Johnson, yes, the very white-skinned
cowboy named Billy Boy Johnson, only son and heir to
the white man who's just said to my people, "no more
fishing," "no more grazing for your cattle," "no more this,
no more that." And I'm Delilah Rose Johnson, of
Kamloops, B.C.

Laughs. Freeze. Fade-out.

*Cross-fade in on the "saskatoon patch" where ERNESTINE
and ISABEL are taking a lunch break. As they take in a
spectacular view of the Thompson River Valley, with its
winding river half a mile "below," they nibble at cubes of
cheese the size of dice, sip at water from small tin cups, and
listen to the bird songs around them. The day is so hot, they
have, alternately, to wipe their foreheads with handkerchiefs
and fan themselves with small boughs of pine.*

ERNESTINE

If Joe Shuswap doesn't have that trout he promised me
sitting on the counter in my kitchen waiting for my
stuffing all fresh and silvery and gleaming in the sun
when I get home, I'll never talk to myself again. (*a long
thoughtful silence as she and ISABEL nibble and bask in the
view*)

ISABEL

This cheese, Ernestine Shuswap of Kamloops, B.C., it's so
... it's so ... so ... salty.

ERNESTINE

(*suddenly pointing in the distance*) Look. A red-tailed hawk
swooping down to the Thompson River half a mile below
us, whooo!

ISABEL

Daisy-May can do much better, don't you think?

ERNESTINE

(*calling out*) Catch me my trout, red-tailed hawk, catch me
my trout, whooo-whooo!

ISABEL

Once she's installed in *my* pasture with its ingenious
irrigation system that Barnabas ...

*The "sign" in the distance "floating" into her descending field of
vision, ERNESTINE's smile melts into a glower.*

ERNESTINE

If I were you, Isabel Thompson, I'd put my own sign up
on my pasture, one that will say something much more
intelligent than that piece of shit over there. Your sign,
for instance, could say, "Our cow is never contented. She
is always striving to do better." (*gleeful*) Ho-ho!

*ISABEL stops chewing and ponders the notion. ERNESTINE,
meanwhile, keeps on chewing and taking in the "vista."
Finally, ISABEL speaks.*

ISABEL

Ernestine Shuswap?

ERNESTINE

Yes, Isabel Thompson.

ISABEL

What in the name of George and the dragon is a Great
Big Kahoona of Canada anyway? (*more silence as they nibble*)

What does he look like, what does he do? Is he old? Is he young? Is he skinny? Is he fat? Does he have halitosis? Does he smoke cigarettes, drink whisky, have a temper, have a family, does he jiggle when he walks, does he wiggle, does he speak many languages, like Barnabas, who can speak not only his native Thompson but Shuswap, Okanagan, Haida, Tsimshian, Tlingit, Klingon, Haisla, Yakima, Santee Sioux, Oglala Sioux, Lakota Sioux, Chalala Sioux, Dogrib, Yellowknife, Blackfoot, Cree, Arapaho, Navaho, Assiniboine, Winnebago, Sauk and Fox, Seminole, Wichita, Choctaw, Cherokee, Chipewyan, Chippewa, Chickasaw, Chickadee, Kickapoo, Boogaboo, Micmac-paddy-walk-give-a-dog-a-bone *and* ten words of English?

ERNESTINE
(*blown away completely*) Wha!

ISABEL
So?

ERNESTINE
According to my husband, Isabel Thompson, there are four kinds of kahoona.

ISABEL
Four? That's ... that's all?

ERNESTINE
You think these ... (*indicates audience*) ... these people out there need *more*?

   Pause. With her great owl eye, ISABEL peers at the audience.

ISABEL
No. So then please, Ernestine Shuswap of Kamloops, B.C. Name them. Name the four categories of kahoona.

ERNESTINE
Alrighty?

As they talk, they put their picnic stuff away, to gradually resume berry-picking.

ERNESTINE

Well you see, first, there's "Kahoona."

ISABEL

Hmph.

ERNESTINE

Then there's "Very Kahoona."

ISABEL

Hmph.

ERNESTINE

Then there's "Extremely Kahoona."

ISABEL

Hmph.

ERNESTINE

And then there's, "pffft!" (*slaps her hands together and slides them across*) "Right out of the picture!" is how Joe counts them.

ISABEL

So this Great Big Kahoona of Canada who's arriving in Kamloops tonight, to listen to this ... this speech, this ... this deputation, this ... memorial our chiefs have been killing themselves preparing for the man these past twelve months, which is he?

And again, they start picking. As they inch their way across the stage and to the "fence," their arm movements, in particular, make them look like dancers in some ritual dance.

ERNESTINE

A Kahoona, you see, is just an ordinary kind of ... of chief, I guess. Kind of like our old Chief Louis who, if you ask me, is ... well ... (*undercover*) Joe would have made a

much better chief, don't you think, Isabel Thompson of
Kamloops, B.C.?

ISABEL

(*loud*) Are you *still* stewing over that election? That was
what now? Ten years ago?

> *ERNESTINE cringes, blushes. Pause. A billow of "river-
> sound," wind. She swallows, rallies.*

ERNESTINE

(*conspiratorial, hard*) You tell anyone I said that, Isabel
Thompson, and I'm barbecuing Daisy-May Kaboom, *live*,
for the banquet tonight. (*back to normal voice*) Anyway, the
point I was getting at is: a kahoona, at the very least, *has*
to be a chief, you see what I'm saying, Isabel Thompson
of Kamloops, B.C.?

ISABEL

Hmph. And "Very Kahoona"?

ERNESTINE

"Very Kahoona," on the other hand, means you have to
have at least five thousand people under your leadership.
That Don Runningwater over in Spuzzum? That unhappy
little man with the nose, and that bum? He's "Very
Kahoona."

ISABEL

Hmph. And "Extremely Kahoona"?

ERNESTINE

Rare. Very, very rare. In fact, the only "Extremely
Kahoona" category of Kahoona we have here in British
Columbia lives away over in Victoria, is what Joe says.

ISABEL

Victoria? Hmph.

ERNESTINE

Joe met him once. But he didn't say much, is what Joe
says. Just stood there looking like a statue.

ISABEL

> And this "Pffft!" (*slaps hands together and slides them across*)
> "Right out of the picture" type of Kahoona?

ERNESTINE

> He rules like a king over millions of people making laws
> left, right, and centre, changing people's lives willy nilly
> billy, is what Joe says. He has so much power, it is said,
> that he can reach into the sky and move the sun about
> like a saskatoon pie, he can change the path of molecules,
> make a man from the rib—of a woman, ha-ha!—he can
> turn saliva into wine, metal into money, delay the
> ripening of wild saskatoons by three whole weeks, just like
> he's done, see? (*holds up a ripe "saskatoon," then pops it in
> her mouth*) In fact, he's probably the kind of Kahoona who
> could very well take your river *and* your pasture *and* your
> saskatoon bushes right out from underneath your feet,
> come to think of it, hmmm … Anyway, this "Pfft!" (*slaps
> hands together and slides them across*) "Right out of the
> picture" type of Kahoona is apparently also absolutely
> frightful to look upon, is what Joe says Chief Louis told
> him. You can't look him in the eye when he passes *or* your
> *oochoochoosimsa* will shrivel up and die. They say, for
> example, that once, this ninety-five-year-old man was fool
> enough to look the Great Big Kahoona of Canada right in
> the eye and, when he got home? His *oochoochoosimsa* were
> so shrivelled up he had to boil them for an hour, he fell
> asleep, and he died.

ISABEL

> Why, in the name of George and the dragon, are you
> scaring me like this, Ernestine Shuswap of Kamloops,
> B.C.?

ERNESTINE

> Because you asked for it, Isabel Thompson of Kamloops,
> B.C. And because you are the kind of woman who *never*
> takes "no" for an answer, even when the word is writ large

across a sign from the devil, then you got your answer, a "Pffft!" (*slaps hands together and slides them across*) "Right out of the picture" type of Kahoona. And that's the type of Kahoona who's coming to Kamloops tonight. And that's who I'm stuffing this so-far-non-existent trout with only the finest of British Columbia herbs, roots, and wild saskatoons for and that's who you're baking 624 saskatoon pies for— and it's way past noon already, and it's way too hot, and they say the Great Big Kahoona of Canada is now only twenty-five miles away—so I'd strongly advise you, Isabel Thompson of Kamloops, B.C., that you get back to work.

ISABEL, however, has come up against the barbed wire "fence" cutting off the field.

ISABEL

Barbed wire, see, Ernestine Shuswap, barbed wire. Oh, Charles Peter Johnson, father of William August Johnson, brand new husband of my little hussy of a sister Delilah Rose Johnson, do you hear me? I will put knapweed laced with iodine deep into a pie, at the banquet tonight you will eat that pie, and then you will *die!*

ERNESTINE

Charles Peter Johnson is simply "low man" on the totem pole, Isabel Thompson, he's just a cog in the machine, a nothing, a pimple on the face of society, is what Joe says. If you poison anyone tonight, why not the Great Big Kahoona of Canada, hmmm? (*ISABEL chortles sarcastically, sustained.*)

They look at the forbidden fruit, ERNESTINE with yearning, ISABEL with rage. Freeze.

Off to the side and a little to the back, two soft lights "breathe up" to reveal, like dreams, two "still lifes." The first "still life" is of ANNABELLE OKANAGAN, standing in her "kitchen" with an apron on, studying what looks like a recipe (but will turn out to be something else entirely), ladle to a large empty pot (the one she just borrowed from

55

*DELILAH ROSE). The second "still life" is of DELILAH ROSE
JOHNSON, still stitching at her tablecloth (which is now even
longer), and looking like a goddess emerging from a river
(the length of white muslin); and again, she is just snipping
at her thread with her bright, glinting scissors. From her
gramophone (or from the faintest "shadow" of her cello-
playing cowboy high up behind her? Or from both?), cello
music starts: unaccompanied Bach slow, mournful, almost
painful. The images of ERNESTINE and ISABEL picking
saskatoons, however, remain very much the foreground.
A billow of "river-sound" and wind, making the shadows of
the saskatoon bushes shimmer across the two women's faces
and bodies which, in turn, makes them look like spirits—the
land is talking, through them. Fade-out, on all. During this
fade-out, the shadows of the bushes "bleed" imperceptibly into
that of a barbed-wire "fence" that "slashes" the four women's
images. Just before complete fade-out, ISABEL shakes the
"fence" with rage. We hear the rattle of metal and the four
women's "war cry," which ends up sounding like the wailing
of a widow at a funeral.*

ISABEL

(*wailing*) Lu-lu-lu-lu-lu-lu-lu-lu-lu ...

*And ... black-out. In the darkness, the cello music rises,
fades, and dies ... as, behind it (or under it), does the river.*

End of Act One.

ACT TWO

From the darkness come the moos of a quite unhappy cow being dragged across a field. They recede into the background, then fade into silence.

Fade-in on ANNABELLE OKANAGAN standing all alone in her "living room," apron on, huge wooden ladle in one hand, sheaf of papers in the other. Poring through the papers (which turn out to be not a recipe but a bureaucratic document), she reads with exaggerated loudness, loud enough, that is, for someone just outside her "door" (and therefore offstage) to hear her.

ANNABELLE
(*shouting*) "Dear Sir and Father ... " that's how our chiefs have decided to open their pitch to the Great Big Kahoona of Canada.

ERNESTINE's voice comes pealing from the "front porch" for she, too, virtually has to shout in order to be heard by ANNABELLE.

ERNESTINE
(*offstage, shouting*) Sounds like a prayer. Makes you feel like grabbing them ole holy rosaries and swingin' 'em around like a kitty-by-the-tail.

ANNABELLE
(*shouting*) "Dear Sir and Father, we take this opportunity of your visiting Kamloops to speak a few words to you ... "

Pooh! Does that beaver ever stink! Maybe boiling it was a mistake.

ERNESTINE

(*offstage, shouting*) Roasting it is worse, trust me. Pee-yew! I can smell it from out here on your porch!

ANNABELLE

(*shouting*) "Sir and Father ... " What Johnny would have said was, "Just call him Wilfrid, for chris'sakes, or Willie. He's a human, is he not, not a priest, not a god?" But anyway it goes on ... (*goes back to her reading*) "We welcome you, dear Sir and Father, to this our beautiful country and want you to understand the conditions under which we live. As head of this great Canadian nation, we expect much of you ... " (*in the background, a moo*)

ERNESTINE

(*offstage, still shouting only, this time, at someone in the distance*) Don't hold her like that. Cows have sensitive nostrils, you know?

ANNABELLE

(*ignoring ERNESTINE, goes on reading/shouting*) "We feel confident that you will see to it we get fair treatment and hope that, with your help, our wrongs may at last be righted ... "

> ERNESTINE *enters, disgusted. The voice she uses, from here on in, will not be shouting but normal/conversational.*

ERNESTINE

That twit, Chicheelia Kaboom. Dragging Daisy-May to Isabel Thompson's pasture by the nostrils. If I didn't have the huge heart I am known and loved for up and down the North Thompson River valley, I'd grab *her* by *her* nostrils and drag her to Isabel's myself. Keep reading. I can listen, talk, and do other things, all at once. Joe and I do it all the time, all the time.

ANNABELLE

I'm sure you do. Anyways, the speech goes on to say: "We speak to you the more freely because you are a member of the white race whom we first met, and which we call, in our tongue, 'real whites' ... " Excuse me a sec. Gotta check my beaver. Stir its juices, poke it, tweak it, maybe even bang it.

She exits to the "kitchen," handing the document to ERNESTINE as she passes her.

ANNABELLE

Here, your turn to proof-read.

ERNESTINE

Where?

ANNABELLE

(*indicates the point in the "speech" where she stopped reading*) Here. (*exits*)

ERNESTINE

Alrighty? Ahem. "One hundred years next year ... "

ANNABELLE

(*offstage, shouting*) Louder. Can't hear a damn thing you're saying.

ERNESTINE

Alrighty? (*shouting*) Ahem. "One hundred years next year, they came amongst us here at Kamloops and erected a trading post."

ANNABELLE

(*offstage, shouting*) One beaver. One miserable goddamn beaver!

ERNESTINE

(*shouting*) You don't know how many times Joe and I went over that line as we'd lie there in our bed late at night examining our lives from one end to the other. He wanted it to say, " ... they came here to Kamloops and

59

built a store," but it just didn't sound ... right. The
rhythm was wrong, somehow. It was me who insisted on
the ... erection ... (*clears throat*) ... of a trading post, not
just a store, it sounds more ... convincing that way, more
exciting, more ... fulfilling, don't you think?

ANNABELLE re-enters.

ANNABELLE

(*normal voice*) One beaver. One miserable goddamn
beaver. That's all my boys, Ron, John, and Tom could get
me for this banquet. All of a sudden, we can't trap, is what
they tell me when they get back from Johnny's old
trapline other side of Lac Dubois. Another new law.

ERNESTINE

(*normal voice*) Charlie Brown? Same thing. They took his
traps and fined him one hundred bucks. Got so mad,
went home, got drunk, banged Sally Brown. On the head.
With a crucifix. Is what they say.

ANNABELLE

Thank gawd, that Chicheelia Kaboom had an extra
beaver. Smoked. Sold it to my sons, Ron, John, and Tom,
for a song and a prayer. The question being: now how the
hell am I supposed to feed two thousand people *and* the
Great Big Kahoona of Canada with just one beaver, huh?
Where's Jesus when you need him?

ERNESTINE

There's my trout!

ANNABELLE

If it ever shows. Is the only person to be eating at this
feast to be none other than the Great Big Kahoona of
Canada? And the rest of us are supposed to sit there like a
chorus line of starving dogs watching him salivate and
drool, chomp, rip, tear, and masticate, chew, quiver,
swallow, and devour, slurp, snort, belch, burp, fart, and

perhaps even shit? (*another moo*) Give me back that speech. (*yanks the document from ERNESTINE*)

ERNESTINE
My trout will arrive, be not a-feared. Joe's been a fisherman since the day he come marching like a bishop from the depths of ole Minny Shuswap's cave-dark womb.

ANNABELLE
(*resumes reading, but in a normal voice now*) Anyways. Ahem. " ... The 'real whites' we found were good people ... " You think the Great Big Kahoona of Canada will appreciate we Indians calling the French "real white" and the English just plain, ordinary ... "white"?

ERNESTINE
The French *love* being considered "distinct," Joe tells me, makes them feel ... wanted. So it's best we humour them, Joe tells me. Just ... don't look him in the eye.

ANNABELLE
Is a frog's kispiox watertight? Anyways, it goes on. Ahem. " ... We could depend on their word." That's the real whites the chiefs are talking about here, not the other ordinary ... whites. (*chuckles*) "They did not interfere with us nor attempt to break up our organizations, laws, and customs ... "

ERNESTINE
The Great Big Kahoona of Canada will *love* being called "real white" so much so he'll give Daisy-May back her pasture, trust me, I can feel it, quote, "deep inside my hot Shuswap Indian capillaries," unquote, ha-ha!

ANNABELLE
" ... Nor did they stop us from catching fish, hunting, trapping, never tried to steal our country, nor take our food and life from us ... " Yup. Johnny woulda loved this part. Wouldn't be surprised, in fact, if he dictated it himself from right there in his grave on the banks of the

61

Thompson River, right across from where old Solomon Owl lives today.

A very loud moo, this time seemingly just outside the door. Beside herself with excitement, ISABEL charges in.

ISABEL

They've moved her, they've moved her, for the love of George and the dragon, they've moved Daisy-May. The dear brown Jersey is now firmly installed smack in the middle of *my* pasture with its ingenious irrigation system that Barnabas designed for me all those years ago. Now her milk, her cream, her cheese, her kurds—their thickness, their texture, their consistency, their aroma, their colour, their vitamins, not to mention their amount!—will improve *and* increase as by God's command, I know it, I know it, I can feel it deep inside my hot Shuswap Indian capillaries. The Great Big Kahoona of Canada will have so much cream on his saskatoon pie at the banquet tonight he will burst and expire, thus leaving behind him everything we Indians are asking him to give us in that speech that you, *as we speak,* are in the singular act of proof-reading, Annabelle Okanagan of Kamloops, B.C., right? Right.

Freeze. A moo of joy. And cross fade-in to …

DELILAH ROSE JOHNSON's "living room" where DELILAH ROSE, yet again, is frantically (though in slow motion) hemming her umpteenth tablecloth (the tablecloth we first saw her working on now four times as long as at the start). The Bach cello suite on the gramophone now balloons out to a full string quartet with hints, inside it, of the "Wedding March." And DELILAH ROSE looks beatific, like the Madonna with child. About one minute into it, and in extreme slow motion, ERNESTINE leaves her grouping on the stage's other side and walks up to DELILAH ROSE's door (this cross-over alone should take at least three minutes). There,

unnoticed, she stands, looking on in silence. At one point,
DELILAH ROSE laughs (nervously, worriedly, almost madly)
and flings the tablecloth out by one end making it billow out,
so that, for about three seconds, it looks like a river—is that
a trout (i.e. a slide) we just saw "inside" it? We can't be
sure. (A gorgeous billow, as well, of "river-sound.") Then she
pulls it back and resumes sewing. The music fades into
silence. Beat. Then ...

ERNESTINE
(*to DELILAH ROSE*) Yes?

But DELILAH ROSE is so hell bent on her sewing that, at
first, she doesn't hear a thing. Or, at least, seemingly she
doesn't.

ERNESTINE
You had a question?

Another lengthy silence. Finally, DELILAH ROSE ties a knot,
snips the thread with her scissors—the scissors glint once,
menacingly, frighteningly, blindingly—lifts her head, and
looks ERNESTINE in the eye. Only then do we realize the
younger woman has been crying. But from joy or from
sorrow, we don't yet know. In fact, she may well have entered
a state of near nervous breakdown.

DELILAH ROSE
(*hesitant*) Can you ... (*pause, then direct*) Can you neigh?
(*silence*)

ERNESTINE
(*startled*) Can ... can I what?

DELILAH ROSE
I said: *can you neigh?*

ERNESTINE
Neigh? You mean, like ... like a horse?

DELILAH ROSE
Yes. Can you neigh? (*silence*)

ERNESTINE

(*disturbed*) Well, I suppose ... I suppose I could try, but ...
Why on earth would I want to neigh? I mean, what good
would it do me? I mean, other than, perhaps ... clear my
passages?

DELILAH ROSE

So then you know exactly how I feel about Billy Boy
Johnson *and* his family, do you not, Ernestine Shuswap?
(*silence*) My eldest sister, Isabel Thompson, *she* wants me
to leave them. My other sisters, *they* all want me to leave
them, "for my good," they say, "and for the good of the
baby." (*touches her belly*) My best friend, Annabelle
Okanagan, *she* wants me to leave them, she didn't come
right out and say it but I know she does. Says the
situation, right now, is just too dangerous. Which is why I
finally sent for you as you are probably my last ray of ...
(*breaks down*) ... hope.

*Suddenly realizing what all these people have been urging
DELILAH ROSE to do, ERNESTINE finds herself affronted. She
spits out her next lines like nails.*

ERNESTINE

This is a Catholic community. I am a Catholic. You are a
Catholic. Catholics do *not* divorce *or* separa ...

DELILAH ROSE

Father Lebeau came here to ask me to leave them.

ERNESTINE

(*indignant*) He did not.

DELILAH ROSE

No, but he did ask me to leave, *with* them.

ERNESTINE

He ... asked you ... to leave ... your own ... family?
(*DELILAH ROSE answers tacitly: "Yes." Suddenly ERNESTINE
flushes livid.*) Why doesn't that ... that old bugger go and

64

ask Charles Peter Johnson to leave Kamloops *and* his family?!

DELILAH ROSE

(*defiant*) Because he doesn't have the guts, that's why.

ERNESTINE just manages to stop herself from slapping DELILAH ROSE across the face.

ERNESTINE

Don't you dare, don't you dare ever, *ever* talk about Father Lebeau that way! Father Hector Lebeau is a true man of God, do you hear me?

DELILAH ROSE

Yes. And God is coming for dinner. Tonight ... (*shrieks out her last word, like a genuine madwoman*) Remember?!

The "remember" echoes and re-echoes, out of which dying cry surfaces that of a loon—the day creeps on, the first "smell" of evening. Long, long silence. Blown away by the notion of God coming for dinner—not to mention by what she vaguely senses is the girl's coming madness—ERNESTINE stands there speechless. And DELILAH ROSE, for her part, goes back to her usual, kind, gentle self.

DELILAH ROSE

Leaving the Johnson family—as I'm sitting here with their child sound asleep deep inside the folds of my flesh, my veins, my spirit, Ernestine Shuswap—leaving them, white as pillowcases as every single one of them may be, Protestant as banks as they may be, *or* leaving you *and* my sisters *and* my family *and* my friends, my community, everything I know, everything I love, well, that would be like me asking you to neigh, Ernestine Shuswap, that would be like me asking you to act like a horse. It just wouldn't happen, would it now?

But ERNESTINE, too, is caught in a Catch-22—her religion or her sense of family, of community, which is she to choose?

She turns away from DELILAH ROSE and to the "window."
Long silence. The loon cries again. DELILAH ROSE resumes
her sewing.

DELILAH ROSE

And your husband? What's he think? Of all this ... this ...

ERNESTINE

Don't know. Haven't seen him since ... since before six
o'clock this morning. Out fishing, even though he's not
supposed to. But I'll bet you a dollar, Delilah Rose
Johnson, I'll bet you a dollar what he'd say is, what he'd
say is: they'll kill him, they'll lynch him, they'll hang him
by the neck from the tallest, most beautiful Douglas fir
they can find between here and Victoria.

DELILAH ROSE

Billy Boy? Or his father?

Another long silence, during which DELILAH ROSE once
again "billows" out the tablecloth she's working on so that,
again, for at least three seconds, it looks like a river. It is a
river ... a river with a "trout" "inside" it. As well, a billow
of "river-sound" surfaces, blooms, and fades. Then, in the
silence ...

ERNESTINE

Harold Jenkins, his name was, English boy so skinny and
with skin so white, people thought he was a ghost when
they first laid eyes on him. Showed up here from out east
one fine fall day, told the chief he was on his way up
north to go looking for that gold we Indians used to think
was about as useful as gills on a human. Said he wasn't
staying but builds himself a house anyway—just for the
winter, this Harold Jenkins says to the chief—*our* chief—
just a little log affair on the banks of the river, round
about the junction, just across from where old Solomon
Owl lives today. House is gone now, of course, they
burned it down after ... well ... anyway, one of Harold

Jenkins's brothers shows up in the spring. And another and another and another. Until there's five of them Jenkins men, with their wives, their children, their dogs. All going north to go looking for that gold, they say. Anyway, the years go by, the years go by, the years go by. And they're *still* on the banks of that river, round about the junction, right across from where old Solomon Owl lives today. And their land is getting bigger and their land is getting bigger and their land is getting bigger and bigger and bigger. Their families, too. Allan Squirrel got the boot, Jimmy Skunk got the boot, Martin Seagull got the boot, so many Indian people lost their land it wasn't even funny, all ended up homeless as vagabonds, living off the charity of their relatives. Margaret Squirrel had so many guests one day that, for dinner, she had to slaughter half her cow, is how legend has it. Until one night, Franklin Coyote got caught stealing a chicken—one chicken, one pathetic chicken!—from Harold Jenkins's middle brother, Don Jenkins Sr. It used to be his coop, for god's sake, Franklin Coyote's children were so skinny they looked like sticks! So Don Jenkins Sr., you know what he did? Came after Franklin Coyote with a gun, and shot him. Shot him dead right there by the river, right across from where old Solomon Owl lives today, shot him in the back. So then you know what happens? Two days later? Franklin Coyote's five brothers all got together. Daniel Coyote, Phillip Coyote, David Coyote, Samson Coyote, Joshua Coyote, they all marched over to Don Jenkins Sr.'s house right there where the North and South Thompson Rivers come together to become the Thompson River proper, Indian Point they call it. They say they threw him on the ground, held his head against a block of wood, and chopped it off, with an axe. And the blood of Don Jenkins Sr. and the blood of Franklin Coyote still hang in the air, like a mist, over the waters of the Thompson River. And they say that inside that mist, late at night, when the moon is out? You can see eyes in them, like lamps, two pairs of them, hanging there waiting and waiting and waiting ... I was six years old, Delilah Rose Johnson. I heard the screams of Don Jenkins Sr. I still hear them.

She pauses. And in that pause, we hear the death screams of Don Jenkins Sr., somewhere far, far away, as though filtered through fifty years of memory. And by now, of course, DELILAH ROSE has stopped sewing, so entranced is she by the tale. She remains sitting, listening to the screams for she can, in her mind, hear them. ERNESTINE remains standing, also listening to the screams. Ever so gradually, we see the "eyes" just described, two pairs of them, like lamps, hovering in the air, on the backdrop, as in a mist. Until, finally, the screams fade away, as do the eyes. DELILAH ROSE breaks from her trance, and resumes her sewing.

DELILAH ROSE
You ... got a trout to prepare, remember?

Her face pale as a ghost's, ANNABELLE enters. DELILAH ROSE and ERNESTINE turn to see her.

ANNABELLE
(*the voice of doom*) It's official.

ERNESTINE
(*disbelieving*) No!

ANNABELLE
Yes.

ERNESTINE
(*disbelieving*) It's been cancelled.

DELILAH ROSE
What? What's been cancelled?

ANNABELLE
The Shuswap language, my dear, our dear Native tongue? *That's* what's just been cancelled. (*ERNESTINE and DELILAH*

68

ROSE are speechless. Silence.) We're allowed not a phrase, not a word, not a syllable, not a vowel, not even a period.

ERNESTINE
We can't ... we can't ... We can't have periods?

Struck by the notion, ANNABELLE stops dead in her tracks. Assuming a tacit "yes" from her, the other two explode. Given their position—exhaustion, sleep deprivation, political tension, major stress—all the women's nerves are tinder-box-sensitive, so one little "spark" is all it takes to "set them off."

ERNESTINE/DELILAH ROSE
Yes! Yes! Yes, oh yes! No more periods!!! No more periods, rah-rah, rah-rah-rah!!! *No more periods!!!*

In their "fevered brains," a full-orchestral version of the song, "Tara Raboom-deeyay" kicks in. And they dance (and sing) a "sock-it-to-'em, kick-'em-in-the-pants" can-can.

ERNESTINE/DELILAH ROSE
(*singing*) Ta ... Ra ... Ra ... Boom-deeyay, Sir Wilfrid Lolly-yay, will he love you today, or will he boom-deeyay. (*shouting*) No more rags!!! No more curse! Good-bye blood! Death, death to the period!!! (*singing*) Da-da-da-da-da-da, da-da-da-da-da-da, etc. ...

ANNABELLE
Ladies. Ladies. (*No response. They keep singing, dancing. ANNABELLE screams.*) Ladies! (*finally silence, stillness*) Unfortunately, kind ladies of the Thompson River Valley, periods in Shuswap are exactly the same as periods in English.

ERNESTINE/DELILAH ROSE
(*groan*) Awwwww ... (*Silence. The women think.*)

DELILAH ROSE
So then what are we ... how are we ...

ANNABELLE
How are we to speak?

ERNESTINE

    Yes, Annabelle Okanagan of Kamloops, B.C. How are we to communicate with each other?

ANNABELLE

    As of five P.M. today, kind ladies of the Thompson River Valley? We are to—ta-da!—neigh.

ERNESTINE

    Neigh?

DELILAH ROSE

    Neigh?

ANNABELLE

    Yes, neigh.

DELILAH ROSE

    You mean like ... like horses?

ANNABELLE

    Just like horses.

    ERNESTINE looks at DELILAH ROSE. DELILAH ROSE looks at ERNESTINE. Both look back at ANNABELLE. ANNABELLE snaps her fingers at ERNESTINE. And ERNESTINE neighs, just like a horse.

ERNESTINE

Neigh-heigh-heigh-heigh-heigh-heigh!!!

    Black-out. In the black-out, not the neigh of horses but the moo of a cow.

    At ISABEL's, a cloud of flour comes billowing from her "kitchen" into her "living room." As well, we can hear ISABEL singing happily away in the background.

ISABEL

    (*offstage, singing*) Tara Raboom-deeyay, Sir Wilfrid Lolly-yay, will he love you today, or will he boom-deeyay. Da-da-da-da-da-da, etc. ... (*continues humming in background*) ...

ERNESTINE comes into view standing at centre-stage proof-reading "the memorial." At first, she reads so ISABEL can hear her from the "kitchen." With all the caterwauling going on in there, of course, she has to shout.

ERNESTINE
(*shouting*) Now remember, Isabel Thompson, as I'm proof-reading this section of the Lolly-yay Memorial, I'm using not human language but horse language, got it?

ISABEL
(*offstage, shouting*) Neigh away. (*sings*) Tara Raboom-deeyay, Sir Wilfrid Lolly-yay ...

ERNESTINE
Alrighty? (*neighs, then shouts*) "When they first came amongst us, there were only Indians here ... "

ISABEL
(*offstage, shouting*) One berry per pie and my twelve children will starve to their deaths but my 624 saskatoon pies will be ready within the hour. (*neighs*)

ERNESTINE
(*shouting*) " ... They found the people of each tribe supreme in their own territory, and having tribal boundaries recognized by all ... "

ISABEL
(*offstage, shouting*) Now all I gotta do is wait for Daisy-May to cream her pail.

ERNESTINE
(*neighing, then shouting*) ... "The country of each tribe was just the same as a large farm or ranch from which they gathered all their food and clothing, fish, grass and vegetation on which their horses grazed ... "

Like a blizzard, another huge cloud of flour billows from the "kitchen." Looking like a ghost, her face just covered with flour, ISABEL emerges from the centre of this cloud. In one hand, she carries a rolling-pin covered in flour.

ISABEL

(*normal voice*) And their cows. Don't forget the cows. They grazed too. (*wipes flour from her eyes so she ends up resembling a raccoon*)

ERNESTINE

(*normal voice*) Screw the cows. The speech is way too long already. Listen. This is what our men have written. (*reads*) " ... trees which furnished firewood, materials for houses and utensils, plants, roots, seeds, nuts, and berries which grew abundantly and were gathered in their season ... "

ISABEL

(*as she looks out a "window"*) Now tell me, Ernestine Shuswap, have you ever seen an udder grow with a speed so astonishing? Three hours in my pasture, and, sproing, Daisy-May Kaboom's is already twice the size it was this morning. (*a moo*) Now *that's* a happy little moo, if I do say so myself.

ANNABELLE enters struggling with a great steaming pot out of which hangs a big beaver tail. As well, a huge wooden ladle sticks out of the pot.

ANNABELLE

That is *not* a happy little moo. (*bangs the pot down on a "chair"*)

ERNESTINE

Oh, for the love of Chicheelia Kaboom and her old brown cow, time is running out. The Great Big Kahoona of Canada is on the outskirts of town already, is what they say. (*neighs and reads*) " ... and water which was free to all ... " (*another moo*)

ISABEL

(*to ANNABELLE*) That is so a happy little moo.

ERNESTINE

(*practically shouting at ISABEL*) " ... without it, the people could not have lived ... "

ISABEL

(*to ANNABELLE*) How dare you tell me that my cow is not mooing happily.

ANNABELLE

It is not your cow. It's Chicheelia Kaboom's. (*takes her ladle out of the pot and brandishes it at ISABEL*)

ISABEL

Pah! Chicheelia Kaboom cares about that cow like she cares about her children. *I'll* show you a moo.

ANNABELLE

Be my guest.

ISABEL

(*she looks out the "window"*) Alright, Daisy-May? (*Claps her hands twice, quickly. Daisy-May moos.*) You see? That's a happy moo.

ANNABELLE

Bullshit. That's an unhappy moo. An extremely unhappy moo.

ISABEL

A happy moo, Annabelle Okanagan, goes up like this. (*ISABEL moos, upward*) An unhappy moo, contrary-wise, goes down like this. (*ISABEL moos, downward*) Daisy-May?

> *ISABEL claps, twice, quickly. In the yard outside, Daisy-May moos, downward. ANNABELLE looks at ISABEL, as in "see?"*

ERNESTINE

(*to audience*) Those two. Like a couple of rez dogs. You never know whether they're gonna fight or *schlu-um.* Watch. While I, Ernestine Shuswap of Kamloops, B.C., keep proof-reading, for tonight's big banquet, in horse language, the deputation to the Great Big Kahoona of

Canada that our men, the Chiefs of the Thompson River Valley now call "The Lolly-yay Memorial." (*neighs*)

ISABEL

Daisy-May? (*she claps*)

ANNABELLE

Daisy-May? (*she claps*)

> As ERNESTINE reads, ISABEL and ANNABELLE continue their (very verbose) argument, in "mime." All we hear, above ERNESTINE's sonorous, orating voice are the alternation of, a) ISABEL's claps and Daisy-May's moos, all of which end upward, and b) ANNABELLE's claps and Daisy-May's moos, all of which end downward. And because the rhythm of these claps and moos is regular as percussion under ERNESTINE's speech, the speech itself ends up sounding like a funky piece of music, ISABEL's and ANNABELLE's movements resembling more and more a dance—a cross between tango and flamenco. As well, ISABEL brandishes her rolling pin, ANNABELLE her ladle.

ERNESTINE

(*neighs*) "Fifty-two years ago, the *other* whites came. They found us just the same as the 'real whites,' only we had more horses, some cattle, and in many places, cultivated the land. They found us happy, healthy, strong, and numerous. Each tribe was still living in its own 'house' or 'ranch.' No one interfered with our rights. We were friendly and helped these whites also, for had we not learned the first whites had done us no harm? Only when some of them killed us we revenged on them. Then we thought there are some bad ones, but surely, on the whole, they must be good. Besides, they are the Queen's people. And we had heard great things about the Queen from the 'real whites.'"

> On the stage's far side, a light comes up on DELILAH ROSE. Dragging behind her the white tablecloth (even longer now)

*that she is working on currently, she is just putting the
needle on a record in her gramophone ... and a gorgeous
tango, played by a string quartet, starts to play, the "music"
ANNABELLE and ISABEL, in their argument, will now
effectively be "dancing" their "tango" to. As does DELILAH
ROSE with the cowboy hat.*

ERNESTINE
"We expected her subjects would do us no harm, but
rather improve us by giving us knowledge. At first they
looked only for gold. (*neighs*) We knew the latter was our
property, but as we did not need it to live by, we did not
object to their searching for it. They told us, 'Your
country is rich and you will be made wealthy by our
coming. We wish just to pass over.' (*light fade-out on
DELILAH ROSE [once again sitting on her "chair" sewing],
though her music keeps on playing*) Soon they saw the
country was good, and some of them made up their mind
to settle it. They commenced to take up pieces of land,
told us they wanted the use of this land only for a few
years, and then would hand it back in an improved state;
meanwhile, they would give us some of the products they
raised for the loan of our land. Thus they commenced to
enter our 'houses,' or 'ranches.' Some of our Chiefs said,
'These people wish to be partners with us in our country.
We must, therefore, be as brothers to them ... '" (*neighs,
then says to audience*) Ha! How's *that* for wild horse
language, huh?

    ISABEL and ANNABELLE's argument rises to the foreground.

ISABEL
    ... and that's thanks to the ingenious irrigation system
Barnabas designed for me ...

ANNABELLE
That's just it, you dork, don't you ever listen? That
ingenious irrigation system Barnabas designed for you, all

those years ago, on the very day you got married, has just been plugged ...

ISABEL

(*gasps, mortally wounded*) Excuse me. Excuse me. What did you just say?

ANNABELLE

I said your irrigation system has just been plugged.

ISABEL

Plugged?!

ANNABELLE

Dammed, jammed, blocked, cut off, kaput, zilch, ka-choing. There's no more water inside it. Charles Peter Johnson, father of your cute, little brother-in-law, frilly-face Billy Boy Johnson—on orders from the Great Big Kahoona of Canada?—is killing your pasture. Daisy-May is dying. All that liquid in her udder is not cream for your Saskatoon pies but the dropsy. Pus, Isabel Thompson, pus.

ISABEL

(*in utter disbelief, whispers, barely audible*) Pus?

ANNABELLE

Yes. It's nothing but an udder full of pus, pus, and yet more pus. (*one last very sad moo from Daisy-May outside the "window"*) You see? Not only is that one unhappy moo, Isabel Thompson of Kamloops, B.C., that is a dying moo. That is a goddawful, miserably unhappy, dying, monstrous moo. There's my beaver. (*bangs her ladle down on the cover of the pot*) Take it or leave it.

> Turns on her heels and exits. The other two freeze.
> ANNABELLE walks around the entire stage, at first, at her normal speed—which is quite fast and aggressive—then slowing down and slowing down and slowing down until it is as if she were walking underwater, in very, very slow

*motion. Until, much eventually, she will reach the downstage
area beside the other three women. All this as …*

*Cross fade-in on DELILAH ROSE JOHNSON now standing
on her "chair" with her tablecloth draped over her head and
shoulders; in effect, a bridal veil now, it is fifty metres long.
She is examining herself in a "mirror" on the "wall." In the
trance-like state that she's in, she looks like a cross between a
bride and a statue of the Blessed Virgin Mary. Slowly, ever
so slowly, she brings out one hand, and stretches it before her,
as if reaching out for Billy Boy's. For his cowboy hat is now
hanging right beside her, at the height of her head, so that we
can almost see the "spirit" of the man himself.*

DELILAH ROSE

I, Delilah Rose Laughingbird of Kamloops, B.C., do take
you, William August Johnson formerly of Manchester,
England but now of Kamloops, B.C., to be my lawful,
wedded husband, in health and in sickness, in wealth and
in poverty, in sorrow and in gladness, in glory and in
shame, in love and in hate, in hate and in love, yes, in
love and in hate, in hate and in love, in love and in hate,
in hate and in love, in love and in hate, in hate and in
love, till death … till death … till death … (*repeats, ad
infinitum*)

*Imperceptibly, the string quartet (with its hint of "The
Wedding March") bleeds in and swells and swells, until,
later, it will drown out all four women's voices momentarily.
For, also imperceptibly, ISABEL and ERNESTINE have come
back to life and are slowly, like zombies, making their way, as
in a stately dance, to the downstage area.*

ERNESTINE

Six o'clock P.M. and my trout has not yet arrived. And
dinner's at nine, for god's sake. The Great Big Kahoona
of Canada will be furious. Six o'clock P.M. and my trout
has not yet arrived. And dinner's at nine, for god's sake.

The Great Big Kahoona of Canada will be furious. Six o'clock P.M. and my trout has not yet arrived. And dinner's at nine, for god's sake. The Great Big Kahoona of Canada will be furious. He'll destroy us, oh, for sure, he'll destroy us. The Great Big Kahoona of Canada will destroy us, oh, for sure, he'll destroy us. I think I'll go down to the river and look for Joe. Yes, that's what I will do. I'll go down to the river and look for Joe. Yes, I'll go down to the river and look for Joe. Yes, I'll go down to the river ... (*starts calling*) Joe! Joe! Jo-hoe! Jo-hoe! (*ad infinitum, her voice weaving in and out of the music [and what will gradually become a gorgeous sonic "collage"]*) Jo-hoe! Oh, Jo-hoe! Yoo-hoo! ...

A giant slide fades slowly into focus, completely covering the backdrop (and splashing, at the same time, imagery across DELILAH ROSE's now fifty-metre-long tablecloth/veil). And, suddenly, ERNESTINE is not only on the banks of the Thompson River, she's in it, walking on its bottom as in a dream ("river-sound" ebbs and flows throughout the scene). And as in a giant aquarium, fish "swim" by her, her trout most evasive of them all, as though teasing her, tantalizing her, "swimming" around her, just out of her reach. And though we sometimes don't hear her voice for all the other sounds, it's still there, going, "Joe! Oh, Jo-hoe! Yoo-hoo! Jo-hoe!" ... NOTE: this dream-like "aquarium/underwater" visual will hold true for the next two scenes as well, i.e. ANNABELLE's and ISABEL's.

ANNABELLE, for her part, now stands before her cauldron, stirring it and stirring it, at the same time as which she is "proof-reading" from the Laurier Memorial, though her voice, eventually, will emerge through the theatre sound system, unreal, dream-like, otherworldly, the document itself, also eventually, nowhere in sight, at least not on stage.

ANNABELLE

" ... The whites made a government in Victoria. At this
time they did not deny the Indian tribes owned the
country. We Indians were hopeful. We waited for their
chiefs to declare their intentions toward us and our lands.
We knew what had been done in the neighbouring states,
and we remembered what we had heard about the
Queen, that her laws carried out by her chiefs were better
than the American laws. Presently government officials
commenced to visit us, and had talks with our chiefs.
They told us to have no fear, the Queen's laws would
prevail, and everything would be well for the Indians.
They said a large reservation would be staked off for us
and the tribal lands outside of this reservation the
government would buy from us for white settlement. They
let us think this would be done soon, and meanwhile, we
would have the same liberties as from time immemorial to
hunt, fish, graze, and gather our food supplies where we
desired; trails, land, water, timber, all would be as free of
access to us as formerly. Our chiefs were agreeable, so we
waited for treaties to be made. We had never known white
chiefs to break their word. In the meanwhile, white
settlement progressed. Our chiefs held us in check. They
said, 'Do nothing against the whites. They will do the
square thing by us in the end ... '"

> *ISABEL, for her part, does the same as ANNABELLE, reading
> from the document at first, then just reciting it, from
> memory, her voice weaving in and out of ANNABELLE's
> until it, too, emerges from the theatre sound system ... and
> the document no longer in sight, at least not on stage. Only
> what she is doing, physically, is, while, at first, holding the
> Laurier Memorial with one hand so she can read from it,
> she is, with the other hand, hauling a string of 624 "pies"
> from her "kitchen," right across the downstage area so that*

79

they eventually will reach right across it, in preparation, as it were, for the "banquet."

ISABEL

" … What have we received for our good faith? Gradually as the whites became more powerful and we less powerful, they changed their policy. Their government has taken advantage of our friendliness. They treat us as subjects without any agreement to that effect, and force their laws on us. They have broken down our old laws and customs. They laugh at our chiefs. Minor affairs amongst ourselves they drag into their courts. They enforce their laws one way for the rich white man, one way for the poor white, and yet another for the Indian. They have knocked down the posts of all the tribes. They say there are no lines, except what they make. They have never consulted us in any of these matters, nor made any agreement, nor signed any papers with us. They have stolen our lands and everything on them. They treat us as children. They say the Indians know nothing, own nothing, yet their power and wealth have come from our belongings. The Queen's law which we believe guaranteed us our rights, the B.C. government has trampled underfoot. This is how our guests have treated us—the brothers we received hospitably in our house … "

ANNABELLE

… They will do the square thing by us in the end …

Then a blinding flash of lightning, a huge clap of thunder, and a downpour from hell (i.e. outside), following which the rain—and the scene upcoming—are punctuated by the sound of more thunder (small and large, distant and close) and people shrieking as they run for cover all around DELILAH ROSE's house and, effectively, all over the village. (These background sounds, by the way, will fade as the scene progresses until, by the end, they are gone completely and silence has been re-established.) And the light on the scene, as

80

*a result of all this lightning, will be lurid, unpredictable,
very unsettling.*

*Snapping back to life, ISABEL, ANNABELLE, and
ERNESTINE scream with horror and rush up to DELILAH-
ROSE who is still standing on her "chair," and beside Billy
Boy's cowboy hat, in bridal mode. For, all of a sudden, we
realize that she is holding her scissors to her belly (and
therefore her child) just one split second from plunging it in.
(NOTE: The little strokes— / —mean the women are
speaking practically simultaneously.)*

ANNABELLE/
(*screaming*) No, Delilah Rose, no! (*echo*) No, Delilah Rose,
no! (*Echo. Repeat.*)

/ISABEL/
(*screaming*) Put those scissors away right now, do you hear
me? (*echo*) Put those scissors away right now, do you hear
me? (*Echo. Repeat.*)

/ERNESTINE
(*screaming*) Delilah Rose, you got a baby inside that belly,
remember? (*echo*) Delilah Rose, you got a baby inside that
belly, remember? (*Echo. Repeat.*)

*ANNABELLE grabs the scissors from DELILAH ROSE but
DELILAH ROSE yanks them away. Then she bursts out in a
long, mad peal of gorgeous, to-die-for, silvery laughter. Either
she has had a nervous breakdown, lost her mind, or is dead
and this is her ghost, we don't know which yet. Leaping off
the "chair," in any case, she neighs. And neighs and neighs
and neighs, galloping up and down the stage like a horse.
Until, gradually, human language starts "bleeding" from
her neighing; it is as if she were speaking in tongues.*

DELILAH ROSE
Once there was a bride who was ready for her wedding.
Oh, she was in love, she was. Oh, she was in love, she was,
she was. In love with a handsome, straw-haired, green-

81

eyed cowboy named William August Johnson, yes, William August Johnson, the white man Billy Boy Johnson. A real fine catch that one, yes, he was a real fine catch, *she* certainly thought so, Delilah Rose Laughingbird did. So now Delilah Rose Laughingbird is about to become Delilah Rose Johnson? First Indian girl to marry a white man, first Catholic Indian girl to marry a white, Protestant man in the Thompson River Valley?

She laughs, long and insanely, then suddenly turns mean, attacking ANNABELLE with the scissors and hissing like a mongoose. The other women scream. A horrified ANNABELLE just narrowly averts getting stabbed in the eye.

ANNABELLE
Sweet Jesus!

DELILAH ROSE
But Delilah Rose's sisters Isabel, Louise, Jeanette, Maria, Florence, and Hermeline Laughingbird and all their husbands and her brothers Henry, Benjamin, William, Raphael, and Thomas Laughingbird and all their wives, they didn't want this Billy Boy Johnson cuz his hair was made of straw, burnt too easily, and thus would kill her or, at least, would kill dead her spirit, they said, Delilah Rose's family did. (*This next line comes out genuinely evil, terrifying.*) Besides, Protestants, they talk to the devil, do they not?

Again, she laughs, long and insanely, then suddenly turns mean, attacking ISABEL with the scissors and hissing like a mongoose. The other women scream. A horrified ISABEL just manages to grab the scissors. But as DELILAH ROSE still holds the other end, the whole encounter becomes a deadly tug-of-war.

ISABEL
(*like a wolverine*) Give me those scissors.

DELILAH ROSE

... then a child came falling from the sky, a child came falling from the sky ...

ISABEL

I said give me those scissors!

ISABEL yanks and yanks but is completely unsuccessful for, for at this point, DELILAH ROSE is preternaturally powerful. In fact, ISABEL gets quite the throwing around, the poor girl whimpering and yelping like a puppy being spanked.

DELILAH ROSE

... that child came falling, falling, falling, landing right in her belly with a doof. But he was white, for the love of George and the dragon, the baby was white, white as a pillow case and not nut brown, not like her. And he, what's more, was a Protestant not a Catholic, isn't that bizarre?

Suddenly, DELILAH ROSE turns chillingly, frighteningly lucid. She addresses her sister/mother, ISABEL THOMPSON, dead on.

DELILAH ROSE

Just like your babies—*my* dear sister dear, *my* dear mother dear—just like your twelve brown babies came a-falling from a Thompson Indian sky down, down into a Shuswap Indian earth. You, a Shuswap Indian woman, married a Thompson Indian man, did you not?

DELILAH ROSE twists the scissors. ISABEL moans with agony.

DELILAH ROSE

Say it. "Yes." (*ISABEL merely whimpers.*) Say it. (*ISABEL merely whimpers.*) Say. It.

ISABEL

(*screams*) Yes!!!

DELILAH ROSE

Yes, what? Yes, what? Yes. What?

ISABEL

I, Isabel Thompson, a Shuswap Indian woman, married a Thompson Indian man.

DELILAH ROSE

So then why are you condemning me—your youngest sister *and* your daughter—for marrying a white man *and* a Protestant, huh? What's the goddamned difference? Tell me. What's the difference, what's the difference, what's the difference, what's the difference? Huh? Huh, huh, huh? Tell me! Tell me, tell me, tell me, tell me!

DELILAH ROSE yanks the scissors away from ISABEL, locks her in a vicious half-Nelson, and holds the scissors to her neck, ISABEL lying there sobbing hopelessly, pathetically. Terrified for ISABEL and for DELILAH ROSE, ANNABELLE, too, finally crumbles, in effect, vomiting six years of suppressed emotion.

ANNABELLE

A white man killed my Johnny. A white-skinned cowboy named Oliver Clapperton killed Johnny Okanagan, my dear late husband. Shot him in the forehead on a Saturday night, yes, at the door to that hell-hole of a bar, Kelligrew's Saloon at Main and Third of Kamloops village six years ago. Killed him for a piece of land, *his* land, Johnny Okanagan's little piece of trap-line, yes. *And* I forgive him, Delilah Rose Johnson. Delilah Rose Johnson of Kamloops, B.C., I, Annabelle Okanagan of Kamloops, B.C., forgive Oliver Clapperton of Chilliwack, B.C. I forgive. I forgive. I forgive Oliver Clapperton … *and his people.* (*she falls to the floor in a paroxysm of sobs*) I just want peace. I just want peace. I just want peace, so I can sleep! Please, God, please, let me sleep! (*sobs pathetically, tragically*)

Suddenly, DELILAH ROSE releases ISABEL, casting her off to the side in a heap. (Through the course of the scene that follows, ISABEL and ANNABELLE will collect themselves and be standing, once again, by the end.) And DELILAH ROSE is back to her "mad" mode.

DELILAH ROSE

So what was she to do, this Delilah Rose Laughingbird, huh? What was she to do? There was a white man in her stomach, yes, a white man in her stomach, a white man who *communed with the devil,* yes, the devil, right there in her stomach, in her stomach, in her flesh, in her veins, in her blood. So what was she to do, huh, what the hell was she to do?

Again, she laughs, long and insanely, neighs three times, then suddenly turns mean, attacking ERNESTINE with the scissors and hissing like a mongoose. The other women scream. A horrified ERNESTINE gets gashed in the arm.

ERNESTINE

Eeeeeeeeee, I've been stabbed, I've been stabbed, oh my God, oh my God, I'm gonna diiiiiiiiiiiiieeeeeeee!!!

DELILAH ROSE

I know, she would cut it out with scissors, yes, she would. She would cut it out with scissors, cut it out, cut it out, cut it out like a little paper doll. And then she would be free, yes, then she would be free, free to return to the land of her ... the land of her ... her what, though? What land, what kind of land, what kind of culture, what kind of country, what kind of world? Huh? Great Big Kahoona of Canada? What kind of land, what kind of country, what kind of world, what kind of life, huh? Huh? Huh, huh, huh, huh, huh?

Suddenly, inexplicably, the scissors are sticking out of her belly. DELILAH ROSE laughs long and insanely. And then neighs, and neighs.

DELILAH ROSE

So she took her wedding veil, stitched it and put it on her head. And thus did Delilah Rose Laughingbird now Delilah Rose Johnson ... and thus ... To this day, a third pair of eyes hang high over the river in the mist, on nights when the moon is out, a third pair of eyes hang high over the river in the mist, like lamps. And to this day, these eyes, they look out over a village, which became a town, which became a city, they look out at a banquet, this woman's head in the mist does, it looks out at a banquet that sits on her veil of pure white muslin, a banquet that sits on her beautiful veil, a veil they call the Thompson River.

Until, finally, she exhausts herself and goes completely limp. As the other three women extract the scissors from her belly, two sets of eyes, like lamps, appear on the backdrop, hanging, as it were, in the mist above the waters of the Thompson River. Then a third set of eyes—DELILAH ROSE's—joins them. And on DELILAH ROSE's veil, the four women set up the banquet, all to the "music," as it were, of the words (coming next) of the Laurier Memorial (or, at least, what's left of it).

On the backdrop (as the speech murmurs on—in effect, it is the river talking), a series of slides comes on, first of Wilfrid Laurier, then of Wilfrid Laurier meeting with the chiefs of the Kamloops area (whatever we can find), one chief ostensibly "reading" it to him, the document now very visible in his hand, *his voice on soundtrack—the only time we hear a male voice* speaking *in the play. (This voice, moreover, is ancient, quavering, yet sonorous, like the babble of a brook, or Gregorian chant—the man could be eighty-five for all we know. Its Shuswap translation, more-over, "circles" the auditorium like a restless breeze.) Meanwhile, on stage, the four women (including DELILAH ROSE JOHNSON) slowly spread DELILAH ROSE's*

tablecloth/wedding veil/river across the downstage area.
And set it up with plates, as in a banquet. (NOTE: they
don't have to be actual plates, they could just be slides of
plates projected *onto the "tablecloth/veil.") ... truly an*
odd, and very disturbing, combination of funeral and ban-
quet.

CHIEF

(*voice-over, in Shuswap with English translation gradually*
becoming prominent) " ... After a time, when they saw that
we might cause trouble if we thought all the land was to
be occupied by whites, they set aside small reservations
for us here and there. This was their proposal and we
never accepted these reservations as settlement for
anything, nor did we sign any papers. They thought we
would be satisfied, but we never will be until we get our
rights. We thought these reservations were the
commencement of some scheme they had evolved for our
benefit, but although we have waited long, we have been
disappointed. We did not know how to obtain redress. We
knew it was useless to go to war. What could we do? Even
your government at Ottawa, into whose charge we have
been handed by the B.C. government, gave us no
enlightenment. We had no powerful friends. The Indian
agents at Victoria appeared to neglect us. Some offers of
help in the way of agricultural implements, schools,
medical attendance, aid to the aged, etc., from the Indian
department were at first refused by many of our chiefs,
because we thought the Ottawa and Victoria governments
were as one, and these things would be charged us as
payment for our land. Thus we got along the best way we
could and asked for nothing. For a time we did not feel
the stealing of our lands very heavily. As the country was
sparsely settled we still had considerable liberty in the way
of hunting, fishing, grazing. However, owing to increased
settlement, this has changed, and we are being more

restricted to our reservations which in most places are unfit to maintain us. Except we can get fair play, most of us will be reduced to beggary. We have also learned lately that the B.C. government claims ownership of our reservations, which means we are landless … "

Until finally, ERNESTINE (still under the above speech/"voice of the river") comes on with her trout on a platter, a great big trout, biggest one you've ever seen. Like a priestess in a ritual, she descends, slowly passes it to ISABEL, who slowly passes it to ANNABELLE, who slowly passes it to the ghost of the very dead DELILAH ROSE JOHNSON, who very slowly comes to place it on the "banquet table" smack at centre-stage down. At this point, the slide show on the backdrop "melts" imperceptibly into The Last Supper, *with Laurier as Christ and the chiefs as the Apostles. Finally, at that exact point where the "chiefs'" recorded speech (above) finishes, the women resume their dialogue, walking off the stage and up the aisle(s) as they do so. Despite themselves, however—that is, from sheer nervous exhaustion—they are giggling. Only the dead DELILAH ROSE-as-bride, stays behind to serve, as it were, the Great Big Kahoona of Canada the trout that ERNESTINE got. She kneels before him. And there, bent in homage to the end of time, she freezes.*

Meanwhile, the other three women whisper/titter/sob their way up the aisle(s) and out the theatre, as though they were tittering/whispering their way out of a sacred space, a church for example, a church with a coffin sitting open with a corpse inside it …

ANNABELLE

So did you look him in the eye?

ISABEL

Oh for the love of George and the dragon, you want my *oochoochoosimsa* to shrivel up and expire?

ANNABELLE

Yes.

ERNESTINE

Oh, well. Mine will surely shrivel up and expire, I guess.

ISABEL

You looked him in the eye?

ERNESTINE

I looked him in the eye.

ANNABELLE

And?

ERNESTINE

Didn't see a thang, not a whisker of a thang. If you really want to know, he's not worth poison.

ANNABELLE

(*derisive*) Pfff! Some Great Big Kahoona of Canada.

ISABEL

Thank George and the dragon Joe Shuswap got that trout he promised you first thing this morning, eh, Ernestine Shuswap of Kamloops, B.C.? Speaking of which, where *is* Joe?

ANNABELLE

Oh, he's still at the banquet, gorging himself on beaver and tits.

ISABEL

But he did catch the trout for Ernes ...

ANNABELLE

Oh no, he didn't.

ISABEL

Well then who ... (*Pause. ISABEL and ANNABELLE turn to look at ERNESTINE.*)

ERNESTINE
(*a twinkle in her eye*) Oh, had enough of waiting for that
tired old bag so I went down to the river by myself. Didn't
bother with a line, didn't bother with a hook, not a sinker,
not a net, no nothin'. Waded in, right over my neck, my
head, my hairdo, and got it with my own sharp teeth!
(*neighs*) Trick I showed Joe thirty-seven years ago, the very
day we got married.

*And by this time, they are gone. And a slow fade-out on the
"collage" and in the theatre. One final time, comes
ANNABELLE's firm, steely voice.*

ANNABELLE
(*offstage*) And she'll be fishing in that river till the cows
come home.

*Then Daisy-May moos ... one final moo, a happy moo, filled
with joy.*

*And last-last—the gurgle of a river surfaces, balloons,
and fades, rich, evocative, the voice of a land, and blackout.*

THE END.

*NOTE I: As the audience leaves, the first movement of
Beethoven's "Sonata for Cello, Opus 69 in A-major" plays
full-out, gorgeous, heart-breaking, the first time in the show
that we hear a piano (that is to say, under the cello). And
not only is the sound almost shocking in its newness because
of this piano, it has a bizarrely-exquisite, strangely-uplifting,
optimistic effect because, for one thing, it sounds like a river,
a river flowing smooth, majestic, dignified, and powerful.*

... In a petition signed by fourteen of our chiefs and sent to your Indian department, July, 1908, we pointed out the disabilities under which we labour owing to the inadequacy of most of our reservations, some having hardly any good land, others no irrigation water, etc., our limitations re: pasture lands for stock owing to fencing of so-called government lands by whites; the severe restrictions put on us lately by the government re: hunting and fishing; the depletion of salmon by over-fishing of the whites, and other matters affecting us. In many places we are debarred from camping, travelling, gathering roots and obtaining wood and water as heretofore. Our people are fined and imprisoned for breaking the game and fish laws and using the same game and fish which we were told would always be ours for food. Gradually, we are becoming regarded as trespassers over a large portion of this our country. Our old people say, 'How are we to live? If the government takes our food from us they must give us other food in its place.' Conditions of living have been thrust on us which we did not expect, and which we consider in great measure unnecessary and injurious. We have no grudge against the white race as a whole nor against the settlers, but we want to have an equal chance with them of making a living. We welcome them to this country. It is not in most cases their fault. They have taken up and improved and paid for their lands in good faith. It is their government which is to blame by heaping up injustice on us. But it is also their duty to see their government does right by us, and gives us a square deal. We condemn the whole policy of the B.C. government towards the Indian tribes of this country as utterly unjust, shameful and blundering in every way. We denounce same as being the main cause of the unsatisfactory condition of Indian affairs in this country and of animosity and friction with the whites. So long as what we consider justice is withheld from us, so long will dissatisfaction and unrest exist among us, and we will continue to struggle to better ourselves. For the accomplishment of this end we and other Indian tribes of this country are now uniting and we ask the help of yourself and government in this fight for our rights. We believe it is not the desire nor policy of your government that these conditions should exist. We demand that our land question be settled, and ask that treaties be made between the government and each of our tribes, in the same manner as accomplished with the Indian tribes of the other provinces of Canada, and in the neighbouring parts of the United States. We desire that every matter of importance of each tribe be a subject of treaty, so we may have a definite understanding with the government on all questions of moment between us and them. In a declaration made last month, and signed by 24 of our chiefs (a copy of which has been sent to your Indian department), we have stated our position on these matters. Now we sincerely hope you will carefully consider everything we have herewith brought before you and that you will recognize the disadvantages we labour under, and the darkness of the outlook for us if these questions are not speedily settled. Hoping you have had a pleasant sojourn in this country, and wishing you a good journey home, we remain,

> Yours very sincerely,
>
> The Chiefs of the Shuswap, Okanagan,
> and Couteau or Thompson tribes
> —per their secretary, J.A.Teit (August 25, 1910)

Two End Notes:

1) Delilah Rose Johnson's tablecloth, of course, does triple-duty as: a) tablecloth, b) bridal veil and, c) river. And though it starts life off as just your ordinary, normal-sized tablecloth (albeit of muslin), it grows and grows in length as the story progresses until, by plays end, it is fifty metres long, maybe more. What has happened in fact, of course, is that all the "extra" length of muslin not seen at first is folded and hidden *inside* Delilah Rose's styrofoam cube/chair (which, of course, will be hollow) and is only very gradually exposed, as becomes necessary, i.e. it should be a gradual, and most wondrous, surprise.

2) Beaver was a staple of the Native diet here in North America for thousands upon thousands of years, as it is still in many regions of northern and western Canada (in Cree, my Native tongue, we call the animal, or dish, "amisk"). Hey, it's not our fault if the English language came along and "appropriated" the term so that it now means something else completely and something completely, some might even say, *inappropriate*. We *still* eat it. It's delish! Try it. You may just like it!

—Tomson Highway

By Steven W. Horn

Sam Dawson Mystery Series

THE PUMPKIN EATER

WHEN GOOD MEN DIE

WHEN THEY WERE YOUNG

Also by Steven W. Horn

ANOTHER MAN'S LIFE

WHEN THEY WERE YOUNG

A Sam Dawson Mystery

STEVEN W. HORN

GPP GRANITE
PEAK PRESS Cheyenne

Cheyenne, Wyoming
www.granitepeakpress.com

GRANITE
PEAK PRESS™

Granite Peak Press
www.granitepeakpress.com

This book is a work of fiction. Names, characters, businesses, places, organizations, events, and incidents either are the product of the author's imagination or are used fictitiously. Any resemblance to actual persons, living or dead, events, or locales is entirely coincidental.

First printing 2017

ISBN: 978-0-9991248-0-2
LCCN: 2017945531

ATTENTION CORPORATIONS, UNIVERSITIES, COLLEGES AND PROFESSIONAL ORGANIZATIONS: Quantity discounts are available on bulk purchases of this book for educational purposes. Special books or book excerpts can also be created to fit specific needs. For information, please contact Granite Peak Press, P.O. Box 2597, Cheyenne, WY 82003, or email: info@granitepeakpress.com.

Printed in the United States of America
10 9 8 7 6 5 4 3 2 1

For her

"Not everything can be categorized, compartmentalized, pasteurized, and homogenized into something that we can swallow."

~*Annie George*

CHAPTER ONE

GIRL

Her face was frozen to the icy ground. Her decomposing scalp had slipped forward in wrinkles above the dark sockets of her recessed eyes. Blonde hair, almost white, spilled over her pallid features as if she were hiding beneath it. His breath caught in the back of his throat. *Just a child,* he thought, *maybe ten or twelve years old.* Her body was curled into a tight fetal position, her wrists crossed under her chin, her knees touching her elbows. She had been cold.

Sam Dawson was cold too. He could taste the Wyoming air, sharp and metallic against the roof of his mouth. His nostrils flared against the sunless hollow, detecting the soft fragrance of pine, the pungent odor of decomposing aspen leaves, and the aroma of sage that drifted across the stream from the open meadows above. Tiny droplets of condensation formed under his nose as his breath escaped in foggy surges. He glanced at L2, who showed no interest in the corpse. Sam, not the dog, had found the girl. "You call yourself a bloodhound," he mumbled softly, without knowing why. There was no one to hear him. The waters of Crow Creek swallowed his words and murmured its own incoherent whispers, the confused gossip of the stream spirits.

Sam leaned his rod case against a snow-covered boulder and placed his wicker creel on the ground. Bending down, he gently pushed her hair from her face. A gray eye, opaque, stared blankly from the blackness of its shrunken socket, a cloudy window to a young soul long departed. Her lips were pulled toward the ground as if sucked down by a subterranean vacuum. Her formless face reminded him of a freshly dipped taffy apple placed on a hard surface to cool. She had not been dressed for a Wyoming winter—black jeans, white sneakers, and a burgundy windbreaker.

Her back was huddled against the cold north-facing slope that rose sharply above her. An embroidered patch appliqué lay upside down next to her. Sam picked it up. It was a gray capital M, with Minnie Mouse standing coyly against the left leg of the block letter. Minnie's red polka-dot bow and oversized yellow shoes added splashes of color. A few broken threads remained along the edges of the patch, and the dark outline of the missing letter was clearly visible against the slightly faded jacket. Tiny oblong pellets—rodent feces—littered the nylon folds of the windbreaker where it met the earth. He had seen several ground squirrels on his hike into the canyon. They scampered among the boulders and pine trees that lined the narrow valley floor. Like Sam, they were eager for spring and were busy assessing winter's toll. It appeared the jerky little rodents had removed the appliqué with surgical precision. Nothing else had been chewed.

Sam sighed. "All I wanted to do was go fishing," he whispered. He looked upstream, then downstream. There was no place more desirable, more rugged or remote within a hundred square miles. He imagined a black woolly bugger, with a flash of red and a gold bead, arcing gracefully over the stream and then back over his head as he placed the wet fly into the swirling eddy behind a boulder. *Why me? Why always me?* he thought. *What is it with me and dead people? I've been here too many times before to think it doesn't mean something.* It was 2008. Only four months had passed since his grisly discoveries in northern Minnesota the previous November. Still, none of it compared to the mess in Colorado more than eight years earlier. *That's why I live in Wyoming,* he reminded himself.

He was only thirty miles from Cheyenne and even fewer road miles from Laramie, as the crow flies. But it would take at least an hour to reach the nearest trail or road. *What were you doing way out here, Little Mouse Girl?* he thought, staring down at her frozen remains. She had been some mother's daughter, some father's little girl. Somewhere, someone missed her. He would have. He knew about little girls. He had raised one. Sidney had been about six when Sam and her mother divorced. Now she was midway through her second year of law school and had become the self-appointed, live-in guardian of her father, whom she viewed as a dangerously inept societal misfit.

Sam pulled the small flip phone from his fishing vest. Sidney had insisted that he take the intrusive little device even though cell service in the area was nonexistent. He held the phone at arm's length and slowly turned in a circle while watching for the little bars to light up next to the satellite dish icon. No bars appeared.

As usual, spring was coming slowly to the Laramie Mountains. Sunny days were separated by bitterly cold nights. Wind-packed snowdrifts streaked the north-facing slopes, while the south slopes portended new beginnings. It was late March, too early in the season for fishing. Sam knew there would be ice and snow. But it was spring break at the University of Wyoming, he'd had his fill of apathetic students, and he desperately wanted to go fishing. He suspected he was at a crossroads in his life, and brook trout would show him the way. Fishing was a diversion, an excuse to be alone, to think, to reconsider, to reconcile, and to change direction. He believed a midlife crisis involved choices, but he couldn't figure out what his were. Poverty had made his life simple. Now a dead girl in the forest was complicating it again.

Sam scanned the area. Dark clouds, almost navy blue, gathered in the west. The temperature was dropping. A huge old-growth ponderosa pine directly across the stream would serve as a landmark. Nearly four feet in diameter, it had escaped the logger's saw back in the 1880s, when the entire area was clear-cut for railroad ties to help push the Union Pacific west through southern Wyoming. The area, which had been too steep and rocky for draft horses to skid logs from, had also proved too rugged for a little girl, cold and lost. He pulled his pocket watch from his vest.

It would take him almost two hours to get to the nearest landline, his house phone. He looked at the dark western sky. It was going to snow. "Let's go," he said, slapping his leg for L2 to follow. He could not make himself look back at the lifeless body of the little girl frozen to the ground.

CHAPTER TWO

HOUSE

Leaning forward, Annie George pressed her nose and lips against the cool glass and exhaled slowly. Stepping back into the room, she watched the foggy smudge disappear. Blowing snow scoured the landscape in hushed confusion. The gray vanes of the windmill spun wildly in the fading light, its galvanized tail thrashing from south to east with each blast of wind. Gnarled cottonwoods, bare and dark, heaved restlessly, groaning silhouettes against the storm's bleakness. Night descended slowly in Horse Creek valley without form or shape, only a blending of earth and sky. Long, swirling waves of snow poured over the Laramie range and descended on the high plains. Annie missed the defined seasons of Iowa. There was no spring or fall in Wyoming, just nine months of winter, occasionally interrupted by a mild day or two that lulled unsuspecting outsiders into thinking the worst was over.

Sam was late. He had promised her a trout dinner. He and Sidney would bring everything; it was to be their housewarming gift. She and Sam had argued about the house. He had made his case for her to remain in the Cheyenne apartment where she had lived since moving to Wyoming a few months earlier. But she wanted to live in the country, and Wyoming had lots of country to choose from. It redefined rural. "The most sparsely populated state in the nation" was an understatement. She had not seen another human being since Sam and Sidney had helped her move in a week earlier. The old one-story ranch house was broken down, a weathered hull of its prewar utilitarian design, with wavy-glass windows and only one entry door. It was all she could afford.

Annie had placed most of her savings into a business account she had established for her new publishing enterprise, Cowboy Press. Sidney was the "big picture" woman, the idea person and marketer. Annie served as owner, editor, chief cook and bottle washer of the fledgling business. An eye for details was her forte. Above all, Annie believed in Sam's artistry. His photographs were more than pictures. They spoke volumes to the viewer— each image a story with a beginning, middle, and end.

But something besides his visual images caused a light feeling deep within her and a shortness of breath. She had made the mistake of a lifetime when she pushed him away eight years before. What had seemed insurmountable at the time, she now viewed as insignificant, considering all they had been through. She thought it funny how time and experience can change one's perspective. Still, there was the fact that Sam was a distant cousin. There was a degree of genetic relatedness that neither of them could take back. She would publish and market his work and help rebuild the career he believed he had lost. In the process, perhaps both of them would find what they were looking for. If it didn't work out, she could always go back to being an environmental microbiologist, or even a waitress again if she had to.

Annie stopped and stared at the cordless wall phone next to the refrigerator. The white plastic reflected dull yellow from the bug-spattered single bulb hanging in the center of the greasy ceiling. She gently picked up the receiver and placed it to her ear. The silence caused the hair on her arms to bristle. The lights flickered once and then went out. Outside, the storm raged.

CHAPTER THREE

BROGUES

The coroner wore black brogues, their wingtips shined to perfection. His tweed sport coat, white shirt, dark necktie, and dress slacks were as out of place as his black Cadillac Escalade parked in Sam's remote mountain driveway. Sam stared at the septuagenarian's shoes. He explained to him they had several miles of rough trail ahead of them that included deep drifts of snow. "What you see is what you get," the old man shouted above the wind as he stuffed a GPS unit into his trench coat pocket.

A nervous deputy sheriff, with all the adornments of his trade hanging from his torso, attempted to take charge by unfolding a topographic map on the wet hood of his truck. Tiny white missiles of sleet ricocheted noisily off the paper. "Sir," he barked at Sam. "Can you indicate on the map, as best you can, where you believe the alleged body of the deceased to be?" Sam stared at him for a long moment, his eyes narrowing, his anger rising. *This guy must have a brain the size of a peanut,* he thought.

Sam had already argued with the dispatcher, then some undersheriff about the location of the body. They had questioned whether it was indeed in Laramie County. He had given them the coordinates, including township and range—right down to the quarter section, as he read from his own topographic map spread over his kitchen table. They wanted it to be in Albany County, out of their jurisdiction. "It's about a hundred yards into Laramie County," Sam had insisted. "It's yours," he finally blurted out, annoyed by their attempt to pass the buck.

Sidney picked up on her father's irritation with the deputy sheriff. She raised her eyebrows and shook her head at him. "Be nice," she whispered as she pushed her thick glasses up the bridge of her nose. Her long dark hair encircled her face. Sam was momentarily caught off guard by her striking resemblance to her mother, Marcie.

Without speaking, Sam shone his flashlight on the deputy sheriff's map and deftly tapped his finger on the canyon. He noted the brown contour lines at forty-foot intervals blurred into a dark knot, as though someone had spilled spaghetti over the pale-green forested sections of the map. The thin blue line representing Crow Creek intersected it.

The coroner pulled out his GPS and started pushing buttons. He turned in a circle, holding the unit in front of him with an outstretched arm, squinting against the bursts of snow. Sam resisted making any comment about placing too much confidence in an electronic device. He preferred a simple compass and a map, no batteries required. Sidney had repeatedly cautioned him that his technophobia wasn't shared by the rest of humankind.

The county search and rescue team, who had pulled up the driveway in a boxy-looking emergency vehicle, strapped on body harnesses, backpacks, and assorted gear that were both noisy and heavy. Sam looked upward to determine how much light remained. An ever-darkening mass of storm clouds had gathered overhead. Flurries were in the process of giving way to a full-fledged storm. It would be dark in half an hour. "If you want out of there before midnight, we should leave now," he said to the deputy. His daughter stood in the doorway of the converted cow camp bunkhouse that now served as home. "Sidney," he said, "call Annie and ask her if she'll take a rain check for tonight's dinner. We're already too late and it's starting to snow. Besides, I didn't catch any fish. Keep L2 inside so she doesn't track us."

"I'll save you something to eat," Sidney called back. She pushed her hair away from her face and glanced at the blackened sky.

Without asking if everyone was ready, Sam pushed through the throng of dark-clad officers and disappeared into the forest. The white-haired old man in a trench coat followed obediently. He wore no hat.

CHAPTER FOUR

BARN

The open doorway of the barn appeared intermittently through the swirling haze. Like the house, the dilapidated structure was without electricity. From the mud porch window Annie tilted her head left, then right, squinting to make out what she imagined to be someone standing just inside the black rectangle of the entryway. She thought of the swampy darkness of the Wapsipinicon bottoms in eastern Iowa, where she had grown up. In fading light, a stump could easily transform into a bear or mythical beast that struck terror in her heart.

Annie knew her fear was irrational, that her mind was playing tricks on her, yet she was afraid to turn away. She continued to stare at the barn, turning her head ever so slightly, hoping her peripheral vision would add clarity. The figure appeared to be wrapped in a dark blanket that covered its shoulders and the back of its head. The specter seemed to fade around the edges, became fuzzy, shapeless, then disappeared completely into the whiteness of the storm. Annie opened her mouth and gasped as if she were drowning in a foggy ocean. It was almost dark, and the storm showed no sign of stopping.

••••

In the kitchen, Annie again lifted the telephone receiver and slowly brought it to her ear. Again, she heard nothing. She thought of her cell phone in her purse, but knew there would be no service, since her bargain provider had no towers in the area. She tried to take a deep breath, but her chest sputtered when she inhaled. The dark house overwhelmed her. She could not swallow. She remembered the old Eveready flashlight in the junk drawer and made her way across the sloping linoleum floor, her hands stretched in front of her like a blind person. She rummaged noisily through the tools, bottle openers, tape dispensers, and other household items that had no place of their own.

The ancient flashlight had belonged to Nana. Annie missed her. When she died, Annie's cousins and their children had descended upon Nana's modest belongings like a plague of locusts. People she barely recognized, with children she couldn't name, had acted like looters following a disaster. There was nothing left to hold Annie in eastern Iowa. She had jumped at the chance for a new beginning, to move westward, be a pioneer.

She pushed the switch forward on the flashlight, and a sick yellow funnel appeared momentarily before blinking out. She shook the metal cylinder, then pounded it against the palm of her hand. Still, there was no light. With her free hand she groped around the kitchen, trying to find the source of an abrupt drop in temperature. The skin on her arms tingled as the cold air enveloped her. She remembered her childhood swimming hole in the abandoned limestone quarry near Maquoketa, where frigid underground springs plumed unexpectedly into the green water, turning her lips blue and covering her young body with gooseflesh. This was even more startling, more chilling.

Suddenly she remembered the gray metal breaker panel on the mud porch. Stepping quietly from the kitchen, she felt the relative warmth of the normally cold entryway. She shook the flashlight furiously and again managed a slice of dusky light, which she pointed at the electrical panel in the corner of the room. Annie yanked open the door and ran her fingers down the unlabeled circuit breakers. All the switches pointed in the same direction. The problem was elsewhere.

Eerie noises from the fireplace flue signaled the storm's intensity beyond the house's dark interior. Flat, flute-like whistles, akin to a giant blowing across an equally large soda bottle, caused the hair on the back of her neck to bristle.

In the living room, Annie fumbled for sheets of newspaper, quickly wadded them up, and stuffed them into the freestanding fireplace, an inverted funnel of black sheet metal. She added kindling and struck a match to the tinder. Instantly the light reassured her. She sat cross-legged on the floor and stared at the flickering orange and yellow flames. She began to take solace from being sheltered while the wind raged outside. The fire was mesmerizing. Genetically encoded from a million years of staring into its enticing glow, she felt predestined to watch it.

A sleepy Annie was no match for the narcotic effects of wind and fire. She heard the whining protests of an old house under siege, the twisting of rafters, the creaking of floorboards. As her eyes began to close, she thought she saw muted reflections in the living room window of something moving across the doorway of her bedroom. She believed her imagination was the source of an oncoming headache, the pain throbbing in her right temple.

At midnight, she awoke to cold silence. The heart of the storm had passed. There was dead calm. Annie went to the mud porch to view the aftermath. A light snow was falling straight to the ground. Huge drifts of white powder lay between the house and barn in an undulating pattern, a blanket covering the bony backbone of a sleeping serpent. A shaft of yellow light spilled placidly from the open barn door.

CHAPTER FIVE

LIGHT

Take your seats, please," Sam said as he glanced at the clock over the classroom door. "Let's go, people. We've got a lot to cover today. We're talking about ambient light this morning." They didn't care. They didn't want to be there; neither did he. It was Monday morning after spring break, and they still had sex, booze, and fun on their minds. "Shelly, put your phone away, please."

"It's a camera, Mr. Dawson," the suntanned coed yawned.

"It's a darn poor excuse for one," Sam shot back. He could tell she wanted to respond that he was a darn poor excuse for a university professor too. This wasn't his idea of a career choice, and the students knew it. He was as temporary as their attention spans. It was another of Sidney's bright ideas. He would teach Introduction to Photography. It would just be for a semester, filling in for a professor who was on sabbatical in Paris, studying nude composition and how to create atmosphere for subtle eroticism. Sam needed a sabbatical too. Losing his publisher—plus most of the advance money on his last book—had put him in an income bracket below the poverty level. Book sales were flat. There was Sidney's law school tuition. Then, he'd used all of his savings to renovate the cow camp cabin into a home. He was forced to accept the university's offer. Now he was a temporary instructor, the bottom of the pecking order at the University of Wyoming. After taxes he made just enough to buy groceries and gas.

"Natural light, available light, domestic light, found light, environmental light are all synonyms for ambient light," Sam began. "Ambient light is real light. If used correctly, it has the potential to create the type of realistic atmosphere that the viewer can identify with. Plus, it allows you to work more freely and be less obtrusive. Lamps, reflectors, flashes, lens flares, diffusers all have their uses, as we have learned, but they take time and money, and they get in the way."

"Mr. Dawson."

"Yes, Brittany?"

"Is this lecture posted on the Web?"

Sam turned to her in disbelief. He had answered the same question at least once a week since the beginning of the semester. "No, you'll actually have to take notes. Which, I might add, requires the use of a writing instrument and paper," he said, noting that she had neither in front of her. She stared at him blankly. He had watched her as she entered the classroom carrying nothing but her smartphone. She had on a pink hoodie and matching sweatpants with the word "Juicy" in bold, black letters across her backside. Her pale blonde hair poking out in all directions was as flamboyant as her attitude. Suddenly,

Sam saw her face pulled grotesquely to the frozen ground, her hair spilling over recessed eyes. She said something.

"Excuse me?" he said, yanking his mind back to the classroom.

"Will any of this be on the final?"

Ah, the final, Sam smiled to himself. That seemed to be the only thing most of them cared about—what's on the test. "Tell me, Brittany, what color is your ensemble in the absence of light?"

"What?"

"What color is your outfit in the dark?"

"Pink. It'd still be pink, I guess."

"Well, that would be the wrong guess," Sam said, raising his eyebrows. "It would be black. In the absence of light, everything is black. There is no color. Your outfit appears pink because of the way in which light is bent and reflected back to your eyes. It's all an illusion, Brittany. Photography is, in a way, an illusion too. It's about the use of light. There's nothing more basic to this art form than light. Whether it comes through a pinhole in a black box or through a thousand-dollar lens, it's light that creates the image."

Her expression was somewhere between total indifference and contempt. Her lips were pulled downward on one side of her mouth. *Like she's mocking the effects of death and gravity on the face of the dead girl,* Sam thought.

"Yes, you can expect several questions about light on the final exam. Better take notes, even if you have a photographic memory. If you can't see it, you can't recall it." Sam turned quickly toward the whiteboard and wrote "blue green." "The human retina is most sensitive to wavelengths between five- and six-hundred millimicrons, the blue-green portion of our visible spectrum. Which receptors in the retina are responsible for color vision?" He turned toward the class, pointing his marker at them, inviting their response. There was total silence. "Anybody?" He waited. "Don't be shy." He waited some more. "Nobody? Does anyone remember the lecture on sensory perception?" Again, nothing. "All right, listen up, *coneheads*," he said, putting particular stress on the last word. "You want to know what's on the final? There will be a question concerning retinal physiology."

"So, what's the answer?" Brittany asked with a wide grin on her face.

Sam's earlier lecture on cones and rods had obviously fallen on deaf ears. He stepped to the lectern, tore a sheet of paper from his notebook, and pulled a ballpoint pen from his pocket. Dodging the tangle of backpacks on the floor, he made his way to Brittany and placed the paper and pen on her desk. "I just told you," he said, smiling.

CHAPTER SIX

MIRANDA

Prairie winds moved the chest-high native grasses in rolling waves across the deserted landscape. The seed heads of big bluestem and switchgrass swayed hypnotically. The Plains Indians believed the Nebraska Sandhills to be the most sacred of all places in their limited world. It was their heaven, where the spirit lived after the body died.

It was July 1985. Mel McDaniel crooned, "Lord have mercy, baby's got her blue jeans on," from the open doors of the bronze Ford pickup. Grass, wind, water, and sky swallowed the music, sucking it from the air, injecting it into the sand and rich loam of the dunes. A short wooden windmill rhythmically pumped sparkling cold water from the birthplace of the Ogallala Aquifer.

Miranda Hofstadter, wearing a short jean skirt and cowboy boots, danced awkwardly next to the round stock water tank. She was tiny for a fourteen-year-old, her growth stunted by the hundreds of gin-and-tonics her mother had drunk during her pregnancy. Miranda's head was small relative to her body. Her eyes were small too, almost Asian in appearance. Her thin upper lip seemed broad and flat, due to the absence of a groove beneath her nose. Red barrettes, one on each side of her head, kept her light-brown hair pulled back.

"Go, girl," the young cowboy yelled as he hoisted his Coors can into the air. The other three teenage boys raised theirs too, joining in the toast.

"Hey, Miranda, you gettin' hot? Wanna go skinny-dipping?" said the tall boy with the huge belt buckle.

The others shouted their approval from the tailgates of their trucks.

"She dances like she's got a bad case of the dry heaves," the stocky kid said, then spat between his worn-out boots, feet dangling carelessly.

"She don't say much, does she?" the lanky seventeen-year-old in the black pickup said, pushing back his straw hat.

"I don't reckon she can talk. I ain't never heard her say a word," the boy with worn-out boots said.

"She can talk. She mumbles like she's got a mouth full of rocks," the first cowboy said. "She's got a weird lisp. Sounds like Sylvester the Cat."

"Hell, that's what *you* sound like after a couple of beers," said the boy in the black pickup. "Maybe the two of you are related."

"We didn't bring her out here to have a conversation with her, for Christ's sake," the tall boy with the huge belt buckle complained. He pulled a small camera from his shirt pocket. "We brung her here to see her dance naked."

They all whooped and hollered and gave another beer salute.

The lanky cowboy in the black pickup jumped down from his truck, carefully placed his beer can on the tailgate, removed his hat, and yanked his T-shirt off over his head. "Hey, Miranda, let's everybody take off our shirts," he said, with a sweep of his hand to signal the others.

The cowboys eagerly complied, scrambling out of their trucks and pulling off their shirts. Miranda smiled guilelessly as she unbuttoned her sleeveless blouse.

"KAAQ, Double Q Country news at the top of the hour" blared from the bronze pickup. "Vice President Bush met today with New Hampshire teacher Christa McAuliffe, who will become the first schoolteacher to ride aboard the space shuttle *Challenger*..."

The wind suddenly changed direction. The Sandhills grass pulsed in agitated rhythm, trapped in the wash of wind currents that pressed them into a thick, writhing mass. The windmill's vane screeched against its springs. From below, Miranda cried out.

"In other news, the Alliance City Council heard arguments last night concerning the placement of trash containers..."

The windmill's blades spun in a maddening cadence. Erratic crosswinds jolted the vane left, then right. Moving metal parts screeched as if in tormenting pain. Water, the essence of life, ejected from the discharge tube.

"And on a lighter note, *Back to the Future* opens at the Rialto Theater with showtimes at..."

Miranda's screams signaled protest and suffering.

CHAPTER SEVEN

THERAPY

Animal behavior therapy demands an understanding of the underlying mechanisms and the adaptive significance of behavior. There are physiological, genetic, developmental, evolutionary, and environmental components that must be considered before therapeutic applications can be made." Dr. Tom Stevens paced confidently across the front of the small classroom at the Cheyenne Animal Shelter. He wore blue jeans, a white dress shirt open at the neck, and a tan corduroy sport coat—a tall academic type with a Tom Cruise smile and Robert Redford hair. His athletic build and tan belied his authoritarian demeanor.

Annie looked across the aisle. Sidney, resting her chin in her palm, pushed her glasses up the bridge of her nose, then shot a glance at Stevens, flicked her eyebrows, and smiled. Annie pursed her lips, widened her eyes, and nodded her agreement ever so slightly. Dr. Stevens was handsome.

"Many of the problem behaviors exhibited by companion animals are psychogenic in origin. These problems are unnecessary in that they are preventable and treatable, using behavior modification techniques. Most often, the cause of an unwanted behavior cannot be established solely with the pet or with its owners, but with the complex pet-owner relationship itself." He looked out over the sparse turnout of mostly women. It was the usual smattering of animal control officers, shelter and humane organization workers, vet techs, breed club members, and housewives who attended his free seminars. Occasionally, a skeptical veterinarian, seeking continuing education credits, would sit through his presentation. He would usually get a couple of referrals, which would more than pay for his time.

"Behavioral therapy involves finding out what the problem is, why it is occurring, and what can be done to solve it. Successful treatment is dependent upon five sequential stages." He held up a thumb. "First, determining the needs of the client." His index finger popped up. "Second, accurate diagnosis; third, developing a treatment program; fourth, the actual treatment application; and fifth,"—all five fingers were now raised—"post-treatment follow-up. We'll talk about each of these stages in detail."

Annie guessed he was younger than Sam by a few years. She would be thirty-six on her next birthday. She thought it funny that—somewhere between forty and fifty—people all become about the same age. She believed Sam was truly in his prime at forty-five, although sometimes he acted older than his years. Lately, he had no patience with her; he seemed preoccupied. Even before finding the dead girl, he had been acting so strangely that she wondered if he was having some sort of career-related midlife crisis. When she complained of being spooked by uneasy happenings in her house, he responded by dropping off L2, a dog bed, and fifty pounds of dog food. On his way out the door, he turned and said, "She has a tendency to chew things. You might watch her a bit." His proclamation turned out to be an understatement.

The dog had started with Annie's personal things— shoes, underwear, a purse—but had now upped the ante to include furniture. The final straw was when L2 ate the arm off the couch. Sam seemed unconcerned and simply said, "Better your stuff than mine." Sidney, however, was her usual compassionate self and offered to help. It was she who had recommended they attend the seminar on animal behavior therapy, advertised in her student newspaper.

With each new question, Dr. Stevens would look at his watch. It was apparent he was having difficulty finishing his prepared remarks. He beamed a smile and was extremely polite with each person who interrupted him. "No, no, it wouldn't do any good to bring the dog to me. With a treatment plan, you have to realize that a pet and its behavior problem do not exist in isolation from its environment. That includes all members of the family— both human and animal—in which the pet resides." Sidney looked over the top of her glasses at Annie, then rolled her eyes. They both knew what Sam's response would be to participating in an in-home therapy program for his bloodhound.

"Look—" Dr. Stevens smiled, but was clearly frustrated by an older woman who continued to monopolize the questions. He started again. "Most problem behaviors are stress-related from either environmental or owner-induced causes. I can only assist the owners in identifying the areas which should be adjusted and then give them the necessary tools, techniques, knowledge, and motivation. Again, the bottom line is that you, not me, have to do the therapy, and it has to be done where the animal lives."

Annie eyed the clock on the wall and wondered if L2 had broken through the baby gate that confined her to the mud porch and was now laying waste to the interior of the house.

"The four big problems I see with dogs are"—he was using his fingers again—"dog-human aggression, house soiling, destructiveness, and barking. About a third of the time the problem behaviors fall into the 'other' category, and these include everything from fear of thunder to eating poop. I once had a client where we identified seven major behavioral issues they wanted corrected."

"And?" a masculine-looking woman in the front row asked.

"We were able to correct all of them. It took a few months and a lot of work on the part of the owner, but I'm happy to report—"

"Do you ever see animals you can't fix?" someone in the back of the room asked.

"Yes and no. I can usually modify the behavior of the animal; it's the owner's behavior, relative to the animal, that is often most challenging. I should add that I've sometimes refused to even develop a treatment plan—when I believed the animal posed a threat to the owners or others. There's not a dog alive that's worth the life or disfigurement of a child. A client once threatened to sue me after I recommended they get rid of their Great Dane, who had repeatedly picked up their infant daughter by the head and taken her from the house into the backyard. Multiple cranial punctures failed to convince the child's parents that the dog should be removed." The audience recoiled. He had their attention. "An eighty-four-year-old woman, who had been sent to the hospital eight times by her one-year-old golden retriever, still refused to get rid of the dog. When I declined to work with her, she threatened legal action. The bond between people and their pets is—"

More hands shot upward and people began shouting out their questions. Tom Stevens looked at his watch again, thanked the group for their attention, gifted them a farewell smile, and announced that there were refreshments in the back of the room. The audience applauded politely, then surrounded him like a pack of hungry wolves.

Annie made a mad dash to the food table. "What do you think?" she said, her mouth full of oatmeal raisin cookie.

Sidney studied her for a moment. "I think you're in heat."

Annie furrowed her brow and sipped her coffee. "What did you say? I like his teeth?" She grinned. "Get his card."

CHAPTER EIGHT

LILLY

Same-day news was hard to come by in the remote parts of Laramie County. Newspapers had to be mailed and would often show up all at once, three or four days' worth stuffed in Sam's mailbox a mere three miles from his house. He faithfully sifted through them as they arrived. The *Wyoming Tribune Eagle* reported that a body had been found by a fisherman west of Cheyenne. The *Laramie Boomerang* identified the fisherman as Sam Dawson and incorrectly assigned him the title of professor at the University of Wyoming. Few other details were given. There was nothing about an investigation, or even an autopsy. There was nothing about the dream Sam had where the Little Mouse Girl's eyes suddenly sprang open, her distorted face still frozen to the ground. Nothing about his wrenching fear of finding another body each time he went into the forest. It had taken him years to recover from the revelations in Colorado. Then his discoveries in Minnesota last fall had renewed the feeling that something was wrong with him. He dreaded that, someday, he would gaze into a mirror and see the faceless messenger of death, complete with a black, hooded robe and scythe.

"Why don't you call the sheriff?" Sidney said as she smoothed peanut butter over her morning toast. "It's been almost two weeks. Surely they know something by now."

"Maybe I'll stop in and see him. I have to go to Cheyenne today and pick up some rat traps. I think Annie's got pack rats in her house."

"That's not what she told me. She said the place is haunted. She was pretty upset."

Sam ignored her. "I need to check on L2 when I drop off the traps. I kind of miss that stink hound."

Sidney slowly screwed the lid back on the plastic jar as if it were a delicate piece of antique china. Her hair was pulled back in a ponytail with a fluffy, red holder. Her hearing aids were clearly visible behind her ears. "Dad, you do know that L2 has some behavioral issues, don't you?" she said, turning around to face him.

"Nonsense." Sam changed the subject. "Says here the pine beetle epidemic may continue for several more years."

"She's a destructive chewer who's ruined a lot of expensive stuff."

Sam lowered the newspaper and looked at his daughter. "She's a dog, Sid. They chew. I don't think it goes much deeper than that."

"Annie and I went to this seminar and met this therapist guy who agreed to meet with us to see if L2—"

"A therapist?"

"Yeah, he's really good at—"

"A dog whisperer?"

"Sort of. He's a—"

"A shrink for dogs?"

"Yes, but—"

"No way." Sam lifted the newspaper and snapped it open.

Sidney could barely see the top of his head shaking with disbelief. "He said it's really important that all family members participate in the diagnosis and treatment phases of the behavior modification program."

Sam lowered the paper. "And how much does this glorified obedience trainer charge?"

"Annie said she'd pay."

"How much?"

"A hundred and fifty an hour. He said it would take a couple of hours to—"

"When pigs fly."

"He'll be here tomorrow night."

••••

Sam discovered that one did not just walk into the Laramie County Sheriff's Office to speak with the sheriff. Thick, bulletproof glass partitions and electronically controlled doors separated the public from their elected official. Skeptical staff treated Sam as if he were covered in cooties. With his ears ready to ignite from anger, he left.

The coroner's office was less than a block away. An attractive woman with a true western accent greeted him with a smile. She listened attentively, nodding her head and jotting down notes. Her eyes sparkled when she leaned over her desk and confided, "You know, hon, everything you've asked for is confidential, 'less of course you're related to the deceased. Are you...related?" She winked and held back a smile.

"You wouldn't believe how many people I'm related to."

"Well, why didn't you say so, hon? That poor young thing left the morgue yesterday, headed for Loveland. We finally got a positive ID on her. She's that sweet little girl that came up missin' in Fort Collins back in December. Surely you heard all the fuss? Her name was Lilly, Lilly Darnell."

"Cause of death?"

"Oh, hon, we won't know until we get the autopsy report from the pathologist. And you know those buggers south of the border with their green license plates. Those greenies wouldn't hurry if their hair was on fire. They'll be doin' everything down there in Colorado."

Sam thanked her and turned to leave. At the door he stopped and said, "Please give the coroner my regards."

"Oh, I think not, hon," she smiled broadly. "You have a wonderful day."

Out in the parking lot, Sam stopped to take a breath and look up. Dark clouds were building over the Laramie range as a reminder the weather could turn at any moment. "Schizophrenic" was how Sam described it. Having lulled you into believing spring had arrived, the Wyoming winter would rebound with a savage intent. He saw Lilly Darnell curled and frozen. The Little Mouse Girl had a name.

CHAPTER NINE

BABY

The oily smell of kerosene mixed with the stench of manure and the scent of hay. The barn kept out the last gasps of winter on the other side of its thin gray boards. Annie lit the lantern that hung from a beam just inside the door. Pounding gusts of wind seeped through the cracks, filling the air with circulating dust particles that shone in the yellow light. She could see her breath.

"Baby," a voice from somewhere deep in the barn seemed to whisper. The hair on her arms and on the back of her neck bristled. Her heart pounded in her chest, and her neck throbbed. A tightening knot seized her stomach, and her legs went weak. She stood motionless, straining to hear against the relentless wind. "Hello?" she managed as she held the lantern above her head. "Is anyone there?"

Annie slowly made her way past worn wooden stanchions that had once held cows for milking, cobwebs tickling her eyelashes and nose. She swept the air in front of her as she went. A strong gust of wind hit the roof, and the entire building seemed to recoil. She stumbled over an empty pint liquor bottle and caught herself on a post, against which were piled several bales of straw. A rusty pitchfork leaned against the dust-covered bales.

The doll lay naked on the floor behind the roughly stacked bales. Its baby face with unmoving amber eyes was cracked in a thousand places; tiny brown lines cloaked its features and bald head with a web of geometric designs. The poorly defined fingers and toes had long ago been reduced to nubs. The moveable porcelain arms and legs were chipped and splintered. Annie's hand shook, and the lantern's glow danced nervously over the doll's face. She gasped as if suddenly remembering to breathe. "Jeez O'Pete," she whispered.

She deliberately circled the straw bales, her eyes straining for light. The stench of human urine and excrement nearly overpowered her as she stepped farther into the darkness. She covered her mouth and nose with her hand in an attempt to subdue the sickening odor.

The door slammed shut with the heavy thump of wood on wood and the jingle of hardware. Annie spun around; the lantern tipped sideways and went out. The wind seemed to cry between the sheets of corrugated roofing, hum among the lifeless cottonwoods, and whistle through the cracks of weathered boards. From the darkness behind her it whispered, "Baby."

CHAPTER TEN

SECRET

Merle Haggard's voice flowed easily from the car's speakers, looking for "A Place to Fall Apart" on a summer morning in 1985. June Hofstadter sang along in an attempt to stay awake. She drove a giant, faded yellow Oldsmobile with a torn black vinyl top. The bug-spattered hood had turned crimson, reflecting the eastern sky; an unnamed lake next to the highway emerged from the darkness as blood-red. The Sandhills loomed in endless shadow. Kangaroo rats dashed into the illuminated path of the car, their disproportionately long tails curving after them. They would turn and dart back before the tires could crush them against the pavement. Deer mice took their chances scurrying toward the far side of the road.

June sucked the last drops of beer from the bottle she had held between her legs, rolled down the window, and flung the empty over the roof of the car into the borrow ditch. There was no place open for miles, nothing to quench her thirst. But she would be home in half an hour. She would make the kids a nice breakfast before they left for school. She lit another cigarette.

••••

"D-don't you tell Mom, okay?" Raymond Hofstadter said to his sister, Miranda. He smelled the milk before pouring it on her Rice Krispies. "She'll have a conniption fit and blab it all over the c-county, and there ain't a thing anybody's g-gonna do about it anyway. Slim's uncle is the sheriff, for c-crying out loud. I'll graduate next year and then we can move away. Are you sure you're all right?"

"Thor," Miranda lisped with a mouthful of cereal.

"I'm sure you're sore, baby girl. But remember, you c-can't tell anybody what happened. Those g-guys will stick together and deny it. And they're mean as snakes. They'll c-come after us, just like they told you. So, not a word to anyone, okay? Especially not to the social worker or your special ed teacher. No one, understand? You want cheese on your baloney sandwich?"

"Yeth."

Raymond made her lunch, as he did every morning. Even when his mother was home, she rarely got up before noon. This time of the month she had money for gas and would run up tabs as far away as Alliance or North Platte. Sometimes she would disappear for two or three days. When the welfare check had been spent, she would make her way home.

"It will be our secret, just you and me. Nobody else, okay?" he said, turning to face his little sister. "You c-comb your hair before the bus g-gets here."

"What about Grandma?"

"She's dead, sweet pea."

"What about Baby?"

Raymond glanced at the ever-present doll that had its own chair at the table. It had been their grandmother's doll when she was a little girl during the Depression. "Only if Baby c-crosses her heart and promises to k-keep our secret. Now finish your cereal and go brush your teeth. The bus will be here any minute."

Miranda picked up her bowl with both hands and drank the remaining milk before grabbing Baby and running to the other end of the trailer. Raymond yelled after her, "And remember, not a word. It's our s-secret, just you and me." The scarlet sunrise out the kitchen window filled his eyes with tears.

CHAPTER ELEVEN

DOMINANCE

You need to establish a clearly defined dominant-subordinate relationship with L2. A dog that understands who it is, relative to the other members of the social unit, is a happy dog. Destructive chewing can result from a host of owner-caused oral behaviors and other stress factors, causing frustration and a need to relieve tension in orally oriented dogs." Dr. Stevens flipped back through the lengthy questionnaire and counted the number of check marks next to categories that meant nothing to Sam. To him they were just nonsense words that the doctor sprinkled into his convoluted conversation regarding a certain bloodhound that had pulled the stuffing out of her dog bed.

Sam leaned back in his aspen log chair. "So let me get this straight," he said, finally taking an interest in the so-called consultation session.

"Dad," Sidney cautioned.

Sam held up his hand to silence her. "None of this is the dog's fault? It's my fault? I've turned her into this biological shredder by creating stress in her life?"

"Sam," Annie interrupted, "hear the man out."

Sam shot her a wounded look. He wanted to shout, "Of course you would take his side. You've been drooling over this guy since he walked through my door."

"I'm sorry if I've given you that impression, Sam," Dr. Stevens said, smiling broadly.

Sam was sure he saw a glint of light bounce off Dr. Stevens' incisor. *Christ, could this guy be any more handsome?* Sam's eyes darted to Annie, then back to Dr. Stevens.

"Let's not worry about assigning blame. Just realize that the genesis of most psychogenic behavior problems is interactional."

"What?" Sam said, grimacing.

Dr. Stevens' perfect teeth were annoyingly bright, and there seemed to be more of them than most humans possess. "Sam, the basis of L2's problem doesn't lie solely with her. Neither does it lie solely with you or the other members of this triad," he said, indicating Sidney and Annie. "It's embedded in the relationship you all have with the dog. We can talk all night about what's caused her unwanted behaviors, but I think what you are most interested in is remediation. How do we reduce or eliminate her destructive chewing?" He paused. "I can't communicate very effectively with your dog, but I can communicate with you. It's a heck of a lot easier for me to modify your behavior than it is to modify hers."

Sam's eyes narrowed. He wanted to tell this upstart just who he was dealing with. Sam had written the book on communications, with a degree in journalism and many years' experience as a press secretary. *You're going to lecture me about communication? You're going to modify my behavior?* he thought.

"So," Sidney said, a little too loudly, seeing that her father was about to blow. "What can we do to solve this?" She shot a pleading look at Annie, raised her eyebrows, and pursed her lips.

Dr. Stevens had noticed how distracted Annie seemed. "Sidney's right, Annie," he said, smiling even more broadly. "In canine language, Sidney's small mouth pucker and direct wide-eye contact are a threat. She's saying you've got to get your head in the game."

"Maybe she's watching the meter go 'round," Sam said, looking at his watch and noting that they were approaching the three-hundred-dollar mark.

"Dad, knock it off," Sidney admonished.

Dr. Stevens' smile was momentarily replaced by a steely-eyed glance at Sam. Quickly regaining his composure, he assumed a gently serious tone. "Sam, like it or not, L2 perceives you as the alpha male in this pack. You've got to commit to the therapy program for this to work. You don't have to understand it or like it, but you must do your part. Otherwise you'll end up undoing the work of Sidney and Annie, and increasing the stress that L2 is attempting to relieve by chewing. And by the way, I own all of your books."

Sam raised an eyebrow.

"I've bought them over the years at full retail price, enjoyed them immensely, and never regretted my investment."

"Oh? Which is your favorite?" Sam challenged.

"I like them all," said Dr. Stevens.

A smirk started to form on Sam's lips.

"But I'd have to say *Colorado Graveyards* is your most evocative," he added.

Sam looked at Dr. Stevens and grinned. "I knew I liked you. Count me in."

"Great. Let's begin," Dr. Stevens said, scooting to the edge of his chair.

Annie was massaging her temples and seemed miles away.

"Annie?" Dr. Stevens spoke loudly.

"Excuse me?" Annie said.

"You ready?"

She forced a smile. "Fire away."

"All right, I'll give you some things to start on immediately. I'll write up a detailed plan of attack and send it to you tomorrow. Remember, the key is consistency and repetition. Sam," he said suddenly, "take a look at L2's forehead. What do you see?"

"Ah, I don't know. Nothing."

"You're absolutely right. She doesn't have a forehead. Keep that in mind. She's got dog brains. Try to think of her as the proverbial black box that experimental psychologists talk about, just stimuli coming in and responses going out. It's really hard not to assign human characteristics to her behaviors, but forget the anthropomorphisms. She's a black box. Consistency, repetition, and communication at her level will make this go much faster. We're going to find the cause, correct it, and reorient the chewing objective."

"Should I take notes?" Annie said, raising her hand.

"No, for now just listen. I'll give all this back to you in writing with much more detail. It will be your instruction manual, and we'll fine-tune it as we go along. First," he said with an upraised finger, "this dog is overly dependent on each of you for social gratification. We've got to reduce her level of dependency and establish a more uniform dominant-subordinate relationship between you and the dog. Until this problem clears up, you must avoid all fondling, coddling, and other solicitous behaviors directed toward her. Instead, you should work on the basic obedience commands of come, sit, down, and stay."

"Obedience? Is that what this is all about?" Sam complained.

Stevens' eyes went blank, but he managed a smile. "I could care less whether your dog is obedient or not, Sam. But simple commands are a good way for you to impose your will on her. It's dominance assertion with the added benefit of obedience. These sessions should be held no fewer than two and no more than…"

Sam noted how quiet Annie was. As he studied her, she looked up and caught him, then quickly averted her eyes.

Dr. Stevens continued his painfully detailed instructions on how to teach L2. "She already knows this stuff," Sam interrupted.

"Don't care, Sam," Dr. Stevens said without missing a beat. "Remember, it's not about obedience. It's about imposing our will and reinforcing the leader-follower relationship." His pedantic manner annoyed Sam, who stifled a yawn. "This type of therapy has the effect of demonstrating to the dog that you, not she, are in charge. Therefore, she need not worry about her environment. Hello—Annie?" he said, waving his hand to get her attention. "Are you all right?"

"Yes, sorry. Just a little headache," she said, straightening in her chair. "Got it. I'm in charge."

"Right. And all this needs to be done at your place too. L2's destructiveness appears more intense there than here, leading me to believe that either she is more stressed at your house, or she has assumed a dominant rank when she's alone with you—or perhaps both."

"Uh-huh," Annie said, staring through him.

Sam contemplated the perfect outline of her face and suddenly felt uncomfortable.

"Maybe, if we weren't so cheap," Sidney said, glancing at her dad, "we could buy her some more toys, something to occupy her when we're not around."

"No, just the opposite, Sidney," Stevens said, his focus still on Annie. "You should remove all the dog's toys and other chewable things and introduce a meat-scented nylon bone. Make this bone the focus of fetch and play sessions at least twice a day for six weeks...." Dr. Stevens turned his attention toward Sidney as he elaborated in great detail about something called "counterconditioning."

Sidney took note of the confusion on Annie's face and the irritation on her father's. "L2 really likes to chew Annie's couch," she suddenly interrupted.

"Tell you what, Annie, what's your address? I'll drop by your place and give you a brief lesson on conditioned avoidance. We can quickly teach L2 to stay away from the couch. The process is pretty simple and painless—"

"If it's so simple, why can't we just teach her to avoid *all* the things she chews?" Sam said, exasperated.

Dr. Stevens raised his voice and spun around toward Sam. "Because it doesn't relieve the underlying cause of her destructive behavior—stress. She'll just go past the couch and move on to the recliner. Plus, the avoidance breaks down in time, and then we would have to pair new unconditioned stimuli with the conditioned stimuli and—" he paused, smoothed his hair, and recovered his smile. "Trust me, it gets complicated."

"I'm not buying it," Sam said, shaking his head. "What stress are we causing? Hell, she only chews things up when we're gone. She's been like this for over eight years."

"Exactly!" Dr. Stevens almost yelled. "It's classic separation anxiety. This dog is so dependent upon you for social fulfillment that when it's denied she becomes almost panic-stricken. Think of it like a drug addiction. When you withhold the drug—in this case, attention— she begins to suffer from withdrawal. Dogs are already incredibly oral creatures. She can't light a cigarette or pour herself a stiff drink to relieve the anxiety. She does what's natural—she chews."

Sam looked at his watch again and slumped forward in his chair as a signal that the meeting was over. "What's your prognosis, Doctor?"

"We'll have an impact on her. L2 is considerably older than the average dog I see, so it might take a little longer. Also, the lack of stability in her environment is problematic. But we can get started, while you folks decide where she's going to live. Destructiveness represents about fifteen percent of my caseload, and the efficacy of my treatment program is very high. Again, success is most dependent on how dedicated and consistent you are in implementing the therapy. That's why I do follow-up. I'll call in a few days to answer any questions you may have. I'll even come back, if necessary. You might want to appoint a contact person who will serve as the liaison between me and the other two members of your group."

"I nominate Annie," Sidney said a little too quickly, her arm raised to reinforce her motion. "Since you're already going to her house," she offered weakly.

Annie looked at Sam, then at Dr. Stevens, and finally said, "I'll call you to arrange a time, Doctor Stevens."

"Fine," Stevens said, pulling an invoice from his notebook and checking the time. He scribbled his tally on the bill, tore off the white copy, and held it up. "Who gets this?"

Again, silence.

"Miss Liaison." Sam nodded toward Annie.

"We'll split it," Sidney offered.

Standing and awkwardly stepping over L2, who lay in a puddle of flesh next to his chair, Dr. Stevens looked squarely at Sam. "Consistency," he said with an emphatic stare.

Obsessive-compulsive control freak, Sam thought. He gave a half-smile and a polite nod.

CHAPTER TWELVE

OSCAR

Annie stood in front of the curtainless bathroom window, a towel wrapped around her. Her hot soak had felt soothing, but now her body burned and itched. The Wyoming winter had robbed her skin of moisture. She slowly rubbed lotion across her shoulders and down her arms, working it into her elbows, then stared at her reflection in the steamy mirror. A few months ago she would have assessed her image and concluded, "Not bad for a woman almost thirty-six years old." But time and worry have a way of eroding youthful things.

Annie put on her robe and tiptoed across the cold kitchen floor toward the mud porch to check on L2, then froze in her tracks. Oscar Roberts was glaring menacingly through the large glass window in the door. It afforded an unobstructed view across the kitchen and into the bathroom, where Annie had stood only a moment before.

Roberts was a large man in his early-to-mid-sixties. His greasy hair hung over his ears, pushed outward by his snug-fitting cowboy hat. His pocked face and small eyes made her apprehensive; the pistol he wore on his hip frightened her. She collected herself and pushed open the door.

"Mr. Roberts—what a surprise. I didn't hear you knock. Have you been waiting long?"

"Long enough," he said, glaring at her.

Annie clutched the neck of her robe and seemed at a loss for words. "Uh, would you like to come in?" It seemed awkward to invite her landlord into his own house. She had met him only once, accidentally, when she delivered her signed lease to his attorney's office in Cheyenne. Roberts was one of the largest landowners in the county. He was also secretive, with a reputation for violence, a hatred of trespassers, and a permanent scowl. Everyone she had mentioned his name to would suddenly change the subject.

"No pets," he growled.

"Excuse me?" she said, tilting her head. The wind gusted through the doorway and threatened to open her robe.

"No pets. No livestock. It was in the lease."

"I'm not sure I understand."

L2's toenails clicked across the linoleum floor of the mud porch, her thick tail waving behind her. She padded up to Roberts and poked him in the crotch. In response, he kneed her roughly in the snout. The dog scrambled backward and stood with a surprised bloodhound look on her face.

"Hey!" Annie objected, drawing L2 to her side. "There's no need to hurt her."

"This is a working cattle ranch. I won't tolerate a dog running my stock."

"She's harmless. Besides, she's not even my dog. I'm just keeping her for—"

"I see her, I shoot her. It's as simple as that. Am I clear?"

"She doesn't chase—"

"Clear?" he repeated loudly. He touched the brim of his hat, turned abruptly, and marched toward his pickup.

"It's just that I'm here alone and—" Annie's voice trailed after him. She was beginning to appreciate having L2 around.

Annie stood in the open doorway, leaning against the jamb, her arms folded across her chest. She watched Roberts' truck bounce slowly over the hill and disappear. Cold air tousled her hair, rushed over her bare feet, and entered the house. Behind her, high in a corner of the living room, a large orb spider crawled silently toward the center of its web, reacting to vibrations created by the breeze. In the north bedroom, a yellowed and brittle strip of wallpaper curled upward above the west window. The wind gave a sigh. Annie stared at the barn.

CHAPTER THIRTEEN

UNDETERMINED

What do you mean, 'undetermined'?" Sam said, gazing out his office window. It was noon, and the students moved like a swarm of ants across Prexy's Pasture toward the student union.

Sidney pulled sandwiches, chips, string cheese, and fruit from her backpack. "Banana or orange?" she asked, holding up one in each hand.

"Orange," he said. "I'm confused. I thought the medical examiner ruled the cause of death as hypothermia—and now you're telling me they don't know?"

"Apparently they found traces of ketamine in her system," Sidney mumbled, holding her hand over her mouth full of sandwich.

"Didn't I teach you not to talk with your mouth full?"

Sidney rolled her eyes and nudged her heavy glasses back up.

"Ketamine?" Sam said. "Never heard of it. What's it used for?"

"It's used mostly by veterinarians as an anesthetic. It's also one of the date rape drugs, like roofies. It causes memory loss."

Sam turned to face his daughter. "Was she molested?"

"According to my source, no."

"So, what was the cause of death?"

"Apparently, the medical examiner had insufficient evidence to determine the cause and manner of death. The sheriff wants to know if it's a homicide. But it seems pretty clear to me that it's a wrongful death at the hands of another. I mean, how did a twelve-year-old get from Fort Collins to the Medicine Bow National Forest in Wyoming? And why would she have ketamine in her system? Something's rotten in Denmark."

Sam smiled at his daughter. "That's my girl. Indict the Danes. What's next?"

"The coroner has asked the forensic pathology staff at the Miami-Dade Medical Examiner Department to review the autopsy findings. They're recognized as the best in the country for determining children's deaths. Tapioca?" she asked, holding up a plastic cup.

He frowned. "Do you have peaches?"

"Nope. When you pack the lunches on Friday, you can put in peach fruit cups. Today it's tapioca."

"Then what?" Sam said, taking the cream-colored glop from Sidney's outstretched hand.

"Well, if *that* review is inconclusive, there will most likely be an inquest. It's usually a three-person jury selected by the coroner to determine the cause of death. They get to consider *all* the evidence gathered during the investigation, stuff the medical examiners don't see, even hearsay evidence that would never be allowed during a trial."

Sam gazed down on the campus. Bicycles wove among the students along the crowded sidewalks converging in the center of Prexy's Pasture. From above, the light-gray concrete walkways looked like the ancients' medicine wheel—the religious, astronomical, or calendrical significance lost on them as they marched toward their next fifty-minute block of instruction. He took a deep breath and slowly exhaled through his nose, realizing that Lilly Darnell would never be among them.

CHAPTER FOURTEEN

AVOIDANCE

An icy draft rolled over Annie's face and shoulders. So abrupt was the change in temperature that she gasped for air. She lay motionless, confused. The blanket, which she had pulled up to her chin, began to recede slowly. She could feel it sliding downward, tickling her ribs, then her stomach, dragging without resistance over her thighs and toes. Something was very wrong, but her muddled brain could not reason. Her confusion quickly escalated into fear. She tried to scream, but there was no sound.

From a distance, Annie heard the distinctive moan a windmill makes when its tail swings into the wind. She forced her eyes open in an attempt to overcome the grogginess of sleep, and listened intently. The windmill moaned, the low-pitched yowl of metal grating upon metal, sounding the early-morning warning that the wind had once again arrived. She lowered her chin toward her exposed body. Annie felt small and unimportant, a woman in her underwear, staring upward at the universe from her bed. As hard as she tried, she could not focus her mind. She wanted to cry.

••••

The first clouds appeared about midmorning—large, billowy cumulus clouds, soft and benign. By noon they had stacked up to the west, piling into each other, creating an ominous, gray horizon. The wind began blowing steadily from the northwest, and the temperature edged downward as the front moved in. Annie knew another snowstorm was brewing. She sipped her peach-flavored herbal tea and gazed out the mud porch window, toward the barn with its slumped roof. The bare cottonwoods blurred slightly as they frantically waved beyond the window glass. The wind's roar rose and fell and seemed to compress the house under its weight. Across the yard, the dark doorway of the barn swallowed the light. The imperfections of the windowpanes, combined with the swaying of the trees, created the impression of movement within the barn's entrance.

Dr. Tom Stevens' Toyota Land Cruiser, bouncing to a stop in the rutted driveway, snapped her out of her unsettling reverie. *He's right on time. Thank God,* she thought, and rose to meet him.

"I was surprised you're living so far out here, by yourself. This place is almost as hard to find as Sam's," Dr. Stevens said, smiling broadly as he walked to the front door.

"You obviously followed my directions," Annie grinned in response. She was glad to see him. She was glad to see anyone, but Tom Stevens had shown an interest in her, and she was flattered. "Please come in. Can I offer you a cup of tea?"

"That would be nice. Thank you."

"I'm sorry about the mess," she said, fidgeting nervously. Boxes of books were stacked in every room, most of them opened with bubble wrap poking out. "I've moved the publishing business here." Hands on hips, she surveyed the room. "Oh, well. I'll get organized one of these days."

"No need to apologize. I work out of my vehicle for the most part. I like the freedom."

Annie busied herself at the sink in an effort to get her emotions under control. She felt confined and isolated in a house that gave her the creeps, and it was now consuming her. "Rent and overhead were killing me. All I really need is Internet access and a phone. I outsource just about everything else." She placed half a dozen Oreos on a plate and laid it on the table. "Now I discover that connections are pretty intermittent out here. Ironic."

L2 managed to get up from her bed in the utility room and lumber across the kitchen to greet the visitor. Dr. Stevens said nothing. He held out his fist, knuckles up, and waited. The dog sat. Bending from the waist, he rewarded her with soft words and a pat as he looked her in the eye. "You've been working with her."

"I have," Annie said as she prepared their tea. "She's pretty stubborn. But so am I."

"What about Sam and Sidney?"

"Sidney's been very busy. She might come by this weekend. Sam, well, he's a different story. Sugar?"

"Please. I'd be lying if I said he was responding differently than most men. Behavioral therapy on a dog somehow belies their machismo. Testosterone blurs their vision. Give him time; he'll come around. I find it interesting that better than eighty percent of my clients are women. They, for the most part, are still responsible for child-rearing, and pets often seem to be lumped into the same category as children."

Annie set his mug of tea on the kitchen table and motioned for him to take a seat. The "eighty percent" thing had stuck in her craw. She was unsure whether it was being categorized as a typical woman, or feeling suddenly thrust into a sexually competitive situation with all the rest of womankind, that rankled her. She sat next to him. "What about you, Doctor Stevens? Any kids?"

"No," he said, pulling items from his Filson briefcase.

She waited; he didn't say anything more. In the long and uncomfortable silence, several questions formed in her mind—all of them much too personal to ask. She returned to the task at hand. "So, what surprises do we have in store for this destructive bloodhound?"

"Did you receive my diagnosis and treatment recommendations?"

"Got 'em."

"Any questions?"

"Not really, but I would guess that Sam will take issue with the half-dozen 'owner-caused factors that fixate older dogs on oral activity,'" she said, reading from Dr. Stevens' letter, which she had placed on the table. "Even

I became a little defensive when I read your twelve causes of frustration and tension-relieving chewing in my orally oriented dog." She ran her finger across the embossed stationery. "I especially liked this one: 'Marked emotional upset of owners, though not directly involving the dog.' And this one: 'Psychological trauma associated with locale or situation.' Now, I agree with some of them. Like this one: 'Barrier frustration at doors, windows, gates, etc.,' but that's only because she lacks an opposable thumb. 'Boredom'—well, she caught that one from me."

Dr. Stevens leaned back uneasily in his chair and looked at Annie. "Are you disagreeing with my diagnosis?" he said with a tight smile.

"Not me."

"Have I missed something?"

"I don't think so."

"Are you taking this seriously, Ms. George?"

"Very."

He sipped his tea, locking his eyes on her. "Are you mocking me?"

"No." She withheld a slight shiver. "Well, maybe a little. Sorry."

"What's the problem?"

Annie thought a moment. "Maybe I was a little taken aback by the...personal nature of what you have identified as stress factors."

His smile relaxed. "Believe me, I have only scratched the surface. From a clinical standpoint I could spend weeks, months, or maybe years uncovering the true source of L2's anxieties. I'm afraid you don't know what personal is."

"She's a dog, Doctor Stevens. Can I call you Tom?"

"Actually, she's a very complex organism, one of the most advanced mammalian species on the planet. Yes, she's a dog and far below our intellectual level, but you shouldn't discount her intelligence. Just because she lacks the ability to verbally communicate doesn't mean she's not taking in and processing information. In reality, she has a very sophisticated communication system; it's just nonverbal for the most part. Her sensory abilities are so much more advanced than ours that we have difficulty even comprehending them." He paused and slowly rotated his mug. "Long story short, L2 is not immune to the many stress factors in your life. Personal? I really don't think you want me to dig that deep. Of course, I could address such things as the obvious sexual tension between you and Sam, the physical disabilities and resultant anxieties of Sidney, or why you want to diminish my professionalism by questioning my abilities or referring to me by my given name. Well, we can certainly go there. It's up to you."

"Jeez O'Pete, are we on the clock here?"

"You betcha." His grin was mysterious, hard to fathom.

Annie paused, then tried to lighten the mood. "How about you knock off the small talk, Doctor Stevens, and get to the point? You were going to teach the dog to leave my furniture alone. Cookie?" she said, nudging the plate toward him.

"It's called 'conditioned avoidance,'" he said, fumbling with the papers he had pulled from his briefcase. "And I'll let you know when you can call me Tom." He bit into an Oreo, then looked up at her warmly. "I'll tell you what, Ms. George. I'll save you a few bucks by skipping all the psychobabble about classical and instrumental conditioning, the pairing of a conditioned stimulus with a neutral stimulus to get an unconditioned stimulus, and the differences between a conditioned response and an unconditioned response. I'll just tell you what time it is, unless, of course, you really want to know how to make that watch. Just ask."

"No. Let's cut to the chase. Just tell me what time it is," she said.

"Great. I'll demonstrate the application." They moved to the living room, L2 padding behind.

Annie watched him carefully. She was fascinated by the way he reinforced important details with facial expressions and hand gestures. She laughed out loud when he scared L2 out of the room with a hissing can of unscented underarm deodorant. "Great withdrawal behavior," Dr. Stevens proclaimed. "Now, without her present, lightly spray those items she has chewed or is likely to chew. She'll associate the scary-sounding can with the novel odor and will subsequently withdraw from any item carrying it."

Annie looked skeptical, but nodded in acceptance.

"Okay," he said. "Just one more thing and we'll call it quits for today. Now, I know you are asserting dominance during your training sessions, but I'm worried the dog isn't taking you seriously. Occasionally, you should simulate jaw wrestling and genital inspection in order to assert dominance."

"Simulated genital inspection sounds a little naughty, don't you think?" Annie said.

Ignoring her, Dr. Stevens called L2 to him and demonstrated the techniques while keeping up his nonstop psychological patter. "These behaviors have little or nothing to do with sex. It's all about dominance and subordination. Nonviolent group cohesion is critical to an animal whose life is dependent upon a social structure where every individual knows who they are, relative to other members of the pack. Bend only from the waist," he said, pushing Annie gently between her shoulder blades with one hand and pulling against her stomach with the other. He reached over her, took her right hand, and covered L2's snout with it.

Annie could feel his leg pressed against her buttocks, the warmth of his hands on her body. Her ears began to burn, and her heart pounded in her chest. She caught the scent of his aftershave. *This can't be his usual routine,* she thought.

"Now, step to her side, but keep hold of her nasal rostrum," he said as he guided her with one hand on her hip, "as you chuck her in the flank. You need to approximate a ninety-degree angle while leaning over her. We call this a Mendelson T-Formation Stand-Over; it's a very dominant thing to do, almost aggressive. Only a rear mount with pelvic thrusting would be considered more dominant."

"If you demonstrate that, I'm afraid I'll have to slap you," she said weakly, her face flushed.

"Again, there's nothing sexual about it," he said, smiling and stepping away from her. "It's simply one dog trying to assert dominance over another dog. Males mount males, females mount females. It's pretty agonistic. I liken it to the human behavior of flipping somebody off."

Annie plopped into a chair and pushed the hair from her face. "Is it hot in here?"

"So, that pretty much covers it. Any questions?" he said as he gathered his notes.

"That's it? No dinner, no movie, not even a cigarette?"

"You've got my directions on counterconditioning, dominance assertion, reducing social dependence, and conditioned avoidance. Call me if you run into any trouble. I really want you to conquer this, Annie," he said, looking deeply into her eyes. "The sooner you solve her problem," he gestured with his thumb toward a confused L2, "the sooner you can call me Tom."

"Excuse me?"

"It's my self-imposed code of ethics. I won't develop personal relationships with my clients. But when you are no longer my client, I'd like to ask you to dinner, if that would be all right."

"I'll take it under consideration, Doctor Stevens." She hesitated, then smiled. "It's complicated."

••••

Annie lay in bed, listening, not so much to the late spring snowstorm that raged in the blackness beyond the windowpanes as to the bone-jarring thumps from the attic that shook the entire house. Her fingers were cramped from the death grip she maintained on the covers that she had pulled up to her chin. The electricity had gone out just after 9:00, and the house seemed to contract as the wind-driven cold sucked the heat from within. Annie ended the day as she had started it, depressed.

CHAPTER FIFTEEN

DISMAL

Though indistinguishable from the rest of the string of broken-down towns that dotted the narrow river valleys of the Nebraska Sandhills, Dismal River was the county seat. White farmhouses, white-steepled churches, white-faced Herefords, and white northern-Europeans-turned-ranchers did little to counter the hopelessness of its name. The crumbling brick facades and boarded windows of main street businesses, along with the dismembered automobiles rusting in front yards, foreshadowed a bleak future. Only the consolidated school district, with its athletic program, was saving the town from total abandonment.

By mid-November 1985, the Dismal River Warriors had gone the way of their Pawnee predecessors. But instead of smallpox, the Oglala Lakota, and the U.S. Cavalry, more civilized factors had decimated their numbers. Agricultural consolidation, vertical integration, mechanization, increased production efficiency, and a shortsighted American agricultural policy had turned what was already a sparsely populated region into a giant sandy ghost town. Six-man football struggled to pull together enough players for weekly games; putting up hay and feeding cattle kept most of them off the gridiron. But on Friday nights, in the dirt parking lot just beyond the lights, young cowboys gathered.

"It was probably Slim," the stocky ranch kid said. His dirty Stetson was pulled down so tight and low that his ears folded in half. He took a drag on his Marlboro, which he cupped in his hand, hiding the glow from any teachers who might be patrolling the area. "He's got a pair of nuts on him like an Angus bull."

"Hell, I didn't think you could knock up something that retarded," another young cowboy said, shaking his head and dangling his boots from the tailgate, the same boots he'd worn back in July.

A third, his face dotted with smallpox-looking acne, joined in. "She ain't said nothin' yet. But she's already startin' to show. My sister saw her in gym class. Folks'll start askin' questions pretty soon."

"Look." Slim stood up in his black pickup bed and spread his arms. "Everybody, keep your cool and stick to the script. Who they gonna believe? My old man will sic Lawyer Daggett on 'em so fast they won't know whether to shit or go blind."

From under the lights a whistle blew, the crowd screamed, and the pitiful Dismal River High School band attempted the fight song.

"Why don't you just man up, Slim, and marry the girl?" the stocky kid said, grinning.

Slim raised his middle finger. "Faggot," he said before spitting in an arc toward his offender. "You should marry her. Ain't she some sort of cousin to you anyway? It'd make your inbred family real happy."

"Screw you."

"Up yours," Slim grinned. "Listen up. I say here's what we do. We set up a diversion. We go on the offensive and pin the whole thing on somebody else."

"Now you're talkin'," the kid with acne said. "How 'bout Principal McDonald? That piece of dog shit deserves it."

"No, I got a better idea." Slim leaned in with a smirk, scanning the dimly lit faces of the other three. "We put it on her brother, Mr. Goody Two-Shoes, the stuttering little twinkie. We tell everybody how we came across them last summer out at Brownlee's stock tank. We watched them through binoculars from the top of the hill. He was poundin' the pork to her like a horny jackrabbit."

The stocky cowboy considered for a moment. "Ain't nobody gonna believe that. Brother and sister don't do that kind of shit."

Slim was unmoved. "Hey, this little turd's a misfit that don't talk to nobody. He skulks around school starin' at the floor all the time. And his sister's a retard who doesn't know diddly squat and just so happens to have a damn good body on her. I'll bet they ain't even related, leastways they don't have the same daddy." His voice lowered nearly to a whisper. "I say it'll work. Tongues will wag all over the county, but ain't nobody gonna be turning over rocks lookin' for us. Who's to say he ain't banging her anyway?"

Slim looked slowly around him at each of the young men, all of whom avoided eye contact. "Are you with me or agin me?"

From above, the playing field of the Dismal River Warriors appeared as an illuminated speck in one of the darkest areas of the continent; a fleck of light that spun dizzily around the earth's axis and raced in an elliptical orbit around the sun. From below, the funnel of coal black sky belied movement. Only the arc of a descending meteor, shedding fiery fragments in its wake, hinted at tomorrow.

CHAPTER SIXTEEN

SHOT

Hello?" Sam spoke wearily into the tiny flip phone as he made his way from the Classroom Building to Arts and Sciences, where his office was located.

"Hello?" he repeated. "You're breaking up. Annie? Hello?" She was gone. Sam snapped the phone shut and slid it into his coat pocket. It rang again. "Hello? I thought that was you. What's—Calm down. I can't understand you—Shot! Who's been shot?" Sam stopped short in the middle of the busy walkway. Students and bicycles hurried past him. "How bad?" His eyes studied the concrete between his shoes. "Where are you now?...I'll meet you there in ten minutes....She's in class. Don't worry about her. Just get to the clinic. I'll leave her a message." Annie sounded hysterical. He could hear a man's voice in the background. "Who's with you?...Who?...I see. Look, I'll be there in ten minutes. Okay?"

••••

L2 had been shot. That much was clear. Between Annie's hysteria and poor cell reception, how badly the dog was injured was not clear. Sam's jaw rippled; his teeth clenched in anger. "Not again," he whispered to himself as he recalled the disturbing final image of Elle, L2's predecessor.

Mountain Vista Veterinary Clinic was south of town; however, nothing in Laramie was more than ten minutes away. He did not see Annie's Subaru in the parking lot, but he recognized Dr. Stevens' Land Cruiser. Blood was splattered against the passenger-side window and windshield.

"She's fine," Annie said, bolting up from her chair in the waiting room. Dr. Stevens, who had been sitting next to her with his arm around her shoulders, stood up cautiously. She had been crying. Annie saw the confused look on Sam's face as he eyed Tom Stevens. "You were in class with your phone turned off," she said, taking a step back. "I couldn't reach you or Sidney. Doctor Stevens was kind enough to help out. He met me at the Tie City Campground. Now we have two cars covered with blood," she said, attempting an awkward joke.

"What about L2? How bad is it?"

"Not bad at all, Sam," Dr. Stevens said. "She took a bullet through her right ear. Not much damage, but a bloody mess. She kept shaking her head. Blood and dog spit flew everywhere."

"Who the hell—"

"Y'all can come back now," the vet tech called from the doorway to one of the examination rooms. Her nurse's smock was decorated with an assortment of dog and cat breeds.

The veterinarian was a pregnant woman with carrot-red hair just brushing the top of her shoulders. She wore the proverbial stethoscope around her neck and seemed no older than the students in Sam's class.

"Tom," she said, greeting Dr. Stevens.

"Allison," Dr. Stevens responded.

"How's my dog?" Sam interrupted.

"She's going to be fine. We have her in the back, cleaning her up a bit. We'll bring her out in a minute. I tried to suture up the hole in her ear, but there just isn't enough surrounding tissue to work with. I mean, I could do it, but she'd be left with an unnatural fold. Which, given all the folds in her face and head, probably wouldn't be noticeable." She chuckled at her bloodhound humor.

Sam was not amused. "Will it grow shut?"

"It'll fill in a bit, but it's probably too large to close up entirely." The vet paused, then spoke in a more solemn tone. "You know, she's very lucky. A slightly different angle, and the outcome could have been much more grim. The ear offered so little resistance that the bullet didn't expand much, if at all." She paused, and Sam realized the full gravity of the situation.

Allison continued more cheerfully. "I cleaned it up really well, gave her a healthy dose of antibiotics, and a little something for pain. You can take her home. Just keep the wound clean and give her these twice a day," she said, handing a bottle of pills to Annie. "If she starts scratching at it, we can put a cone on her. She's got a perfectly round thirty-caliber hole through her ear. I've seen bigger ear piercings on campus." Again she laughed.

The back door to the exam room opened and L2 pulled yet another young woman in. The dog's nails clacked on the linoleum floor as she tried to gain her footing. Her thick tail waving, she plowed her way through the throng of humans and buried her head in Sam's lap. He squatted down to greet her.

"Sam," Annie warned with a wide grin, "no coddling, fondling, or other solicitous behavior toward the dog unless she has responded appropriately to some directive given by you."

Dr. Stevens revealed his toothy smile. "Do I really sound like that?"

"Yes," Sam and Annie said in unison, without looking at him.

Dr. Stevens breathed a laugh. "Love your dog, people. This is an exception. But this emotional outpouring is for you, not her. So keep it brief," he added sternly. "Remember, she's just a black box. Keep this up, and she'll develop a condition known as sympathy lameness."

"Do you really believe that, Tom?" Allison said, looking slightly flushed as she rubbed her hand over her extended abdomen.

Dr. Stevens regarded L2, who now appeared to be hugging Sam's neck. "While I know she's this creature with no concept of self who makes no distinction between herself and people, then I see something like this—All the anthropomorphisms aside, I have to say *that* is a sentient being." He nodded in her direction.

Sam gently held out the dog's ear to examine the reddened wound. "Since it is not hunting season, I'm ruling out mistaken identity and assuming that someone tried to kill my dog," he said, anger creeping into his voice.

"It was Oscar Roberts," Annie said, still wiping tears from her eyes. "I saw the son of a bitch drive away."

Sam lifted his head with surprise—it was not so much at the revelation as the fact that he had never heard Annie swear. He had thought her incapable of profanity. For that matter, he could not remember ever seeing her cry. He wanted to take her in his arms and comfort her, but that was no longer an option. His attention shifted to Stevens, who had placed his hand on Annie's shoulder.

The door swung open and Sidney burst into the already crowded room. She, too, had been crying.

Throughout the clamor, Sam crouched low and contemplated L2. He wondered what this dog with a conscious mind was thinking, and whether revenge and jealousy were concepts that only humans understood.

CHAPTER SEVENTEEN

PHOTOGRAPHS

Oscar Roberts is as bad-tempered and cantankerous as they come," Undersheriff Piccard said, twirling the left side of his moustache between his thumb and forefinger. "He's got a thing against trespassers."

"My dog wasn't trespassing," Sam insisted. "She's staying with my friend, who rents a house from him."

"Was the dog off her property at the time of the incident?"

"She was within a hundred yards of the house and barn when he shot her." Sam was starting to feel the burn of irritation at the tops of his ears.

"Was she off her property?"

"I have no idea. She has no idea. She's a dog, for crying out loud."

"Are you from Wyoming, Mr. Dawson?"

Here it comes, Sam thought, *the old Code of the West crap that outsiders can't understand because they weren't born here six generations ago.* "I live here," he hedged.

"Then you are probably aware that dogs running livestock may be killed, and the person doing the killing is not liable. That goes for livestock and big game, alike."

"My dog was not chasing livestock or wildlife. She—"

"Are you aware, Mr. Dawson, of the law that states that anyone who permits their dog to run livestock outside a radius of a hundred yards from their property, can be fined up to seven hundred fifty dollars or imprisoned for up to six months—or both?"

"Are you going to arrest me?" Sam was nearing his boiling point.

"Are you admitting guilt, Mr. Dawson?"

Sam stood up. "I'm sorry I wasted your time, Deputy Piccard."

"Undersheriff," Piccard corrected.

"But I'm sorrier that I wasted my time. I should have known that the largest landowner in the county would enjoy diplomatic immunity from animal cruelty laws."

Piccard remained unfazed. "Are you aware that it's a public nuisance for dogs to be running at large in unincorporated areas? If Roberts files a complaint, we can issue a summons and sock you fifty bucks for the first offense and a hundred for subsequent violations."

Sam exhaled loudly in frustration and anger.

"Ain't that the shits?" someone said from behind him.

Sam turned to see the imposing figure of a tall, well-groomed cowboy standing in the doorway—creased blue jeans, a crisp white shirt open at the neck, and a ten-gallon Stetson tilted at a rakish angle. An automatic pistol was tucked into a holster high on his hip.

"Just when you get to thinking you're a law-abiding citizen, somebody tries to arrest your ass." He smiled broadly and strode toward Sam with his right arm extended. "Sam Dawson, it's a pleasure to finally meet you. I'm Harrison O'Malley."

Sam hesitated, then shook the sheriff's hand, assessing his penetrating pale-blue eyes. "The sheriff himself," he said.

"Undersheriff Piccard treating you all right?"

"Swell. He was about to pistol-whip me," Sam said with a sideways glance at Piccard.

"You can stand down, Francis. I'll take over from here."

"Yessir," said Piccard. He shot a lethal look at Sam and retreated from the office.

"I wanted to thank you for your help in recovering the body of that young girl up in the forest," said O'Malley.

"Lilly Darnell. She had a name," Sam said, surprised at his defensive tone.

"That's right. I didn't know her name had been released to the public just yet."

Preferring to keep his source at the coroner's office under wraps, Sam did not respond.

The sheriff seemed to be sizing him up. "I was told you never accept 'Go to hell' as an answer. Tony Garcia down in Pueblo speaks highly of you. He's fixin' to retire this year. He never fails to ask about you when we get together at our annual sheriffs' association meetings. And you know, I got a call last fall from Sheriff Whitehorn up in Minnesota…" He gazed into the distance, into Sam's past.

Sam was trying to figure where Harrison O'Malley was headed with his walk down memory lane.

"You seem to have a knack for finding dead people and those who made them that way."

Sam continued to probe the man's unsettling eyes.

"I hear you've been sniffing around the coroner's office." He waited in silence for a reply that never came. "Any ideas?" the sheriff said finally.

"About what?"

"Lilly Darnell."

Sam sidestepped the question. "That's not why I'm here."

Again there was silence, except for the background clatter of a busy office seeping in from down the hallway.

"Tell you what. I'll send a deputy up to the Rocking R to have a talk with Oscar Roberts. But my advice is not to cross that old boy. He's mean as a snake and smart as a fox. You best keep your dog off his property." With that, he abruptly turned and disappeared down the hall.

••••

"Dad," Sidney nearly shouted as she burst into Sam's office. "Guess what!"

Sam had been grading the most recent test from his introductory photography course and was in no mood to guess anything; his students seemed to do that better than studying. Also, he knew he didn't have to ask. She would tell him.

Sidney exhaled deeply. "Oscar Roberts has been arrested."

"That's a good thing," said Sam, holding his red pen in midair. "What for?"

"My mole in the DA's office said there's a whole host of charges pending, but they got him on possession of child pornography."

Sam carefully placed his red pen on the desk and waited. Sidney had his undivided attention.

"Apparently, he threatened a sheriff's deputy with a rifle—a thirty caliber, I might add. After the arrest, and with probable cause, the deputy searched Roberts' truck and found photos of naked children in his glove box."

Sam let the information sink in. "You said there were other possible charges?"

"Sure," she said, still catching her breath. "There could be first-, second-, or third-degree sexual abuse of a minor, or sexually exploiting a child. I don't know what the photos depicted, but if he was taking immoral or indecent liberties with a minor, we could be talking major prison time. Even if he wasn't making child porn, possession carries a penalty of up to ten years. But wait, here's the kicker. Are you ready?"

When he looked at Sidney, Sam still saw his little girl—not the blossoming defender of the law she had become. "I'm ready," he beamed proudly.

"One of the photos was a picture of Lilly Darnell."

Sidney continued to talk, her words and gestures fading into incoherent jabber. Again, Sam was haunted by the image of the Little Mouse Girl curled into a fetal position, cold and alone, her face turned downward, frozen to the icy ground.

CHAPTER EIGHTEEN

NOISES

A quiet dawn gave presence to the uneven geography of the Laramie range. The wind seldom blew during the early morning hours, regaining strength for the busy day ahead. The sun rose as a fiery red ball, the sky grading to hot pink as darkness bled from the night sky along the northern and southern horizons. "Red sky in the morning," Annie whispered.

There was no spring in Wyoming. An occasional warm, sunny day would be followed by a blizzard that seemed to combat the innovations and intrusions of man into a land not meant for habitation. Isolation was no longer a benefit. She had become increasingly apprehensive about being alone, especially at night. The noises in the attic had intensified to nightly occurrences. The thumping would start over the spare bedroom to the south, then bang and crash across the living room ceiling, stopping directly over her head in the north bedroom. They vibrated through her body, waking her, while the windows rattled in their frames. When the moon shone, it cast a cold bluish light and an eerie shadow into her drafty room.

Sam had dismissed her complaints, saying that pack rats were probably tossing around the spoils of their thievery. Unless they had the strength of Mighty Mouse and could lift bowling balls, something much larger and more disturbing had taken up residence in the attic. She had never believed in things that went bump in the night, but she was desperate to accept any alternative to the possibility of mental illness.

Annie sat at the kitchen table, hunched over her coffee mug. She inhaled the fragrant steam. "Sit," she commanded. L2 was a puddle of dog flesh on the throw rug in front of the sink, a giant oozing dumpling that smelled like a dirty sock. The dog raised one eyebrow, but made no effort to respond. She, too, was tired. The nightly noises had forced her to seek refuge on Annie's bed. Sometimes she would jump up and spin around as if someone had stepped on her tail. Then she would stand, her head cocked, listening, trying to hone in on the location of the disturbance.

"L2, sit," Annie demanded in a stern voice. The one thing in her life that she should be able to control ignored her. Tom Stevens had told her that, if she gave a command, she had to follow through by demanding and achieving compliance. She hoped that he would call soon to check on her progress. She was drawn to him—more than she should be, and that frustrated her. The awkwardness she felt in his presence had become obvious. She was sure that Sam had noticed it too. Yet Sam failed to say or do anything that would suggest he had feelings for her. "Sit, damn it," she said, rising from her chair, pointing at L2 for emphasis.

Equally frustrating was that she had a job to do. She had accomplished little or nothing since establishing

Cowboy Press less than five months earlier. Sam's book sales had been stagnant for more than a year, long before she became his publisher. Now, printing costs had reached a breaking point. Book returns to the distributor from the bookstores were killing them, since the buybacks were charged to her as his publisher. She was out of money and forced to deduct the cost from Sam's royalties. It was no wonder he was acting cold to her. *Or, maybe it's the Little Mouse Girl that's bothering him. The poor guy does seem to have a knack for finding dead people,* she thought.

She grabbed L2 by the collar and yanked her to a sitting position. "When I tell you to sit, I mean sit. Do you understand me?" she snarled with her face inches from the dog's nose. L2's eyes darted from side to side. "You don't have a clue, do you?" Frustrated, Annie released her grip and stepped back. As she did, she moved through a cold draft that made her shiver.

The sudden drop in temperature reminded her again of the unexpectedly freezing underground current in her childhood swimming hole. She clutched at the neck of her bathrobe and searched for the source of the draft. There was no movement of air, no apparent source, no rhyme or reason to it. Rather, it was a dank, bone-chilling air mass that occupied an isolated, defined space just north of the center of the kitchen. By extending her arm into the cold, she felt her way around it. Leaning into it, she could see her breath.

The unexpected sensation that someone was watching her suddenly swept over her. She looked over her shoulder and saw nothing. She could see across the living room, through the large window, to the hillside on the west side of the house. She craned her neck backward to peer through the kitchen door, across the mud porch, and to the outside door. Again, there was no one. It was not merely someone watching her; it was someone standing within inches of her. Never in her life had she sensed so strongly the presence of another. She wanted to bolt for the door. Instead, she stood petrified, trapped in the acute nothingness of air. Fear clutched at her stomach and roiled slowly upward into her throat. The sound of her breath rushing through her nostrils seemed amplified. Goose bumps again spread down her arms and across her chest.

A cross between a whine and a growl came from L2. She stood with her feet together and her back humped, facing the same empty space. Her tail was tucked between her legs to make herself look smaller. She held her huge ears back as far as possible and pulled her lips back into what Stevens called a "submissive grin." He had taught Annie to recognize the postures and facial expressions of fear-induced aggression. The dog was scared.

The clapboard house trembled noisily as if bracing itself for battle. The wind had rallied for another attack.

CHAPTER NINETEEN

RABBITS

The towering silver spruce of Grandview Cemetery cast long dark shadows in the morning sun. The traffic noise from West Mountain Avenue had already begun as Fort Collins greeted another busy Colorado day. From across the cemetery, it appeared that someone was kneeling with their head bowed, as if in prayer, perhaps mourning at a gravesite. Sam made his way through the maze of monuments, trees, and shrubs.

Lilly Darnell's grave was fresh. Dark wet soil was mounded in a rectangle beneath the newly placed red granite monument. Floral arrangements in varying stages of decomposition were piled neatly on the dirt and against the headstone. A large purple and yellow Easter bunny sat on the grave, its head bowed toward the gravestone, long ears drooping almost to the ground. The sad Easter bunny took his breath away. He turned, straightened his shoulders, and swallowed hard in an attempt to regain his composure. He seldom photographed new graves, but this one was personal. He brought the camera to his face. He saw Little Mouse Girl curled in a fetal position, her pale blonde hair spilling over her frozen face. He could not click the shutter.

"She had a thing for rabbits," the woman said.

Sam spun around, startled. He had not seen the woman sitting on the stone bench in the shadow of a looming cottonwood tree. He stepped on a pinecone and stumbled forward as he came to face her. "Excuse me?"

"It was the biggest rabbit I could find on short notice. It's actually an Easter bunny. She was getting too big for Easter stuff, but she still liked her rabbits."

Sam studied her. She was perhaps forty, round-faced, and overweight. Tear-streaked mascara ran below each eye. She wore a Denver Broncos insulated jacket and an orange stocking cap that was twisted so the team's logo was slightly off-center.

"You wouldn't happen to have a smoke, would you?"

"Sorry," Sam offered simply.

"She kept a hutch full of rabbits in the backyard, New Zealand Whites crossed with Californians. She sometimes crossed the does with Flemish Giant bucks. She could produce a four-pound rabbit in eight weeks. Took second last year at the county fair. She was in 4-H, you know."

"Mrs. Darnell?"

She looked up at Sam with sad eyes. "I'm not sure," she said in a high voice. "Ever since her disappearance, we haven't said ten words to each other." She looked toward the sound of a truck gearing up on West Mountain. "But don't print that. The article should be about Lilly, not us."

Sam squinted at her and cocked his head. "I'm sorry?"

"You're with the press, right?"

"No ma'am."

She looked up at Sam and studied him with one eye almost shut. "I saw the camera and just assumed…Who are you then?"

"My name is Sam Dawson."

"Why are you here, Mr. Dawson?" Her tone had a slight edge to it.

It was a simple question that surprised him. Being in a cemetery at dawn was normal for him, but she did not need to know that. He hesitated. "I-I'm here to pay my respects."

"Did you know my daughter?"

"No ma'am."

Her face became hard as she studied him.

"I'm the guy who found your daughter, Mrs. Darnell," he said quickly. There was so much more he wanted to say to her, to tell her he understood her loss; that he had a daughter too; that he had lost his sister and her body had never been found; that he could not explain why he felt compelled to drive for more than an hour and a half in the predawn darkness to see the grave of a girl he did not know.

"The fisherman?"

"Yes, ma'am."

Her eyes filled with tears. "You found my baby?"

Sam nodded.

Tears slowly streaked down her cheeks. Her bottom lip quivered and her nostrils flared. Her eyes darted back and forth across his, searching. She held back.

Sam turned away. He studied the Easter bunny slumped over the little girl's grave, its ears arching downward in despair. He held back too.

CHAPTER TWENTY

INFINITY

Splitting wood was the therapy Sam needed. He had briefly considered buying a used hydraulic splitter, but knew it would not give him the relief that swinging a six-pound splitting maul would. Sweat glistened from his face; the neck and underarms of his long-sleeved T-shirt were dark with perspiration. He wiped his brow with the back of his leather glove as he watched the sheriff's cruiser bounce slowly over his rutted driveway.

"Well, well," Sam said, smiling. "This must be serious. The sheriff himself. What brings you clear up here on a Saturday morning?"

"I'm thinking maybe you framed Oscar Roberts by planting pictures in his truck in order to get even with him for shooting your dog."

"I'm fine, thanks. Yes, it's a beautiful morning in the Rocky Mountain west. How about a cup of coffee?"

"Don't mind if I do." The sheriff grinned broadly and tipped his Stetson back on his head.

The two men walked to the house without speaking.

"Sidney," Sam called, "we've got company."

"Hi," Sidney greeted him as she came into the kitchen. She clutched an open book titled *Criminal Law* to her chest. Her hair was pulled back, exposing her hearing aids.

A yellow pencil was tucked above her ear. She offered her hand. "Sidney Dawson."

"Harrison O'Malley," the sheriff said, removing his hat and turning his head sideways to read the title of her book. "Will you be representing the accused this morning?"

"Only because I have to. I'm the appointed public defender. He'll get what he pays for. Sit down, Sheriff. Can I get you a cup of coffee?" Sidney quickly yanked off her scrunchie, allowing her hair to spill over her ears.

"Please."

"How do you take it?"

"Black as a politician's motive, thanks."

"The sheriff thinks that maybe I set Oscar Roberts up by planting incriminating photos in his truck," Sam said, pulling a chair from the table. "He thinks maybe it's me because I have an axe to grind over him shooting L2."

"In that case, as your counsel, I'm advising you not to respond until you've had a good laugh and a second cup of coffee," Sidney said, handing them each a mug. "How about some fresh-baked banana bread, Sheriff? It's on the table."

"That sounds wonderful, Sidney. Thanks." O'Malley looked around the room. "Where's your dog?"

"She's still staying with my publisher, Annie George, over by Horse Creek," Sam said, sipping his coffee.

"Is she all right?"

"The dog is fine. Annie, on the other hand, is still a bit shaken."

The sheriff picked up a slice of banana bread and leaned over the table as he took a huge bite. "This is excellent. Thank you, Sidney."

"I heard Roberts made bail," Sam said.

"He's got more money than God. He's lawyered-up big-time with a well-known defense team out of Denver. At this point, the only thing he's being charged with is possession of child pornography and assault on an officer. Since he has no criminal record and isn't a registered sex offender, I don't expect he'll do time if convicted. What I'm most interested in, of course, is the picture of Lilly Darnell, and if he's connected in some way to her death."

"Will somebody cowboy-up and call it murder?" Sidney interrupted from the kitchen counter. "Call a spade a spade, for crying out loud."

"I'd call it a freaking shovel if I could get a positive cause of death," the sheriff said, twisting in his seat to look at her.

"I'm assuming this isn't a social call," Sam said, leaning back in his chair. "What do you want from me, Sheriff?"

"Two things. First, your expertise as a photographer. The photo of Lilly seems different than the rest. I need to know how it's different. Second, you know this country as well as anybody. I need to know where the photo was taken. Would you be willing to take a look at the pictures we found in Roberts' truck?"

"Wait a second," Sidney protested. "You've got the photos with you?"

"Yep." The sheriff pulled a manila envelope from inside his coat.

"These are the originals? What about chain of custody?" Sidney said, stepping toward the table. "They should be locked up in an evidence room somewhere."

"They were. I checked them out. DCI has already examined them and collected everything they wanted from them. But to be on the safe side, you should put these on," he said, taking a pair of latex gloves from his jacket pocket and offering them to Sam.

Sam looked at Sidney.

She nodded.

"My attorney says it's okay," Sam said. He gingerly accepted the gloves from the sheriff and pulled them on. He opened the clasp on the envelope and carefully slipped the photographs out. There were only a half dozen. Sam flipped through them quickly. He stopped at the last one, studied it longer than the rest, then placed them back in the envelope. He removed the gloves and made a move to sip his coffee, but placed the mug back on the table untouched.

"Well?" O'Malley said, fixing his eyes on Sam.

"I assume the pubescent blonde is Lilly?"

"You recognize her?"

"No. Just the hair color; it's almost white."

"What else?"

"It's pretty obvious," Sam smiled. "The photo of Lilly is different than the others. First," he said, "it's the only black-and-white photo in the bunch. Second, she's older than the other children. Third, she appears to be unconscious. Fourth, she's not posed in a pornographic posture like the rest. And fifth, the photo was taken by an amateur using a built-in flash, with a camera that has a focal length fixed at infinity. The others were all taken with more complex cameras and lenses that could adjust focal length. The complete absence of shadows in the color shots tells me that somebody knew how to use reflectors, bounced light, and background control. They were professional or semiprofessional photographers who shot those. They're probably all digital. I can't tell you the pixel count, but the color photos are of a much higher resolution, more suitable for enlargement. The paper is all the same. You can buy it at Walmart, stick it in your home printer, and download pictures from anywhere in the world."

"The world is a big place, Sam. Can you narrow it down for me?"

"Your guess is as good as mine," Sam said. He started to lift his coffee mug to his lips again, then abruptly set it back down on the table, the coffee sloshing over the rim from the uncontrollable shaking of his hand.

••••

A face-numbing April wind hissed through the ponderosa pine, causing the limbs to bow and bend. The swaying branches danced above Sam's upturned face. It was 2:00 a.m. He had seen satellite photos of Wyoming at night showing the absence of light from the sparsity of man. But from below, the light show was overwhelming. He stood fixated on the radiant glow of the milky swath of stars spread over the sky from horizon to horizon, the galaxy of which Earth is a part in the infinity of space. He wished he could erase from his mind the image of Lilly Darnell, lying naked on the filthy mattress in Annie's bedroom.

CHAPTER TWENTY-ONE

VAPORS

Darkness flowed down the Horse Creek valley, a black ooze in the wake of another spring squall. Annie stood on the mud porch watching the slow-moving storm roll over the valley. It had started as a light rain and then turned to sleet that beat upon the corrugated tin roof with a deafening clatter. She could not remember ever seeing lightning during a snowstorm, but as the puffy popcorn snow gave way to giant flakes, horizontal sheet lightning ricocheted between the dark clouds. Periodically, the barn appeared through the white veil of snow, illuminated by erratic flashes of lightning. It was as if someone were thumbing through a giant flipbook, a slow-motion animation of a menacing structure standing sentinel over a sinister place.

Annie had hoped the electricity would not go out, but it abruptly ended with the first flashes of lightning, along with the cordless telephone. She thought how good a hot bath would feel before going to bed. There was enough hot water in the insulated electric water heater. But she decided to conserve whatever water pressure remained in the tank under the windmill for a last flush of the toilet, and maybe a glass of water.

She forced L2 outside one more time. She watched as the dog, caught in the sickly yellow beam of her flashlight, hurriedly squatted in the snow just off the landing. She locked the deadbolt and checked it repeatedly as if she suffered from some obsessive-compulsive disorder.

The yellow and orange flames danced above the burning wood. Annie undressed by the warmth of the fireplace and stood there with her nightgown in her hands. If the phone worked, she would call Sam and apologize for pushing him away. She would beg his forgiveness and ask that he reconsider their relationship. She would be sincere, even misty eyed, as she revealed her true feelings for him. He would listen without interrupting her, ask if she knew what time it was, and hang up. She would then wake Dr. Stevens and call him Tom when he answered. With feigned interest in something like canine dominance assertion with simulated genital inspection, she would ask him to talk her through it on the phone. Midway through his lecture she would casually mention that she was naked.

••••

Annie could not tell if she had been asleep. She had no idea what time it was. The clock radio was as dark as the room. There was no wind. An eerie silence had settled over the house. She was cold. She pulled the covers up to her chin, rolled onto her side, and brought her knees up in an attempt to conserve heat. Sleep surrounded her.

The impact upon the roof shook the entire house. Annie bolted upright in bed. Disoriented, she was uncertain if she had dreamed the bone-jarring noise or if it had really occurred. She had been dreaming of when she was a little girl. She and several other children and her long-dead dog, Pepper, were running and leaping through a field of wildflowers, mostly daisies—white petals with yellow centers. She could still smell the scent of flowers and grass on a hot Iowa summer day.

The sound of something heavy striking the roof was totally out of context with her dream. She sat motionless, listening for anything that might help her determine whether she had actually heard something. In the storm-darkened night, she could see the outline of L2 standing at the foot of the bed. She too was motionless, frozen in an alert posture. Her head was cocked to one side. Annie could see she was staring at the ceiling. Annie's heart began to pound in her chest, and the metallic taste of fear formed in her mouth as she realized L2 had heard it too. She fought off panic.

The vivid image of the deadbolt on the mud porch door flashed in her mind. *Did I lock the door?* She could not remember. She quickly reviewed the things she had done before going to bed. *Did I lock the damn door?* She remembered putting L2 outside. She recalled the repetitions of locking and unlocking the deadbolt. "Yes," she whispered aloud.

Quietly, Annie turned back the covers and slid her legs from the bed. She grabbed the old Eveready flashlight from the nightstand. L2 growled a low rumble that graded into a high-pitched whine. "Hush," she whispered sternly.

"You stay," she commanded with the palm of her hand brought sharply to a stop in front of the dog's nose.

The smoldering coals from the fireplace shone faintly as she tiptoed through the living room, the floor creaking.

The mud porch was cold and damp under her bare feet. Finding the deadbolt with her fingers, she froze in terror. It was in the unlocked position. She quickly pushed the sliding button upward. The spring-loaded bolt slammed closed. Her hand found the light switch by the door and flicked up the toggle, reaffirming that the electricity was still off. She cautiously peeked out the window in the upper half of the door and held the flashlight against the glass, but it was useless. Its narrow beam extended only a few feet.

In the wake of the storm, a dense fog had rolled into the valley. Billowy wisps of vapor floated and rolled above the snow-covered ground, creating a dreamlike illusion in the moonless night. A faint, yellowish glow shone intermittently through the murkiness. At first she thought it was her imagination again. She turned her head slightly and strained to peer between the shadowy plumes of haze. For a brief second, an unobstructed corridor appeared from the house to the barn, revealing a dingy, yellow column of light filling the barn doorway.

CHAPTER TWENTY-TWO

SPOLIATION

Most of the missing children were girls. The skewed sex ratio jumped out at Sam almost immediately as he scrolled down page after page of kids' pictures, occasionally clicking on a child's web page to see the specifics of their disappearance. Racial minorities were also overrepresented, especially Hispanics. On the National Center for Missing & Exploited Children website, he got the impression that all missing children were exploited children. The Polly Klaas Foundation, on the other hand, made him think of undiscovered bodies of dead children. They were listed chronologically from the time they disappeared. He stared at twenty-year-old pictures of children and wondered what they looked like today.

So many innovations had occurred with the advent of the Internet. It was no longer a matter of grainy posters tacked to a telephone pole or a single-color outline of a child on a milk carton. He wondered if his own sister might have been found if AMBER Alert had existed in 1975. The National Crime Information Center, maintained by the FBI, appeared to be the main database on which law enforcement agencies depended when looking for a missing person, but it was inaccessible to him. He was not sure what he was looking for, but hoped that something would jump out at him. The stories of man's inhumanity to the young and defenseless were heart-wrenching.

"If you don't talk to me, I can't help you," Sidney said from across the breakfast table. Her cheeks were puffed full of Froot Loops. She gazed at him through the distorted lenses of her Buddy Holly glasses. The thick, black temples, wedged between her hearing aids and skull, caused her ears to stand out; the morning sun shining behind her turned them pink.

"The Internet is a time sink," he complained. "It's white noise with information overload. You ask a simple question and you get taken for a long, bumpy ride to someplace you didn't want to go. And for the most part, it's too general to be of much value."

"What do you want to know?" she said, adjusting her glasses on her nose with the same hand that was holding her spoon. Milk dripped from the spoon back into her cereal bowl.

"I'm not sure," Sam said, turning his gaze inward. "Some things just don't add up."

"Like what?"

"Like, why Lilly Darnell?" he blurted out.

"Opportunity." Sidney dabbed the corner of her mouth with a paper napkin. "Like most crimes. We just aren't seeing the connection."

"What opportunity? She lived in Fort Collins—a different state, for crying out loud. What opportunity would a crusty old rancher like Oscar Roberts have?"

"He may have seen her in a restaurant, playing in the park, or walking to school. Maybe her picture was in the paper for something. Maybe she was a relative. Who knows how these predators operate?"

Sam pinched his chin between his thumb and forefinger. "He just doesn't fit my image of a sex offender. Isn't there a pattern of behavior or something? Besides, she wasn't molested."

Sidney studied him. "Evidence, Dad. They found a nude picture of the victim in his glove box. That, alone, qualifies as sexual abuse. It seems a little beyond a reasonable doubt. You know they're going to find DNA— or something else—that ties Roberts to this."

"If they had hard evidence, he wouldn't be out on bail. Besides, why would he be driving around with an incriminating photo that tied him to a dead girl right on his own property?"

Sidney's juice glass didn't make it to her mouth. She cocked her head and said, "Nobody said anything about his property." She probed him with her eyes. "You recognized something in that photo, didn't you?"

"If they're so damn sure they have their man, they'll stop looking, and my gut tells me they need to keep looking."

Sam's actions and their legal implications hit Sidney all at once. "Oh my God, what have you done, Dad?"

Sam did not respond. He closed the laptop and gave her a hapless grin.

"You've withheld evidence in a murder investigation? What were you thinking? Spoliation of evidence can have serious consequences. If there's either statute or relevant case law, you could be in a heap of trouble. You could go to jail."

"Trust me, Sid, there's something hinky about all this."

"Something hinky?" She leaned over the table. "*Something hinky?* That's no defense. I gotta tell you, Pop, sometimes being related to you is a real challenge."

Sam smiled at his girl attorney. "I know."

CHAPTER TWENTY-THREE
EVICTION

I have a signed lease," Annie said, her arms folded firmly on her chest. She ignored her hair blowing across her face, determined to hold her ground.

"Show it to a judge," the sheriff said.

"I've paid my rent. I have the canceled checks."

"If you choose to challenge the eviction, you'll have the opportunity to appear at a hearing to answer the complaint."

"A hearing? You mean I have to go to court?"

"No, you can move out. You have three days to vacate the premises."

"Shouldn't I have gotten some kind of notice? You just can't show up here—"

"I'm sure he convinced the court that he had given you notice. Otherwise, they wouldn't have issued this," he said, handing her an envelope.

"What's this?"

"It's a summons. He filed a complaint. It has the time and date for a hearing, if you want to contest the eviction. The judge will listen to both you and Roberts and make a decision."

"But I don't have the money to move right now. Why is this happening? I haven't violated the lease." She repeated, "I don't understand why this is happening."

Sheriff O'Malley covered his crotch as L2 rooted him in the groin. "I'm sure that has something to do with it," he said, nodding toward the bloodhound.

"Do I need an attorney?"

"That's up to you. We do have some free and low-cost mediation services that handle landlord-tenant disputes. I'll bet Sidney Dawson could help you. She's pretty sharp."

"How do you know Sidney?"

He smiled at her, but did not respond.

"And why is the sheriff himself serving an eviction notice? Surely you've got a whole horde of deputies that could have driven all the way out here to hand me a summons."

"That's true, Ms. George. I haven't delivered one of these in many years. Let's just say I have ulterior motives."

Annie looked at him; her eyes narrowed and her brow wrinkled.

"One of which was to meet the publisher of Sam Dawson's fine books. I'm a fan."

"How is Sam involved?"

"I don't know, but from what I've seen and heard of that guy, he's up to his eyeballs in something related to this. He's an interesting character who holds his cards pretty close to his chest. Tell you what, for a cup of coffee, I'll give you my opinion about why you're being evicted."

"Oh my, where are my manners?" Annie demurred. "Just because I'm being evicted, it's no excuse for a lack of hospitality."

"Look, I'm just the messenger," O'Malley smiled.

"I'm sorry, but I've never been evicted before, or summoned, for that matter. Please come in," she said, standing away from the doorway.

From the moment he entered the house, Annie noticed a change in the sheriff's demeanor. He carefully placed his Stetson down on the table. His glib attitude became serious, reserved. Annie busied herself at the kitchen counter. "Do you take anything in it?"

"Just black," he said, but his voice came to her from another room.

She turned around and saw him standing in her bedroom doorway, his back to the living room. "Feel free to have a look," she said sarcastically. "I would have picked up a little had I known you were going to snoop around."

"Sorry," he said quietly, continuing to stare into her bedroom.

"You were going to give me your theory as to why I'm being evicted."

"Yes." He attempted a smile as he turned and walked across the living room to the kitchen.

"Have a seat," she said, studying him. She set a mug down across the table and cupped hers in her hands.

O'Malley settled in his chair and covered his mug with his hand. "Oscar Roberts didn't file the complaint. His attorney did. Your eviction isn't just a landlord-tenant dispute. Primarily, it's a diversion his defense team came up with. They're asserting that you planted those photos on account of he threatened to cancel your lease because your hound was chasing his livestock—and as revenge for shooting the dog. They're building a case that bad blood existed between the two of you, and you got even."

"He shot the dog!" she almost yelled.

"He warned you he would if he caught it running his stock."

"So, you're here to investigate me, not just serve an eviction notice?" She glared at him. "This is unbelievable. You don't really think I—"

"It doesn't matter what I think. What's important is what a jury thinks if this goes to trial. The defense is simply trying to establish your or Sam's motive for planting evidence in Oscar's truck. To me, the bigger question is, who took the photo of Lilly Darnell?"

"I can't believe this is happening. A child molester—a murderer—is blaming me?"

"Or Sam. The dog was his, after all. He wanted revenge. And, he's a photographer," he added.

"Again, do I need an attorney?"

"That's totally up to you."

"I think you better leave now," Annie said, standing abruptly.

The sheriff retrieved his hat, stood, and walked toward the door. He paused and again looked toward her bedroom. "I hope your day turns out better than it has started, Ms. George."

Annie watched his unmarked pickup disappear over the hill west of the barn. Her throat felt painfully constricted. Her eyes began to burn as she fought the urge to cry. She surveyed the boxes of books on the mud porch, the dishes and utensils in the kitchen, the furniture in the living room. She exhaled forcefully. "Three days," she whispered. "I'll be glad to get out of this miserable place."

CHAPTER TWENTY-FOUR

SHUNNED

June Hofstadter lit a cigarette off the butt of the one she had been smoking. "Better hit me, Jimmy," she said, her eyes squinting through the haze. She ground out the butt in the glass ashtray on the polished bar.

The bartender ignored her and continued his conversation with the only other patron, who sat at the opposite end of the bar drinking an orange Nehi and eating a bag of potato chips. The afternoon sun knifed through the smoke at an oblique angle, illuminating the worn-out floor of the tavern. *General Hospital* flickered from the television above the bar, competing with the gaudy assortment of neon beer signs. The smiling Hamm's bear held up a Big Bear Drinking Brotherhood placard that urged patrons to join today—March 17, 1986.

June held her frosted tumbler in the air and shook the ice cubes. "Jimmy, what's a girl gotta do to get a drink in this place?"

The bartender and patron both glared at her. She recognized the balding manager of the NAPA Auto Parts store from Mullen. She had generously offered him sex in exchange for a rebuilt alternator a couple of years back. How was she to know he was also the pastor of the local Church of Christ?

"What are you looking at, limp dick? Change your mind yet?"

The bartender picked up his bar rag and slowly walked toward her.

"One more for the road, Jimmy," she said, pushing her glass toward him.

"No more, June. You're done."

"Whaddaya mean, done? Hell, I'm just getting started."

"Do yourself a favor and go home. Do us all a favor and get the hell out of Hooker County," he said, tossing the rag on the bar.

"What? Leave Dismal River? This town's a going concern, I tell ya. I ought to buy this dump and fire your ass. Now give me another gin and tonic."

"The whole town's talking, June. Do us all a favor and move on, and take those degenerate kids with you."

"Don't you ever say nothin' about my kids." She slammed the tumbler on the bar. Ice cubes sprayed in all directions. "I'll have your goddamn job. Your boss and I go way back."

"Don't threaten me, you trailer trash bitch. I'll call Chief Zimmerman. He's lookin' for any excuse he can find to run your sorry ass out of town."

June Hofstadter glared at him. The neon Schlitz beer sign above the bar blinked intermittently, proclaiming it was "The Beer That Made Milwaukee Famous." "What the hell are you talking about? I ain't done nothin' to piss off the chief."

The bartender glared back at her. "It's not so much you as it is that boy of yours."

"Raymond?" She attempted to focus on Jimmy's face, but her head seemed too heavy for her neck to support. "He's a good boy." She tucked her chin and frowned at the bartender.

Twenty-six years of tending bar had taught Jimmy the futility of arguing with a drunk. "Yeah, he's a good boy, June." He glanced at the lighted clock behind the bar. "He oughta be getting out of school in a few minutes. Why don't you go home and fix him a nice dinner, maybe some Ding Dongs and a Fruit Roll-Up—and a Twinkie for dessert."

June Hofstadter stuffed her cigarette in the corner of her mouth, ashes sprinkling the bar. She gathered her change and slid off the stool. She glared at Jimmy and thrust her hand toward him with her middle finger raised. "And the horse you rode in on," she growled.

••••

Twenty-three to the right, fifty-one to the left, thirteen to the right…Raymond Hofstadter's hands shook as he frantically pulled up on the locker's latch, but again it would not open. He looked up and squinted at the locker number. One seventy-eight. It was his locker. He spun the dial two revolutions to the right as he furtively glanced left, then right. Students stood in tight little groups, their books clutched to their chests. They stared at him and whispered to each other. He wished they'd all disappear. Suddenly, the catch released with a loud metallic clang. A color snapshot slid out onto the polished linoleum floor. It was a photo of Miranda dancing naked in front of a stock tank. "P-p-pervert," someone said loudly from behind him. Everyone laughed.

CHAPTER TWENTY-FIVE

SYNDROME

You're asking the wrong person, Annie," Sidney said. "I've been poked, prodded, shocked, and bled—tested and tortured for years. I'm going blind and deaf, and there isn't much I can do about it. Do you know I take a hundred-fifty-thousand international units of vitamin A every single day? It's like eating polar bear liver in hopes of slowing the progression of rod cell degeneration. You talk about seeing things? You wouldn't believe what I see at night—blinking and shimmering lights. I can't drive after dark anymore. It's like looking through a toilet-paper tube. You say you're seeing things out of the corner of your eye. Well, I've lost almost all of my peripheral vision. Heck, my central vision is starting to play tricks on me because my cone cells are croaking. I can't even tell you what color blouse you're wearing. And as far as hearing stuff, forget that too. I can't hear thunder, let alone whispers."

Sidney shrugged her shoulders and exhaled loudly. "Sorry, you didn't need to hear me rant. The short answer is no. I won't stay here overnight—and neither should you. I believe you. There's something weird about this place, and I don't want to know what it is. Pack a bag; you're coming home with me. After classes tomorrow, Dad and I will come over and get the rest of your stuff. You can live with us until we figure out what to do."

Annie smiled. She reached across her kitchen table, took Sidney's hand, and squeezed it gently. "Thanks, but I couldn't impose on you like that. Besides, your dad would have a cow."

"No he wouldn't."

"Yes he would. I think he wants me to fail and move back to Iowa so he can say, 'I told you so.' And you know what? I think he might be right."

"That's not true," Sidney said, pushing back her glasses.

"Yes it is. The business is about to crater. I had no idea it was in such bad shape. I'm almost broke—personally, and can't support it. People aren't buying books. Whatever bookstores are left are selling coffee and celebrity kiss-and-tells to survive. Publishers keep consolidating and dictating market trends. Without a major house to provide distribution and buy shelf space, and a decent advance against royalties, Sam will continue to circle the drain. Face it, he's a regional author in a market flooded with self-published books, all vying for the attention of a public that only wants to look at their phones."

"We can talk about this later. Right now, I think we need to concentrate on getting you out of Hill House, or Amityville, or whatever the heck you want to call this place. How about Horse Creek Creepy?"

"Look, I've got three days. I'll stay here till I get packed up. Then I might bunk with you guys for a few days while I try to determine what to do."

Sidney seemed to be considering her next words carefully. "You know, having Usher syndrome has forced me to develop some of my other senses. I hope you don't think I'm out of line, but you and Dad have feelings for each other. It's as plain as day. I see it whenever you are together. I see it when you're apart. The both of you might as well be wearing those sandwich board signs with something written on them, like 'Can't you see I love you?' or 'Pay attention to what I do, not what I say.' And what's with you and Doctor Stevens? You don't have to be deaf and blind to recognize the old jealousy ploy. You won't win that one. Dad is as stubborn as they come. Shoot, he'll walk you down the aisle and give you away at the altar before he'd admit his feelings for you."

Annie smiled and relaxed in her chair. "I asked you to come over and look at this eviction notice," she said, lifting it from the table. "Instead, I get Dear Abby's advice for the lovelorn."

"Like I keep telling Dad, you get what you pay for," Sidney grinned. "As far as the eviction process is concerned, I recommend you not contest it. It's a blessing in disguise. The faster you get out of Horse Creek Creepy, the better. Besides, I miss my dog," she said, nodding toward L2, who lay on her side by the sink like a roadkill doe. "Come stay with us," Sidney said earnestly.

Annie forced a tight-lipped smile. "It's complicated," she said.

CHAPTER TWENTY-SIX

PERCEPTION

Perception necessitates reception, but the converse is not true," Dr. Tom Stevens said, nodding earnestly as if to say, "Do you get it?"

Annie stared at him blankly. Sometimes he operated on a plane that both mystified and irritated her. He seemed to be stuck in some academic gear that she had not experienced since graduate school. She liked Tom Stevens. He was handsome, smart, compassionate, and was obviously interested in her, as evidenced by the fact that he called her almost every day under the pretense of checking on L2. She believed she was genuinely attracted to him, in spite of what Sidney thought. Why else would she take him up on his invitation, drop everything, and drive all the way to Laramie to meet him at Crow Creek Coffee? She had told him she was coming to town anyway to pick up more boxes and packing tape. Actually, she had jumped at the chance to get away from the unnerving events at the house.

"Let me explain it another way," he said, smiling. "I call it the 'I see dead people' phenomenon."

"Excuse me?"

"Remember the line in the movie *The Sixth Sense* with Bruce Willis when the little boy confides in Willis, his psychiatrist, that he sees dead people?"

"Uh-huh," she muttered over the brim of her coffee mug. She was uncomfortable with where this was going, and now regretted telling him of the strange happenings at her place on Horse Creek. But the circles under her eyes attested to another sleepless night, as a result of the inexplicable events in a house that now frightened her, and she could no longer explain things away.

"I think that some people may have the ability to experience things that others don't. Maybe you're one of them."

"Oh God, I'm Odd Annie from Iowa."

"Maybe so," he grinned.

"It takes one to know one," she shot back.

"Touché." He blinked and raised his eyebrows as if he had not expected her rebuttal. "Look, we're constantly bombarded by sensory stimuli. We only detect those things that come to us above a certain threshold. Perhaps some people have slightly lower thresholds. Did I ever tell you that I did my master's research on the psychophysics of canine vision?"

"If you did, it didn't make it over my threshold for comprehension."

"Cute, but you understand the concept. Anyway, I was interested in scotopic sensitivity. I wanted to determine what dogs could see at night. To do that, I needed to know what their absolute scotopic threshold was for light sensitivity. I used a complex behavioral technique that involved a Skinner box, and a purely physiological technique on anesthetized animals where I looked at electroretinographic potentials. Long story short, I found very distinct differences between what their retinas were capable of receiving and what the animals actually perceived."

"Like afterimages from a flashbulb?"

"No, afterimages are a result of a chemical process in the retina that requires a strong source of electrical stimulation. But you might be onto something there. You said you have seen things only in your peripheral vision. With a high density of rod cells in the peripheral retina, it may be possible that these cells are receiving and responding to stimuli outside the visible spectrum. But it's borderline. It's moving back and forth across the threshold for perception. We know that the human retina receives and responds to a lot more stimuli than we actually perceive."

Annie perked up; Dr. Stevens had piqued her interest. "What you are saying is that if some stimulus is on the borderline between our ability to receive and perceive, moving into the perceptual plane only for fleeting moments, then we may be able to see things that are not really there?"

"No, I'm saying just the opposite," Stevens said, smiling with excitement. "It allows us to catch quick glimpses of things that really are there but, for the most part, are lying outside our ability to perceive them."

Annie took a deep breath. "Well, I was only scared before. Now I'm terrified."

"Don't be. You're an environmental microbiologist. You can't see giardia in the crystal clear water of a mountain stream. It doesn't mean they aren't there. Put a little stain on them and slap them under a microscope and—presto chango, there they are. It's the same concept. Before van Leeuwenhoek developed the microscope, we had no idea that giardia or red blood cells or spermatozoa even existed."

"So, if I had the right tool, some ghostbuster-type machine, some paranormal sensing gizmo, I might be able to see the things that go bump in the night?"

"Perhaps. Or if you consulted a medium or used a Ouija board, or other such nonsense, you could make contact with the spirit world. You know, there was an entire religion, Spiritualism, founded on the concept of conducting séances?"

"You don't believe in any of this stuff, do you?"

"Of course not. I'm a scientist. Show me the empirical evidence."

"Whew, you had me going there for a minute. Next thing you know, you'll be telling me how to communicate with my dog." Annie smiled broadly, feeling the pull of attraction toward him.

Tom Stevens leaned across the table. He rested his chin on his open palm and gazed at her. "What do I need to do to make a believer out of you?"

Annie twisted her mouth to the side and rolled her eyes upward as if considering his question. Refocusing on him, she said, "Can you levitate something?"

"I believe I'm in the process right now."

They both laughed. It was then that Annie noticed someone standing at her side. She turned her crimson face upward and met Sam Dawson's disapproving eyes. "Sam," she exclaimed a little too loudly.

"Annie," he said flatly, then turned toward Tom. "Doctor Stevens."

Stevens started to get up, but instead offered his hand. "Good to see you, Sam."

"I didn't see you come in," Annie said. "Won't you join us?"

"Thanks, but I can't. I've got a faculty meeting at three," he said, glancing at the clock behind the counter. "I just need a shot of caffeine to get me through it." He wanted to say, "Besides, two's company, three's a crowd," but resisted.

"Sidney came by this morning," Annie said.

"So she said," Sam nodded. "Looks like I'm going to get my dog back."

"She told you about my visit from the sheriff?"

"Yep."

"I'm looking for a place that doesn't require a long-term lease."

"Uh-huh, and how's that working out for you?"

Annie's ears had turned as red as her cheeks at the realization that she had less than three days to vacate her house and she was sitting in a coffeehouse with Tom Stevens, laughing and flirting.

In the momentary silence, Sam shifted self-consciously from foot to foot. "When you find a place, Sid and I will come over with the truck and help you move. But it will have to wait until after the storm."

"What storm?" Annie and Stevens said in unison.

Sam looked at them incredulously. "Big snow headed this way. Supposed to start sometime after midnight. They're really hyping this one, talking up to twenty inches here and a lot more in the high country. Fifty-to-sixty-mile-per-hour winds will shut down the roads."

"It's May ninth, for crying out loud. It's sixty-five degrees out there," Annie complained.

"It's Wyoming," Sam shot back with a smile. "Gotta run," he said, stepping away from their table. "Food, water, candles, and firewood, Annie. That's what you'll need. I expect phone and electricity to go down. Use the downtime to get packed up. I suspect you'll miss your eviction deadline, but the sheriff will have higher priorities." Sam glanced at Dr. Stevens. He wanted to suggest that Stevens rise to the occasion and save the damsel in distress, but thought better of it. "We'll be there to move you when the roads open up." With that, Sam turned and made his way to the counter.

"What can I do for you?" the barista said without smiling. She wore a wool stocking hat pulled over her ears, in spite of the uncomfortable heat behind the counter.

Wash your hair, take out your disgusting nose and lip rings, and cover up the ridiculous tattoo of Tweetie Pie on your neck. "Regular coffee, small," he said, trying not to stare at her.

He wondered how long it would take the police to get there if he kicked over a few chairs, flipped the table that Stevens and Annie were sitting at, and tossed the good doctor through the plate-glass window onto the sidewalk.

"Leave room for cream?"

"No, thank you," he said pleasantly. "I'll take it black." *Same color as her heart.* He glanced over his shoulder at Annie.

CHAPTER TWENTY-SEVEN

SOMETHING

Giant clouds, the big fluffy kind, appeared in her rearview mirror as Annie reached the summit on I-80. By the time she turned off the Horse Creek Highway and headed down the long, winding two-track toward the house, the clouds had stacked up to the west—black and blue on the horizon, sore looking. When she finished unloading the packing materials and supplies she had picked up at Walmart, it was almost dark. The wind was blowing steadily from the northwest, and the temperature had edged downward as the front moved in. She busied herself filling pitchers and pots of water, bringing in armloads of firewood and stacking it on the mud porch. She even brought in the old hurricane lantern from the barn, after carefully filling it with kerosene from the can she found in the barn workshop.

She tried not to think about the embarrassing confrontation at the coffee shop. She was angry with herself for hurting Sam again. The fact that he was visibly upset spoke volumes about his feelings for her. Yet he refused to act on those feelings. Lately he seemed withdrawn and edgy, always cynical. She could not determine if his disappointment and frustration were with his or her career. Perhaps neither, she reasoned. She had noticed that he seemed edgier since finding the little girl's body. She had been exposed to more death and carnage after meeting Sam than most people experience in a lifetime. She believed it had to affect both of them. Now adding insult to misery, she had thrown Tom Stevens into the mix, rubbing salt into an already festering sore.

She caught her reflection in the window above the kitchen sink and stroked her forehead and cheek in surprise. She looked tired, drawn. Worry was taking its toll. The room had suddenly grown cold. She folded her arms to ward off a shiver. She had done the same thing in Laramie when Tom walked her to her vehicle. He had leaned in to kiss her, or to peck both cheeks as in a European goodbye—Annie wasn't sure which. Something unexplainable made her pull back. Instead, she thanked him profusely for the coffee and exaggerated her concern for getting home ahead of the storm. After all, she had a dependent bloodhound to care for.

She looked past her reflection to the beginnings of the storm. The wind whipped against the house, sweeping over the roof, creating swirling masses of snow that pelted the darkened west windows. Ice crystals danced against the panes, producing a soft crackling sound with each intermittent gust.

"A hot bath will warm your gizzard," her Nana used to say. She missed her grandmother. She missed Iowa with its defined spring weather. She missed Sam. *Maybe a steamy bath would relax me,* she thought. Backing away from the sink, she moved through a cold draft that caused her to shudder. *Not again,* she thought. She backed up through the cold spot again, then checked around the kitchen for the source of the frigid air, but couldn't detect a draft.

As before, she was overcome with the sensation that someone was watching her. She craned her neck to see into the living room, then across the mud porch toward the outside door. No one was there. Still, the intensity was startling. She fought an impulse to bolt for the door. Instead, she turned and grabbed onto the sink. Fear clutched at her stomach and rolled slowly upward to her throat. Her heart raced, and her breath came in staccato jerks. Gooseflesh spread down her arms and across her chest. She turned to face the intruder, but again there was no one there, though she still felt a palpable presence. She pushed the hair away from her face with trembling hands. She felt weak with fear and fought the urge to cry out. Leaning her head back, she inhaled deeply in an attempt to regain her composure. The wind roared over the chimney with a deafening howl and caused the house to contract and expand with each frigid assault. Every darkened corner held a threat, something ominous, something foreboding. The lights blinked. She hated this house.

••••

L2 lay sleeping by the fireplace, the flickering firelight reflecting off her soft brown fur. She was dreaming. Her eyelids twitched, her lips quivered, and her paws flexed and extended as she chased her imaginary prey.

Annie undressed by the warmth of the fire. Standing in her underwear, she pulled her hair back into a ponytail and secured it with a rubber band. There was something hypnotic in the red flicker of the coals, something primeval. She turned slowly, allowing the invisible fingers of heat to caress her entire body. She wished Sam were there to hold her, and scold her for letting her imagination get the better of her.

She slipped on her robe and went to the mud porch to check the storm's progress before taking her bath. The linoleum floor was cold and damp under her bare feet. The wind buffeted the house in harsh, intermittent fits, whistling through the cracks around the doorjambs. A sheet of corrugated roofing flapped and banged from the roof above the door. Beating against the side of the house, a torn screen was suspended by only one corner. She flicked on the switch for the outdoor light. At least the electricity was working. Tumbleweeds, trapped in the wash of wind currents that plunged over and around the house, had found agitated refuge at the front door. They were piled upon each other in a thick, writhing mass. Compelled to escape their tormented wanderings, they pressed against the window glass, as though struggling to break into the house, away from the relentless forces of nature. The snow and wind were unyielding. She turned off the porch light. Absently groping for the deadbolt with her fingers, she found it unlocked. She froze in terror. She distinctly remembered locking the door after bringing in the lantern from the barn. Quickly, she pushed the sliding button upward. The spring-loaded bolt slammed closed. *My God, why is this happening to me?* Her hand trembled as she checked the lock a second time, then a third.

The kitchen floor protested loudly when Annie crossed it on her way to the bathroom. The porcelain-coated cast iron tub felt like a block of ice. She turned on the tap and steam filled the tiny room. She slipped the hook on the door through the eye on the jamb and hung her robe on the back of the door. Easing herself into the chipped and stained claw-foot tub, the warmth immediately relaxed her. She slid down, closed her eyes, breathed deeply, and covered her face with a hot, wet washcloth.

She heard the doglike yelping of the tub's hot water faucet being opened fully and the sound of rushing water. Annie struggled to a sitting position. Steam spiraled upward, cloaking the room in gauze-white vapors. She grabbed the faucet handle and turned it counterclockwise, but it spun loosely in her hand. Scalding hot water continued to pour into the tub. Annie squirmed up and out of the tub, her skin rubbing noisily against the slick surface, like fingers scraping a balloon. The water level rose to half full. Again, she twisted the faucet handle, to no avail. Panicked, she looked around the room for a shutoff valve. There were two under the sink and one behind the toilet, but nothing for the tub. She remembered the hot water heater in the laundry room and visualized the red-handled gate valve on the top of the tank.

Swirling clouds of steam condensed on the enameled door. She flipped up the hook, grabbed the doorknob, and pushed. The door did not budge. She put her shoulder into it, but it held firm. She kicked with a bare foot at the bottom of the door, but the door wouldn't give, as if it had been nailed shut. Reaching into the searing water, she felt for the stopper and pulled upward on the beaded chain, but the chain pulled loose, leaving the plug in the drain. She grimaced in pain as she yanked her arm from the water.

Annie put on her robe and stepped to the window. She released the latch and pushed her palms upward against the sash. Like the door, it did not move. She could see layers of dried paint smeared carelessly along the framework. The window had not been opened in years. Again, she tried the door. It was no use. She turned toward the tub. She pulled the bath towel from the rack above the toilet and wrapped it tightly around her fist and wrist. She punched the window squarely. Shards of glass exploded outward, followed by an inward torrent of cold air. She pushed out the remaining daggers of glass and swept the broken pieces from the sill. She poked her head through the window to gauge the distance to the ground. Wind-driven snow pelted her face and ears. It was about a five-foot drop. Awkwardly, she backed through the window and slid roughly to the snow-covered ground. Her robe caught on the corner of the sill and was pulled upward to her armpits.

The frigid air and driving snow assaulted her exposed body. She felt an immediate burning numbness in her toes as she hurried along the darkened east side of the house.

Climbing the three steps at the southeast corner of the mud porch, her toes felt as if they were about to split open. She clawed at the tangle of tumbleweeds piled against the door, grasped the doorknob, twisted, and pushed. The deadbolt held firm. "Oh God, this can't be happening," she said, the words swallowed by the roar of the wind. Her feet began to throb as she turned her back to the door and jabbed at the glass with her elbow. On her third attempt, the glass shattered loudly. She reached carefully through the jagged hole and fumbled with numb fingers to rotate the deadbolt. She did not feel the glass cut deeply into the bottom of her right foot as she stumbled through the door and across the mud porch.

Water was beginning to flow from under the bathroom door as she swept madly at the air for the string attached to the light chain in the laundry area and yanked it hard. The single bulb illuminated the two pipes at the top of the white water heater. Only one of them had a shutoff valve. She twisted the handle clockwise and listened carefully for the water to cut off in the bathroom. The valve seated reluctantly, and the sound of running water stopped. "Thank God," she whispered as she stepped to the bathroom door and twisted the knob. The door opened easily. Swirls of blood flowed in the water away from her foot, dissipating lazily over the linoleum floor. She stood motionless, captivated by the word "Baby" scrawled in graffiti-like fashion in the steam of the bathroom mirror. She cocked her head slightly and studiously tracked the droplets of water that slid sanguinely downward from the *B* and the *y*.

CHAPTER TWENTY-EIGHT

COMPLICATED

I t's complicated," said Sam.

"That's exactly what *she* said." Sidney was honed in on her computer screen.

"You mean you already invited her?" Sam said. He looked over the top of the *Popular Photography* magazine he was reading but not reading. Instead, he had been listening to the storm assail the roof. He glanced at the huge stone fireplace he had built in the center of the house, separating the living room from the kitchen. It was a Russian-style masonry heater that warmed the entire log home. He had not installed a furnace.

"Of course I did. You would have done the same thing."

"Not a good idea, Sid."

"You can charge her rent, if that's what you're worried about."

"How would that work? She's my publisher—a publisher with one client, mind you, who hasn't paid me a royalty or given me an advance in five months. You honestly believe she could pay me rent?"

"She's paying rent to Oscar Roberts."

"She signed a lease for a year and gave him six months in advance. I'm telling you, she's broke or darn close to it."

"Great! You're both broke. See? You have something in common. Maybe the two of you can figure out how to turn this business around," Sidney smiled. Her eyeglasses had slipped down.

"She hasn't a clue." Sam slapped the magazine down on his lap. "She's killing me. She thinks regional book signings on weekends are somehow going to bail us out. The Tattered Cover, and Barnes and Noble could care less about her profit margin. I usually sell a dozen books at a signing, but they've ordered fifty, knowing full well that they'll return the unsold books back to the distributor. You know they won't keep anything on the shelf for more than a week or two."

Without moving her head, Sidney glanced at him over the top of her glasses. She pushed the tiny button on the top of her right hearing aid to change the program. Her father's voice had gotten louder.

"So, my brilliant publisher gets to pay for thirty-eight books that are returned to the printer and destroyed. Following standard procedure, she passes on the loss to the author by deducting it from the advance on the royalties. She should have done exactly what Pat did to me last fall—drop me like a hot potato. But my foxy little publisher just keeps booking more signings."

"You really think she's foxy?" Sidney said.

"You're missing the point."

"No, Dad, I'm not missing the point. I've heard it a hundred times before. The business is totally unfair. But you think Annie is foxy? Why don't you call her up and tell her that?"

Sam looked at his daughter and sighed.

"Was that a sigh of exasperation?"

"Uh-huh."

"Well, two can play that game." She sighed loudly. "You're not the only one in this family who is frustrated. You whine, whine, whine about your failing business. Yet, you keep doing the same thing over and over again, expecting different results. How insane is that?"

Sam hastily changed the subject. "What have you found out about ketamine?"

Sidney squinted at her computer screen. "The problem with ketamine is that it leaves behind metabolites. A toxicologist is going to pick it up easily."

"Good to know," Sam said. "But why is that a problem?"

"If you're going to use an anesthetic drug during the commission of a crime, you want one that metabolizes into something that's normal, that doesn't raise a red flag."

"And?"

"The coroner found ketamine in Lilly Darnell, but couldn't determine the cause of death. He suspects that it might have been a combination of asphyxia and hypothermia. But what if—and this is a big what if—the ketamine was administered to either throw off the toxicologist or to point authorities toward someone with access to ketamine?"

"So now you're defending Oscar Roberts? That bastard shot my dog." Sam squirmed in his chair.

"Look. Ketamine renders the victim very compliant, especially during a sexual assault, right?" Sidney said. "It's a date rape drug. But I keep going back to the fact that the coroner says Lilly probably wasn't physically molested. He didn't find any postmortem evidence of genital trauma, even though he also said that it's hard to detect after decomposition. Also, it's hard to kill someone with ketamine. If her attacker's goal was to kill her, he'd have to use a lot of ketamine to do it."

"Where are you going with all this, Sid?"

"I don't know, Dad. What if Lilly wasn't a random victim?" She adjusted her glasses and looked at her father. "Why was she killed? What's the motive here? There's a reason. There's got to be a reason. This is all starting to sound a little too elaborate. What if there's a pattern? What if we're not dealing with an isolated act here?"

"Are you talking about a serial killing?" She had his attention now.

"I don't know, maybe. It's a stretch at this point. I'm just thinking out loud, considering all the possibilities. I need a modus operandi that can be traced back to an individual to see if there's a pattern of behavior that has cropped up before. I'm still worried about the trace metabolites. Everything leaves something behind."

"You're making a case for some degree of sophistication on the part of the killer," Sam said, pinching his chin in thought. "Maybe the killer used the ketamine to control the victim until he could murder her in some other fashion or take her to another location."

Sidney hunched over her computer screen and resumed tapping the keys. "Here's an epiphany: What if you used a neuromuscular paralytic drug that leaves behind metabolites that are normally found in the body, something a toxicologist might overlook if only small elevations above normal were found?"

"Is there such a thing?"

"The one that keeps popping up is succinylcholine chloride, or 'sux' for short. In surgery, it's used as a part of anesthesia, usually for endotracheal intubation."

"Say what?"

"That means stuffing a breathing tube down your throat. It's a drug that's really fast acting. You become completely paralyzed almost immediately. Even the muscles used for breathing stop functioning. You'd suffocate pretty quickly if someone wasn't there to keep you breathing. The bad news is that the patient doesn't lose consciousness—there is no sedative effect unless they've already been anesthetized, which is how it's used in a medical procedure. Otherwise, they feel everything that's being done to them. Pretty scary! It was even used on prisoners as an aversive conditioning agent back in the 1960s, but was too psychologically terrifying on the subjects, and the practice was abandoned.

"Here's something that's interesting," she said leaning even farther forward toward the screen. "A peculiar thing about sux is that it is one of the few drugs known to cause something called 'malignant hyperthermia' in susceptible people. That's when the patient can't control their body temperature and all sorts of bad stuff starts happening, like a huge buildup of calcium in the muscle cells causing severe contractions. The body can't get enough oxygen and you basically suffocate after your circulatory system collapses. High levels of potassium usually indicate some kind of cardiovascular death, and they definitely accompany malignant hyperthermia. There's a genetic predisposition to this, but it's rare, like one in thirty thousand people. By the way, it has been described as the perfect poison or perfect murder weapon and has apparently been used as such in the past. They're working like crazy to come up with a test that will detect sux in suspected victims."

"Is there a trade name?"

"Yep, it's sold under Anectine and Quelicin," she said, sounding out the names like a child reading.

"Who'd have access to the drug?"

"Just about anybody in the medical profession has access to sux. Doctors, dentists often have it in their offices. Even airlines have it in their emergency first-aid kits. From what I've read, it's the murder weapon of choice for nurses with domestic problems. It takes about four milligrams per kilogram in an intramuscular injection. That, alone, can be problematic. Even a young girl would require a pretty big dose, if given intramuscularly. A good medical examiner would find the injection site. It would be better to give it intravenously using something like a tiny insulin needle."

"What about the ketamine?" Sam said, squeezing his chin.

"That's a little tougher to come by since it's a controlled substance. You can buy it on the street. They call it Special K. Vets use it a lot as an anesthetic, and they're pretty notorious for not keeping track of things. Have you ever looked in the back of one of those mobile clinics? It would be easy to snatch stuff out of there. Some researchers at the university use it in animal research. I know they can order it from pharmaceutical supply companies."

The lights flickered again. Sam looked toward the blackened windows. "Did you say you fed Daisy?"

"You already asked me that. Yes, Dad, I fed my horse. Did you gas up the generator?"

Uh-huh," Sam nodded. "It looks like we're going to need it." The portable generator was only big enough to power the well, the freezer, and the refrigerator, but that was all they needed to get through most power outages.

"I'm worried about Annie," Sidney said in an attempt to bring the conversation back to its starting point.

"I'll call the coroner tomorrow to see if he's heard back from the forensic folks at Miami-Dade. Didn't you tell me they were reviewing the autopsy results?"

"I said, I'm worried about Annie who's alone in an all-electric, creepy old ranch house out on Horse Creek."

"She's got my dog," he mumbled as he gazed at the fire. The photo of Lilly Darnell came back to him. She was spread-eagled on a filthy mattress, lying on the bedroom floor of the house that Annie was now renting. The peeling wallpaper with its floral design was unmistakable. "You would think they'd be able to test for some of the things you've been talking about."

Sidney sighed and pushed up her glasses. "You're impossible," she said. The lights went out and the refrigerator in the kitchen abruptly stopped humming. The storm continued to rage against all that was made by man.

CHAPTER TWENTY-NINE

TELEPHONE

Annie drifted in and out of a restless sleep. She had been hesitant to allow herself to slide into that vulnerable state of unconsciousness. Confused, she was unable to determine if something had awakened her. Like a repetitive dream, she looked for the familiar red numerals of the clock radio on the nightstand next to the bed, but there was only darkness. She closed her eyes and listened. The house groaned under the burden of wind and snow. It seemed to twist right, then left, moaning with discomfort. She pulled the covers over her exposed shoulders and snuggled deep into the featherbed liner atop the mattress. She could feel the numbness of sleep as it swept over her, then she slowly faded into the transition between the real and the unreal.

As before, the impact upon the roof shook the entire house. Annie bolted upright in bed. Disoriented, she was uncertain if she had dreamed the bone-jarring noise or if it really had occurred. This time she had been dreaming of a grassy meadow on a hot summer's day. Small white butterflies filled the air. They landed delicately on her hands and arms, and surrounded her as she lay on her back, staring upward at the blue sky and billowy clouds. She could hear the gentle rustle of the aspens that surrounded the meadow. Sam was there too. He stood above her, his camera obscuring his face. "Take off your dress," he said, his voice quivering slightly. The camera's shutter clicked repeatedly.

In the cold darkness, Annie and L2 stared at the ceiling, as they had before, in a nightmarish déjà vu. A vision of the deadbolt appeared in her mind. She distinctly remembered locking it, after covering the window with cardboard and duct tape and sweeping up the broken glass. She fought off panic at the notion that flattened book boxes taped over two windows did not present a barrier to someone or something trying to get in.

Holding on to L2's collar, Annie led her across the dark living room. The cold kitchen floor felt almost wet. She tried the light switch by the door, but there was nothing. Across the mud porch, she fumbled for the deadbolt. It was in the unlocked position. Her eyes began to sting with tears; her bottom lip quivered. Fear descended down her neck and across her shoulders. A gust of wind lifted a sheet of corrugated roofing above the mud porch and slammed it down with the rippling screech of a train that had jumped the track. There was a flash of light from the direction of the barn, interrupted by swirling squalls of snow. It was the same as before. It was always the same. She stood transfixed, and strained to peer between the curtains of spiraling snow that swept across the landscape, eroding and depositing. The barn loomed as a symmetrical piece of slate, jutting upward from the earth, cryptically blending into the storm-blackened night. The lighted rectangle of its open doorway flashed menacingly in the distance.

The cordless telephone stuttered an abbreviated ring. The lights flickered and then went out. Annie felt nauseous as she turned and stared at the phone, its white plastic body reflecting what little light was available. She stood motionless, her body tense with anticipation. Cold air swirled around her legs and rose upward under her nightgown. She gently picked up the receiver. It felt cold and artificial as she wrapped her fingers around it and slowly placed it to her ear. There was no dial tone. Instead, there was the crackling sound of static electricity, popping and snapping crisply within a cotton-soft background of diffuse white noise. As she was about to hang up, she thought she heard a distant voice, a strained whisper of something unintelligible.

"Hello?" She paused and pressed the phone harder to her ear. "Hello?"

The response was weak and slightly garbled, but unmistakable. In a strained, drawn-out guttural whisper with the accent long on the first syllable, the voice amid the static murmured, "Ba-a-by."

CHAPTER THIRTY

BULLSNAKES

By late May 1986, the daytime sun warmed the asphalt that connected the undulating hills of sand and grass in the Nebraska Panhandle. Radiant heat, stored in the oil-darkened sand and gravel, had pressed the blacktop into long flat ribbons. The road linked the abandoned hamlets of the Sandhills to civilizations east and west and, to a lesser extent, north and south. Ashby, Bingham, Ellsworth, Lakeside appeared and disappeared along Highway 2, as they had done before. Wet valleys always surprised June Hofstadter. Shallow reed-choked lakes and narrow corridors of cottonwoods and junipers would magically appear in the lowlands of the grassy desert.

On chilly nights, the highway was a warm respite for bullsnakes. Their mouths were fixed in a permanent smile as they stretched and flattened their belly scales against the heat-soaked road. Large creamy-yellow snakes with blackish dorsal blotches were no match for the four thousand pounds of Oldsmobile 88, creamy-yellow with a blotchy black roof, that hurled westward away from Nebraska. June could have avoided them, but with a beer in one hand and a cigarette in the other, it was too much effort. Miranda slept next to her, her head wedged against the passenger door, her flabby, postpartum abdomen exposed from under her too-small T-shirt. She never mentioned her stillborn child. Instead, she nurtured the filthy porcelain-faced doll she clutched to her breast.

Everything they owned was piled into the backseat and trunk. There were no suitcases, boxes, or order. The Oldsmobile sat back on its axle; the shock absorbers had lost their will. The grill angled proudly upward. It, too, was fixed in a permanent smile as the tires rolled over the bullsnakes without noise or emotion. Red was added to the cream and black writhing mass, the chrome and glass disappearing into the future.

They would start over in Wyoming. The Lutheran minister in Dismal River had paved the way for them. She and Miranda would make a good life for themselves. If she played her cards right, she might even make a little extra from the cowboys during Cheyenne Frontier Days. She wouldn't tell social services about the twelve hundred dollars she got for the trailer. Raymond was no longer her son. He could rot in hell, for all she cared. Besides, the little chickenshit had run off, didn't even attend his graduation ceremony from his precious high school. A lot of good all those A grades did him. Miranda still stood by her brother, insisting that the baby was their little secret. *Goddamn kids! You can't take your eyes off them for a minute.* June lit a cigarette off the butt of the one she had been smoking, steering with her elbow, her beer in her left hand. She tossed the butt out the window in a shower of sparks. *Life is good,* she thought. From the radio, Kenny Rogers cautioned Ruby not to take her love to town. Alliance—19 miles.

CHAPTER THIRTY-ONE

RADIO

The time is nineteen minutes after the hour and this is *Open Air.*" Her voice was low and melodious, like most of the public radio announcers Sam had heard in other states. He had sat next to her in the faculty dining room earlier in the semester. She was younger than he had envisioned—mid-to-late twenties, he guessed. Dressed in blue jeans and a V-neck pullover, she was as relaxed as her voice. Her long, flaxen hair was flattened by her bulky headphones. He envisioned her studying an assortment of VU meters, whose needles jumped spasmodically in contrast to her soothing voice. "We're very fortunate today to have as our guest Doctor Tom Stevens, who will be talking with us about animal behavior therapy. Welcome to *Open Air*, Doctor Stevens."

"Thank you for having me, Ursula. It's a pleasure to be here."

"Animal psychology is, to say the least, not a widely recognized profession," Ursula cooed. "As one of only about a dozen practicing animal behavior therapists in the country, I can imagine that many people are puzzled when they hear about your work. Do you frequently hear comments, like 'Oh, I didn't know there was a psychologist for animals' or 'How can you psychoanalyze a dog? Do you put it on a couch or something?' or 'How do you talk to them? Do you analyze their dreams?'"

Tom chuckled. "I think the picture most people have of a behavioral therapist comes from television and movies. They see a psychologist or psychiatrist sitting in a paneled office, books on the shelves, attempting to help their client understand what troubles them. Radio, too, has had its share of call-in personalities who recommend canned solutions to troubled listeners. Consequently, you can imagine the strange images that people conjure up when I tell them I'm an animal behavior therapist."

"Do you think he'll mention the hundred-and-fifty bucks an hour he charges to unlock the secrets of your dog's personality?" Sam quipped as he pried up the edge of the eggs in the frying pan and peeked under to gauge their progress.

"Shush," Sidney cautioned. She was adjusting the antenna of the portable radio she had placed on the kitchen counter. They were still without electricity, and the storm continued. She poked at the buttons of the device she wore around her neck in an attempt to increase the volume of her hearing aids. "Dad, we really need to trade this Radio Shack relic in on something with Bluetooth so I can stream."

Sam looked at her blankly. "Sounds expensive. Sit down. Your eggs are ready."

"Tell me about it. Here I am living with my father on the dark side of the moon. Ticktock, ticktock."

"What about the veterinarian?" Ursula asked, her voice like warm butter.

"In the past, people have looked upon the veterinarian as the panacea for all the woes of the animal kingdom," Dr. Stevens said. "This has, in my opinion, placed an unfair burden on the veterinarian. Animal behavior therapy is a complex field that requires years of specialized training that, in most cases, the veterinarian does not have the time, money, or interest to pursue. Vets, for the most part, are interested in the proximate questions about the mechanisms responsible for a behavior problem. They are concerned with the physiological, genetic, and developmental bases of behavior, the 'how' questions. The behaviorist, on the other hand, is typically interested in the ultimate or evolutionary reasons an animal does something, the 'why' questions. For example, dogs alive today carry genetic information that, in the past, generally conferred a reproductive advantage to the individual that possessed it."

"What the hell did he just say?" Sam shook his head as he dished two over-easy eggs onto Sidney's plate. "This guy needs a public information officer."

"Shush." Sidney frowned.

"I should call Will Gottlieb down in Fort Collins and get his take on all this. He's a real vet."

"Dad," Sidney warned again.

"What about the obedience trainer? Do they recognize the role of the animal behavior therapist?" Ursula asked.

"Yes and no," Dr. Stevens stated. "They've been a little slower than veterinarians in recognizing the importance of behavioral therapy to remedy certain emotional and behavioral troubles in pets. It's no longer a question of disobedient pets that need a whack with a rolled-up newspaper or a jerk from a leash attached to a choke chain. That Victorian approach to raising both pets and children often does more damage than good. People are now beginning to recognize that pets, like children, can develop emotional and psychosomatic disorders."

The Aladdin lamp in the center of the kitchen table glowed brightly as Sam joined his daughter for breakfast. "Horsefeathers," he said. "A good whack with a newspaper worked for me."

"Dad, I'm trying to listen to this," Sidney pleaded.

"Do you think the public is ready to accept behavioral therapy for their pets?" Ursula said.

"I think that twenty years ago most people would have ridiculed this type of therapy and certainly would not have envisioned the area of pet psychology becoming an established practice. Such ridicule, based on the attitude that the family can take care of its own problems, has changed considerably today. Families seek counsel for problem children, marital difficulties, exercise and diet issues, you name it. Since the extended family structure and sense of community have all but disappeared in our society, especially in urban and suburban nuclear families, outside help is a necessity. It's no longer a luxury reserved for the wealthy."

"That's easy for him to say," Sam muttered. "He's not the one forking over a hundred and fifty an hour."

"Doctor Stevens, can you tell our listeners how you differ from a clinical psychologist?"

"Certainly," he said. He paused for effect. "I'm not a psychologist. Rather, I'm an ethologist, or animal behaviorist. The difference is that I deal with different problems, using different techniques, drawing from different information, and most of all having a decidedly different outlook. For example, in order to deal with an animal's behavior problems, you have to stop trying to determine what the animal is thinking or feeling and start paying attention to what the animal is doing. There are several advantages to this type of approach. First, it is very objective, more in accord with what you are actually seeing. Second, you avoid attributing anthropomorphic judgments—human emotions, such as fear, love, anger, frustration, jealousy, et cetera—to an animal. By confining yourself to observing what stimulated a particular action and then the resultant behavior, you make fewer errors in interpreting what is happening."

"This all sounds a bit complex."

"With animals, we often know what the releasing stimuli are, both endogenous and exogenous, for most of the fixed action patterns of behavior we observe."

"This guy couldn't say poop if he had a mouthful of it," Sam suddenly declared.

"Dad, why don't you call Annie and tell her you're jealous as hell and you're not going to take it anymore?"

"Excuse me?"

"You heard me. Call her up and invite her to come live with us while you two sort out your feelings for one another."

"I can't believe I'm hearing this from my own flesh and blood. Besides, you've already invited her. Did she accept? Is she coming here or not?"

Sidney stopped him with a raised hand. "Wait, I want to hear this," she said, turning the radio up.

"Eighty-one percent of the people seeking assistance for an animal behavior problem are women," Dr. Stevens said.

"I can see why," Ursula shot back.

Dead air followed.

"That didn't come out right," Ursula said. "I apologize, Doctor Stevens. What I meant to say was: Are pets treated like children in most families where women assume the role of caregiver?"

"For Pete's sake, she's flirting with him too," Sam complained.

"Hush." Sidney was grinning from ear to ear.

"At the risk of sounding sexually chauvinistic, I sense that women are still role-oriented in our society," Dr. Stevens said. "Family pets are lumped into the same category as children. In a typical family situation, it is the woman who assumes most of the child-rearing duties. This includes seeking medical or professional attention for both children and pets. Conversely, men appear to hold to the philosophy that they can handle behavior problems themselves. To engage the services of an animal behavior therapist would betray their machismo and subject them to ridicule by their peers."

"You have no peers, pal. You're in a league of your own," Sam muttered as he placed his dishes in the kitchen sink. He leaned forward and looked out the window. The ponderosa pine boughs drooped to the point of breaking under their heavy loads. They bounced dangerously in the wind that drifted the snow between their trunks. He estimated that more than two feet had already fallen. "I'll start the generator so we can do these dishes and flush toilets."

"The average age of my clients is thirty-four point five years, and outwardly appears to represent the middle class in socioeconomic status," Dr. Stevens droned on.

Sam looked at the clock above the sink. Sidney was right. He should call Annie.

"Dogs make up eighty-eight percent of my caseload, with cats representing the remaining twelve percent."

"Why is that?" Ursula sounded sincere.

"I'll bet she has a house full of cats," Sam said over his shoulder. "I'll bet public radio staff has more cats per capita than ancient Egypt. I'll bet—"

"Dad, call Annie. She was noncommittal with me. I think she's waiting for you to invite her."

"I believe that this statistic represents the common belief that dogs are more plastic than cats, with cats being too independent to shape," Dr. Stevens explained.

"God help us," Sam said.

"This same reasoning may explain why dogs are seen, on average, at two point nine years of age as opposed to cats at four point three years. I think that people are more willing to accept unwanted behaviors for longer periods of time with cats because they feel little or nothing can be done. Additionally, there may be a correlation between sexual maturity in dogs and the onset of certain behavior problems."

"Oh, here we go," Sam laughed. "Let's blame the gonads. Did you ever consider that sofa pillows just might be sexually attractive to bulldogs? They sort of look alike."

Sidney shook her head in disgust. "Earth to Dad, can we focus here? I get it that this guy irritates you. And it's not because he's drop-dead handsome, intelligent, and compassionate. It's because he took the initiative to show an interest in Annie. She's flattered, as most women would be. That's all. It doesn't mean—"

"Sid, you're treadin' where you ought not to be treadin'. Look, we've been there. We had our chance and it didn't work out. Let it be. Okay?"

Sidney knew by the tone of his voice that the discussion was over. She fell silent, her lips pursed in frustration.

They both listened to the radio.

"The incidence of a particular behavior being brought to my attention is probably the result of the level of tolerance that people have for that behavior. The moral and legal consequences of dog-human aggression provide for a low tolerance level by most people. The economic consequences of house soiling and destructive chewing also tend to reduce tolerances. Barking almost invariably involves low tolerance levels by someone other than the owner."

Sam looked at the radio and smiled. "I have a low tolerance for pseudo-intellectual pet shrinks, that's all."

Dr. Stevens' voice had become as rhythmically serene as his interviewer's. "Many problem behaviors appear to be stress-related from either environmental or owner-induced causes. The animal behavior therapist can assist the owners in identifying the areas which should be adjusted and then give them the tools, techniques, knowledge, and motivation necessary to deal with the problem behavior."

"I'm afraid we are out of time. We have been talking today with Doctor Tom Stevens about animal behavior therapy. One of the many thought-provoking messages shared with our listeners today is that both hope and help exist for pet owners who are experiencing problems with their pet's behavior. You owe it, not only to yourself, but to your loyal animal companion to consider behavior therapy. Thank you, Doctor Stevens, for being with us today on *Open Air*."

"My pleasure, Ursula. Thank you for having me."

"My pleasure, Ursula. Thank you for having me," Sam mimicked in a whiny voice and clicked off the radio.

Sidney picked up the cordless phone and held it to her ear. She punched the talk button repeatedly. "You're in luck, buster. This thing doesn't work without electricity."

"Somebody thank Jesus," Sam muttered under his breath.

"I can read lips, you know." She picked up her smartphone and began following it around the room as if it were a divining rod. "Nothing," she said a little too loudly. "Why is it that I'm not surprised? Let's take a little tally: The roads are closed, the electricity is out, the phones are dead, my eggs are ready, there's no cable, no satellite, no TV reception. Oh, wait, we don't even own a TV. It's the tenth of May, and there's a blizzard raging. Again, why is it that we live on the dark side of the moon, the land that time forgot?"

Sam settled back in his chair, smiled, and picked up his magazine. "Isn't Wyoming great?"

CHAPTER THIRTY-TWO

SANCTUARY

Annie awakened from a deep sleep and immediately became vigilant, listening for hidden sounds. The warm bed offered sanctuary from the wind as she lay nestled within the frigid room. The coolness of the pillow reinforced the contrasting warmth of the covers. The room was illuminated with the uniform grayness of morning. Annie did not move. She was lost in time and place. She wondered if primitive man had felt the same way as the wind lapped at the entrance of his cave. Genetically encoded from a million years of listening, she was predestined to take comfort from her shelter.

Annie knew that sleep was again near as the heavy dullness of unconsciousness swept upward from her brain stem, an anesthetic blanket creeping over her cerebrum. Annie was tired. She had lain awake much of the night, listening, waiting for the repeated whisper of the one clearly enunciated word she was sure she had heard in the hissing static of the telephone.

Too tired to resist, she fluttered between the conscious and the unconscious. She saw herself lying naked on a cold beach. The surf was rushing to shore, washing its cold water up over and between her legs, stopping at her breasts, and then receding with a gentle tugging on her lower torso. She felt the sand beneath her hips erode from under her as the waves gently pulled her to the sea. Her arms and legs felt heavy and numb. She wanted to cry out, but her voice would not come, only useless puffs of exhaled air. She tossed her head from side to side to free the scream from her throat. The smell of wet sand and decaying flesh invaded her nostrils. "Help," she whispered feebly. "Help me." Her voice became a little stronger as she forced the words from her lips. When she attempted a final desperate scream, another wave swept upward over her body, rushing over her chest and neck, filling her ears, and plunging into her open mouth. Her scream was drowned in a frantic gasping as she fought vainly to expel the water and extract one more life-giving measure of air.

Annie stared at the ceiling, listening to the wind. Her arms ached as the feeling in them slowly returned. She became aware that she was partially uncovered and weakly raised her hand in an attempt to pull the sheet and blanket upward.

The weight of the covers pressed down uncomfortably over Annie's feet. L2 had been cold too, and had sought warmth between Annie's lower legs in defiance of her training. The dog was cradled in the depression between her ankles. Annie slowly extended her big toes against the weighty resistance of the covers. The dog stretched with an almost fluid movement that flowed from head to tail, then again settled heavily between Annie's calves.

L2's high-pitched yawn sounded an alarm in Annie's brain. It was the same attention-getting yawn the dog used when she needed to go outside. But there was something out of context, something amiss. Confused, yet sensing that someone was watching her, Annie slowly turned her head to the left. L2 sat on the floor next to the bed, staring at her; her giant bloodhound nose only inches from Annie's face. Fear, like an electric shock jolted every nerve in her body with the realization that something else was nestled between her legs.

CHAPTER THIRTY-THREE

FAMILIAL

Forty-two inches on the level, with wind gusts of more than sixty-five miles per hour was the official storm tally. The day was warm and sunny, but Southeastern Wyoming had come to a standstill. All attention was on I-80. Trucks were backed up as far east as Sidney, Nebraska, and west to Rawlins. Rotary plows were brought in from the more mountainous counties to cut a swath through the fifteen-foot drifts. Finals week had started, and the university was closed. Sam had been considering Sidney's question of why they lived in Wyoming. It was not for the mild climate.

The 1950 John Deere bulldozer was the classic Johnny Popper, a two-cylinder workhorse that could move mountains. Sam had used the little MC Crawler when renovating the cow camp and constructing the road that connected him to the outside world. He had replaced the mouse-eaten seat with one he had taken out of a wrecked school bus in a Laramie junkyard.

The double seat allowed Sidney to ride next to him as he chugged slowly down the quarter-mile driveway. Tons of snow rolled easily ahead of them. The forest was in continuous motion, large dollops of snow sliding from the bent ponderosa limbs as the morning progressed. Sidney laid her head on her father's shoulder and beamed.

••••

After several false starts, power was restored by early afternoon. The telephone produced a dial tone at four o'clock. Sidney tried to call Annie, but the busy signal seemed to indicate her exchange was still down.

Plowing snow had given Sam time to think. He was anxious to find out if the coroner had received the results from the Miami-Dade review. He drew a blank from the coroner's office—the coroner was stranded in Fort Collins. But the same woman who had leaked Lilly Darnell's name to him said that the Miami-Dade review had arrived days ago. She was not at liberty to divulge its contents, since a murder investigation was underway.

"Work your magic, Sid," Sam said. "Call your mole in the sheriff's office and see what you can find out."

Less than ten minutes had passed when Sidney stepped into Sam's study. "Potassium and lots of it," she said. "There was cardiovascular failure as a result of huge amounts of potassium in Lilly Darnell's system, most likely from being injected with succinylcholine. But listen to this: They found a heap of intracellular calcium, which would have caused horrible muscle contractions, revving up her metabolism to a degree that would've consumed monster amounts of ATP—adenosine triphosphate— and generated lots and lots of heat. She couldn't process it the way normal people do—"

"Bottom line?" Sam interrupted.

"Bottom line is that she suffered from malignant hyperthermia. How rare is that? One in thirty thousand in the general population. Apparently there's a familial link."

Sam stood and walked to the window. He stared at the heavy white blanket of snow that had softened the rugged terrain. Had he not found Lilly Darnell, her body would once again have been covered by nature's relentless attempts to cleanse itself. "I don't get it," he said, turning to face Sidney. "Didn't you tell me that paralysis is immediate with this drug? That the victim collapses in a heap, unable to move or breathe, and that they are conscious while they slowly suffocate?"

"Yeah, it's a horrible death. That's why a sedative is always given first when sux is used in surgery. Knock 'em out before you paralyze them. Sux is one of the drugs in the three-drug cocktail sometimes used in executions. First, they get a barbiturate like sodium pentothal, then a paralyzing agent like succinylcholine, and finally potassium chloride to stop the heart. Not very humane, in that potassium chloride causes a heart attack, and that hurts. I think it has been deemed cruel and unusual."

"So, how did Lilly end up deep in the forest more than a mile from the nearest two-track? A twelve-year-old is a bit heavy to carry that far."

"I suspect her killer walked her there, then injected her with sux." Sidney frowned. "Remember, they found trace amounts of ketamine in her system. She was drugged just enough to keep her from escaping. Add sux to her bloodstream, and Lilly would have dropped like a sack of potatoes. I think the killer staged the scene after her murder to make it look like an accident—lost child freezes to death in the mountains."

Sam squeezed his chin between his thumb and forefinger. "I still don't get it. Why not just shoot her and dump the body somewhere more convenient?"

"Don't ask me. I didn't kill her," Sidney shrugged.

"It just seems a little too elaborate. And why the nude photo at Annie's place? I don't think there's anything random or spontaneous about this. There's motive written all over it."

"Speaking of Horse Creek Creepy," Sidney said. "I'm worried about Annie." She pushed up her glasses and viewed Sam through distorted lenses.

"Me too, kiddo," he said quietly, picking up the phone and dialing.

A tight-lipped smile formed on Sidney's face and she blinked her approval at her father.

"Mrs. Darnell, this is Sam Dawson in Wyoming," Sam said, turning away from his daughter.

CHAPTER THIRTY-FOUR

WHISPERS

The world had been born the night before. Now in daylight, it rested. There was quiet, no wind. Annie's ears rang from the silence. No hum from the refrigerator or crackling from the baseboard heaters competed with the monotonous singing of the single note that emanated from deep within her ears. The fireplace, black and cold, stood silently in the corner of the living room. She had burned the last of the wood the night before. She could see her breath. She lay fully clothed on the couch, her knees pulled up to her chest. Disoriented, her eyes searched the room. Boxes and crumpled newspapers littered the floor. Her stomach rumbled. She had forgotten to eat as she busied herself packing. She glanced at the bedroom door. It was still closed. She would not go in there again, ever.

Her body felt numb. The sensation was simply one of pressure. It was the same feeling she had experienced upon awakening to find her hand totally numb with sleep resting on some portion of her body. The touch was not cold, nor was it warm, simply foreign. Fingers were resting lightly on her neck just below her jaw. She could feel the bitter cold of fear wash over her as she realized that both her hands were stuffed between her thighs in an attempt to warm them. Again, she felt the overwhelming sense of another's presence. It seemed to hover above the couch. The foreboding perception swept over and through her, chilling her flesh, stinging the skin of her exposed face and neck. Her heart raced, and the hair follicles on her arms tightened their defensive grip as her skin crawled at the realization that an extra set of fingers rested on her neck. *Maybe I am going crazy after all*, she thought.

"No!" she screamed as she leaped from the couch. She tore at her neck as if a large, hairy spider had crawled down her blouse. L2 scrambled to her feet and leaped into the kitchen, her nails clawing noisily against the linoleum floor. Standing in the center of the room, Annie smelled the repulsive stench of rancid death and human excrement. Her eyes narrowed and her upper lip curled against the sensation of having fresh feces stuffed up each nostril. The taste on the back of her tongue produced a heavy involuntary retch. She clutched at her stomach and tried to suppress the urge to vomit. She pressed the back of her hand to her mouth and nose. An invisible fog of icy air seemed to envelop her, descending down the back of her neck and sliding over each shoulder, then down her spine.

Two large stereo speakers that sat at each end of the couch emitted a fuzzy crackling of amplified static electricity. "Baby" was again the one-word proclamation she thought she heard hissing in the background. Annie stood motionless in the middle of the room. Her eyes darted quickly to the VU meters on the stereo receiver. She frantically sought confirmation, reassurance that the voice actually existed, that she had not imagined the sound. But there was still no electricity.

She stumbled backward toward the kitchen, pushing boxes and newspapers from her path. She tried to breathe, but her breath came in sputtering spasms. At the open doorway to the kitchen, she reflexively reached behind her for the light switch on the kitchen side of the wall. Disbelief raced up her arm, across her chest, and settled in her brain stem at the realization that her groping hand had encountered someone else's hand covering the light switch. The unmistakable bony protuberances of knuckles beneath cadaverous skin stretched tightly over tendons, sent a heart-stopping shock through her body. She jerked her hand away with terror and repulsion. "Jesus!" she yelled.

"Baby" was the promptly whispered reply from behind her.

Annie spun around and faced the wall phone. It was only half a ring, an incomplete electrical response. She waited, anticipating the next full ring, but it did not come. Perhaps it had not rung at all. She was not sure. Maybe she had imagined the sound. She slowly reached for the receiver, but pulled her hand back reflexively. She knew what she would hear.

The house creaked. At first she believed it was the weight of the snow or that the wind had finally arrived. But it was too systematic. A crescendo of tortured shrieks and groans, force and loudness combined in a frightening finale. Annie believed the house was shrinking. The air seemed to have been sucked from the room. She was breathing noisily, her mouth wide open. Lightness swept upward past her knees and waist. Her hair seemed to float outward, gravity suspended. The frosty vapors of her breath momentarily clouded her view. Her knees trembled—no, they vibrated. She looked at the floor between her feet and watched the floor quake. Tremors oscillated upward through the soles of her shoes. She was not trembling, she realized—the house was. Overhead, the fly-spattered plastic light fixture vibrated as it slowly rotated around the stationary bulb.

A blinding flash illuminated the house. The light did not radiate from a single source, but emanated from the length and breadth of the entire structure. It lasted only a millisecond, just long enough to produce the disturbing blue halos of after-images in Annie's retinas. Suddenly, all was quiet and still. Her left arm throbbed with fatigue from holding something clutched to her chest. With cautious repugnance, she slowly turned her face downward toward the object she held to her breast. The cold, dark eyes amid the thread-like fractures of the porcelain face stared vacantly in return. "Baby," a voice seemed to whisper.

CHAPTER THIRTY-FIVE

CONNECTIONS

The question had been simple, yet it seemed to catch Dorothy Darnell off guard. She would ask her husband and get back to Sam. It was a hunch, nothing more. One of Sam's curious questions that often seemed to have no context.

The phone rang just before dark as Sidney dried the dishes, which Sam had washed and placed in the drainer next to the sink. Sidney could hear her father's muffled voice in the next room.

"Interesting," he said, returning to the kitchen.

"All right, I'll bite," Sidney said without looking at her father.

"It's probably nothing, but Mrs. Darnell's husband—Lyle Darnell—had an uncle that died during routine gallbladder surgery some forty years ago, a guy by the name of Hofstadter."

Sidney pushed her glasses up on the bridge of her nose. "Uh-huh. And?"

"An otherwise healthy man died on the operating table before they even had a chance to remove his gallbladder?"

"Where are you going with this?"

"Probably nowhere," said Sam, "but I'm still troubled by the fact that we haven't been able to establish a motive for Lilly's murder. I guess I'm just trying to get the puzzle pieces on the table."

"So, are you thinking that the great uncle had an adverse reaction to the anesthesia, something like malignant hyperthermia—from the sux, maybe?"

"I don't know. It seems possible. I doubt if there's any connection, but I think I'll do a little digging."

Sidney recognized that faraway look in her father's eyes. She could see the wheels turning. There would be no deterring him. "Don't stay up too late. I'll bet they get the highway open sometime during the night. That means the university will reopen too. But first things first. We need to check on Annie."

Sam tugged at his chin and stared blankly at the dark window above the sink.

"Earth to Dad. Come in, Father," she waved her hand in front of his face.

"What?" Sam said, a surprised look on his face.

"I said, where did he die?" she lied.

"Oh, Lincoln, Nebraska, but the family lived in someplace called Dismal River. It's in the Sandhills of western Nebraska."

CHAPTER THIRTY-SIX

MISSING

The sun crept incrementally above the eastern horizon of the Horse Creek valley. At ground level, there was no perception of depth or shape, just a uniform whiteness. Above, the branches of the cottonwoods, the symmetrical lattice of the windmill tower, and the lumpy appearance of the weathered barn with the sudden upcropping of the jack-o'-lantern house, all provided a measure of relative size and distance.

Overnight, the roads had been cleared, but there was no one on them. Ranchers were busy plowing feed lanes with giant four-wheel-drive tractors. Dark bunches of cattle had drifted against fences in protected arroyos. They waited. Sam was able to get the Willys to Horse Creek via Cheyenne, but Annie's quarter-mile driveway was drifted shut.

Sam's breath surged through his puckered lips as he fought for balance on the antique snowshoes, their bent ash and rawhide lacings keeping him atop the deep drifts. He rounded the hill and made his way toward Annie's house, stabbing army-surplus ski poles into the snow with each opposing step. He was beginning to perspire. He carried Sidney's aluminum and nylon snowshoes strapped to his back.

Sam had rehearsed in his mind what he wanted to say to Annie, but knew he would not. Instead, he would likely criticize her for something unrelated to how he really felt about her. Visions of taking her in his arms and kissing her deeply were pleasant daydreams that, for unknown reasons, never came true.

The reasons why they were no longer together were obscure. Foggy remembrances of illogical discussions that bordered on arguments, played repeatedly in his mind. They had been through so much together. She knew his secret. It was her secret too. The Colorado revelation seemed a lifetime ago. He had buried the master ledger that showed their twisted pedigree, the coded descendants of the false science of eugenics. But he could not bury Annie's perception of wrongdoing. Unions between cousins were depravity. He had argued, unsuccessfully, that their relatedness as second cousins once removed was minimal from a genetic standpoint. They shared only a fraction of their genotype, a mere one sixty-fourth. He presented the case that his cut-and-tied vas deferens made the entire issue moot. But she said it was no consolation for unrighteousness.

Sam loved the tiny wrinkles at the corners of Annie's eyes when she smiled, the buried dimples on each side of her mouth. He loved her long, flawless neck that demanded to be kissed. He loved her perfect hands, slender and smooth. He loved the smell of her hair. Sam took a deep breath that seemed to sputter as he inhaled. He probably loved Annie George, but he knew he had a tendency to give away his heart too easily. She had rejected him, and it made him bitter. He could not allow that to happen again.

Only a portion of the roof of Annie's green Subaru protruded above the giant drift of snow extending from the house to the barn. A shovel stood upright in a pile of snow that had been cleared from the driver's door. At first, he did not understand why she would attempt to dig out a buried car that had no chance of going anywhere. Tracks led from the house to the car to the barn, lots of tracks that created waist-deep corridors in the wet snow.

Cardboard and duct tape covered the window in the door to the house. Sam removed his snowshoes and opened the door. Broken shards of glass littered the floor. The window had been smashed from the outside. "Annie," he called. There was no response. He quickly checked the other rooms, his voice becoming harsher as fear rose in his throat. His hands began to shake with the discovery of a second broken window in the bathroom. He hurried back to the kitchen and noted his breath condensing in the icy air. He flipped the light switch on his way out, but nothing happened.

Sam plowed his way back to the car. The windows were encrusted with ice on the inside. Panicked, Sam forced the door open. *Surely she knew not to start a car whose muffler was buried beneath four feet of snow.* The backseat had been folded down. A pillow and blankets indicated that she had sought refuge in the car. *But why? Why sleep in the*

car when she had an entire house to sleep in? It did not make sense.
Surely, the house would have been warmer than the car.

A kerosene lantern sat upright in the snow. Instinctively, he picked it up and kicked his way to the barn. L2 almost knocked him down when he pulled open the door. She wiggled from the tip of her nose to the end of her tail, all the while grunting and poking her bloodhound nose into Sam's face as he knelt and hugged her. "Yes, yes, I'm glad to see you too," he said. She shied when he accidently tousled her injured ear, which still appeared red and slightly swollen. "Sorry, girl, sorry," he said as he hugged her again. "Where's Annie? Where's Annie, girl? Go get Annie." He suddenly felt like he was commanding Lassie to find Timmy in the well. L2 responded by lumbering to her dog bed and fetching her tennis ball. Sam noted the large bowls of food and water placed near a broken bale of hay. He replaced the lantern on its hook by the door and scanned the dusky interior. The silence was eerie. Dust particles floated in the shafts of sunlight that filtered in between the battens of vertical siding. He called Annie's name, his voice absorbed by hay and snow. He was beginning to panic. "You stay, girl. I'll come back for you."

He burst outside and called again and again, his voice small and insignificant. A painful lump had formed in his throat as he followed a foot trail around the north side of the house. Snowmobile tracks snaked away from the house along the valley floor like the fossilized path of a giant worm, and disappeared in the distance.

••••

Smoke drifted lazily upward from a slightly crooked brick chimney atop the slumped ranch house. An assortment of outbuildings and corrals sat back from a line of giant, bare cottonwood trees that followed the meandering course of Horse Creek. In the distance, calves bawled for their mothers. Granite hills and bluffs surrounded the Rocking R homestead. An ancient shepherd mix with cloudy eyes and arthritic joints struggled to its feet when Sam burst into the house unannounced. Sweat ran down his cheeks as he surveyed the kitchen. The sweet aroma of burning cottonwood filled the room.

"Sam," Annie said loudly as she stood up from the kitchen table. A gilded picture of Jesus and his disciples at the Last Supper hung on the wall behind her. "I certainly didn't expect to see you way out here. How did you know where I was?"

Sam ignored her. Instead, he kept his attention focused on the man who sat across from her.

Oscar Roberts rose stiffly from the table. He frowned at Sam suspiciously. His small, piglike eyes appeared black, and his greasy hair hung over his ears. White beard stubble could not hide his pocked cheeks.

"Oscar, this is Sam Dawson," Annie said politely. "Sam, this is Oscar Roberts."

Neither man said a word. Instead, they stared at each other blankly.

"Most people in these parts knock," Roberts said without diverting his gaze.

"You shot my dog," Sam said, his eyes narrowing.

"I generally hit what I aim at," Oscar responded.

Both men continued to stare at each other.

Annie shook her head. "Are you two done with your male displays of aggression? Go pee on a tree or something and then let's be civilized."

Oscar and Sam looked at her, then back at each other.

"You're trespassing, Dawson," Roberts sneered.

"Screw you, Roberts. If you want to add another assault charge, make your move."

The standoff continued.

"Isn't she a little old for your taste?" Sam said, nodding toward Annie.

"You trying to provoke me, Dawson?" Oscar's eyes narrowed. "I could shoot your ass and be justified."

Sam wiped away the sweat from his forehead and began to unbutton his coat, but did not take his eyes off Roberts. "Were you justified when you killed Lilly Darnell, you sick bastard? Go ahead and make your move, old man. I'm not a defenseless twelve-year-old girl. I'll tear out your stinking liver and stuff it in your mouth."

Annie made no attempt to stifle her laugh. "Mr. Roberts came by looking for cattle that had pushed through fences during the storm. He was kind enough to bring me here until the power is restored. I was getting pretty cold. Did you come to rescue the damsel in distress?" She smiled, looking eagerly at Sam.

"I came to get my dog back," he said, immediately sorry for covering up his true feelings for her. But this was no place to discuss matters of the heart. He thought she looked tired. Dark circles had formed under her puffy eyes. "Cold aside, what the hell are you doing here?" Sam said sincerely. "You voluntarily run off with the guy who has been arrested for possession of child pornography? The guy who's a prime suspect in a murder case? The guy who evicted you? The guy who shot my dog?" Sam was out of breath.

"You can't prove I shot your dog," Roberts said matter-of-factly.

"And the rest of it?"

Roberts stared at him for a moment. "I have my faults, Dawson. Molesting and killing children are not among them."

"You'll have your day."

"We'll all have our day when we stand before the Almighty. There'll be no escaping His justice."

"I hope to hell He's got a dog," Sam shot back. "Get your coat on, Annie. We're leaving."

Annie looked up at Sam. Her smile had disappeared. "First, you're being a jerk. Second, you can't order me around like I work for you or something." She paused as she searched Sam's face. "Third, where are you taking me?"

"You're coming to my house."

"Why?"

Sam hesitated. "Because Sidney wants you to stay with us until we get this sorted out."

"Sidney wants me? What about you?"

"I want my dog back."

Annie looked away and inhaled deeply. "How are we supposed to get there?"

"The Willys is parked on the highway near your place. If we leave now we can be there before dark."

"I'm not going back in that house."

"We'll come back and get your stuff in a few days when we can get down the driveway."

"What about L2? She's in the barn."

"We'll pick her up on the way back. Here, put these on," he said, pulling Sidney's snowshoes from the sling on his back. "Let's go."

"The Hofstadter place—er, her rental," Roberts corrected. "It's more than a mile away," he warned.

Sam froze. He looked at Roberts, but said nothing. That was the second time in the past twenty-four hours that he had heard that name.

CHAPTER THIRTY-SEVEN

ESSAY

Final grades were to be posted in the morning. Sam had underestimated the time required to assign a somewhat arbitrary rating to the students' terminal project. There was no final exam. Instead, each student was to muster everything they had learned in the class to tell a story with pictures, the proverbial photo-essay. Lens choice, focal length, exposure, shutter speed, depth of field, light, composition, and all the other tools and techniques they had learned during the semester were to be used in presenting an original essay. No text or captions were allowed. He had spent most of a lecture on the differences between picture stories and essays. The kicker was that they were limited to a dozen photographs. Clarity and point of view must be defined and effectively influence the viewer. Each photograph had to convey both information and emotion. Sam had thought he was being clever. He looked at the mantle clock and sighed. It was 1:15 a.m., and he was only half done grading the visual gibberish that had obviously been slapped together like a baloney sandwich the day before the project was due. He wished he had given them a multiple-choice exam instead.

L2 popped her head up suddenly and oriented toward the outside door. She emitted a low, throaty growl, her usual warning to indicate the presence of strangers long before Sam or Sidney would see their vehicle pull into the driveway. Sam glanced at the clock again. It was 1:40 a.m. "Easy, girl," he cautioned, sliding from his chair and walking to the door. He cupped his hands around his face and peered out the window in the door. Scanning the driveway where the Willys was parked, he saw nothing. "Probably a raccoon or your close relative, the skunk," he said, walking back to the kitchen table. "Go back to sleep."

Annie padded softly to the refrigerator at 2:00 a.m. At the sound of the door opening, L2 raised her head from the rug in front of the fireplace. The interior light of the refrigerator shone through the thin, worn shirt Sidney had given her to wear as a nightgown. Sam watched her as she bent slightly into the fridge, scanning the shelves, her perfect shape clearly outlined beneath the fabric. Her hair fell off her shoulders when she bent to look behind the pickles. She settled for a glass of milk, which she brought to the kitchen table, where Sam was grading the essays. She sat down with one leg crossed beneath her.

"You're working late," she said, taking a man-sized gulp of milk, then licking the white moustache from her upper lip.

Sam smiled at her. "That storm last weekend put everybody a little behind."

"What are you working on?" She leaned over the table to look at the photographs spread between them.

"I'm grading their final project. They're photo-essays." He looked up at her. The top two buttons of her shirt were undone, and he could see the rounded top of her right breast. He smelled the light citrus fragrance of her freshly shampooed hair.

"What's this one about?" Annie pointed to a cute little boy holding up a ribbon in the middle of a rodeo arena. He wore a dirty cowboy hat pushed back on his head, a broad smile on his face. Dozens of other children surrounded him.

"It's about a kid's dream of becoming a rodeo star. It's one of the better essays, actually. Here we see him starting out at an early age, competing in a catch-a-calf event at a small-town rodeo. He then moves on to mutton busting." Sam pulled out a photo of a helmeted boy riding a sheep. "The story progresses through different age levels, always using dark-haired boys, then men to portray the same individual. There's the saddle bronc stage, followed by the bareback event, and finally bull riding. His success is depicted by the silver belt buckles the young man proudly displays after each of the action shots. Good composition with a nice blending of foreground and background. Lighting is a bit tricky."

"How does it end?"

Sam shuffled to the end of the stack of pictures. A lifeless cowboy lay facedown in the arena as a rodeo clown was desperately trying to divert the attention of the huge bull that was about to gore the young man. Dirt was flying and people were running, panic on their faces.

"Oh my God!" Annie gasped. "How tragic."

"Great," Sam smiled. "He got an emotional response out of you. That's the goal. I didn't think the little goofball was paying attention. All semester he acted like he was bored stiff, and then he turns in something like this."

"Are they all this good?"

Sam chuckled. "Heck no. Here, look at this one," he said, sorting through the stack of assignments. "She's my little religious fanatic. She turned in a dozen black-and-white shots of white churches on the plains. I have no idea what the essay is about. It could be architecture, desolation, purity, steeples. Who knows?"

Annie leaned a little closer to him. Sam stole another look at her exposed neckline. "Check this one out," he said. "This is Brittany's essay. I secretly call her 'Juicy' because that's what it says across the rear of her sweatpants. I think it refers to her cerebral cortex. Anyway, here are a dozen pictures of tattoos and tattoo parlors, and more than I needed to see of Juicy Brittany." He pulled the last photo and slid it toward Annie. It was of Brittany standing naked in front of a full-length mirror. Several tattoos adorned her otherwise nubile body.

"Jeez O'Pete, Sam. Did she get an emotional response from you?"

Sam raised his eyebrows. "I hadn't thought of that. I might have to pass her after all."

Annie stared at him. "Is that what it takes?"

Sam cocked his head to the side and narrowed his eyes. "I'm not sure I follow you."

She smiled broadly; her eyes shone mischievously. "What if I told you that I had a tattoo?"

Sam replaced the cap on his red Sharpie. "I'd be curious," he said, holding her gaze.

"Is that all, just curious?"

"I'm not sure what you're saying, Annie. Do you want me to ask you if I can check you for tattoos? Is that it?"

"Maybe," she said coyly.

Sam shook his head. "I know where this bus is headed. It's the bus bound for frustration, with a stop at disappointment. I took it once before, remember?" He paused then added softly, "I think I'll pass."

Neither of them spoke for a long, uncomfortable moment. "What happened to us, Sam?"

He took a deep breath. He wanted to tell her what had happened to them, how she had rejected him at a time when he was least prepared to deal with it. How she had broken his heart when she gave hers to another. And now, her cruel courtship ritual with Tom Stevens, the doggie shrink, was like holding him on his back and plucking out his legs one by one. He was tired of the game.

"Look, I think we need to establish some ground rules while you're here. And, let me be clear, you're welcome to stay with us for as long as it takes to find a new place of your own. We'll move you out of Horse Creek as soon as I can finish up at the university. But as long as you are here, I think it's best that we—"

Annie slid her chair back from the table. Tears had welled up in her eyes. She attempted a smile, but her quivering lips betrayed her. She turned and quietly disappeared into the darkness of the house.

CHAPTER THIRTY-EIGHT

RUNAWAY

Winter persisted at the summit. It was the highest point on the transcontinental Interstate 80 and had its own microclimate. Tractor-trailer rigs often littered the boulder-strewn buffers between the highway and the canyon walls—like lemmings. Glimpses of Laramie, in the valley below, would occasionally appear as the road snaked its way down the fifteen-hundred vertical feet from top to bottom. The road's surface varied from wet to snow-packed to icy as Sam piloted the Willys onto the interstate. He slipped the Muncie overdrive into high and watched the tachometer bounce back to two thousand rpms. The heater hummed, and the windshield wipers lurched at the mist thrown up by the eighteen-wheelers.

The morning sun was shielded from the highway where the road descended into the steepest part of the canyon. Its surface was covered in black ice. He wished he had locked in the hubs at the summit. But the deteriorating highway conditions could not compete with his thoughts about Annie. She occupied every available space inside his head. He was in love with her. He had always been in love with her. *I'm going to come clean with her and tell her how I feel,* he thought. He had his chance the night before. Instead, he rebuffed her advances and continued the charade of keeping her at arm's length. *Tonight! I'll tell her tonight.*

A Colorado greenie swished past him. Sand and ice pelted the windshield. "Idiot," Sam said aloud. On the open highway, Coloradans seemed to have a death wish. He wondered if he had been so reckless when he lived there. *Post the grades, clean out my desk, drive back to Cheyenne, see O'Malley, then go home and tell Annie I want to spend the rest of my life with her.* Sam smiled to himself. It would be a good day.

Up ahead, the greenie began to slide sideways. A chain reaction of brake lights flickered up the canyon like a progressive neon sign. Sam eased his foot onto the brake pedal and noted his speed. Nothing happened. The pedal collapsed to the floor without resistance. He was on the steepest grade of the canyon.

A string of semitrailer rigs stretched down the hill in the right lane. He reached for the overdrive gearshift. The rpms approached twenty-six hundred. Taking the Willys out of overdrive at this speed would certainly send him into a tailspin. Likewise, downshifting to third at sixty miles per hour would have the same effect. He would become a pinball bounced between jackknifed semis. He glanced at the useless emergency brake handle to his left. He visualized the cable as it wound its way toward the rear brake drums, the ball-like knobs bobbing up and down, unattached to the braking mechanisms. It was one of those things he had never needed and he was always too busy to hook up. Now he wished he had.

Sam saw the runaway truck ramp a quarter mile ahead. It had been crudely carved into the canyon wall by giant D9 Caterpillars when the interstate swallowed the old Highway 30 years earlier. He had never seen it used. Steep and narrow, it looked like Evel Knievel's launch pad to self-assisted suicide.

He was gaining speed as he passed the giant trucks that were lined up in the right-hand lane, the lane he would need to be in if he hoped to exit onto the ramp. The truckers left little space between their rigs. The timing would have to be perfect for Sam to swerve between trucks and onto the ramp—glare ice made such sudden moves treacherous. He glanced to his left, at the concrete barrier that separated the westbound and eastbound lanes. The oversized tires on the Willys would grab at the wall and force him into—and possibly over—the barrier. At best, he would roll the Willys and ricochet into the trucks, causing a massive pileup with him at the bottom. Ahead, semis occupied both lanes. Sam was out of options. He skated right, nearly clipping the giant chrome bumper of the Peterbilt pulling tandem trailers. The trucker blasted his air horns, the sound deafening as the Willys filled the space between trucks. Snowplows had left a wall of snow along the edge of the road that presented a barrier to the runaway ramp. He would probably roll, but in a direction away from the trucks. He pulled the loose end of the seat belt tight across his hips and steered the Willys hard right toward the center of the ramp. The wall of snow exploded with less resistance than he anticipated. The Willys was engulfed in a blinding spray of snow as Sam slammed into the steering wheel. Dreamlike silence followed. He wondered if he was conscious. He waited for pain.

••••

Sidney would blow a fuse when she found out. She would be less concerned about Sam or the Willys than the road charge. The tow truck bill was, by design, just under his insurance deductible. The ticket for careless driving from the state trooper was an insult added to misery. "My driving was superb," Sam had argued. "I had no brakes."

"You were operating an unsafe vehicle that resulted in an accident," the young trooper said. His Smokey the Bear hat looked comically uncomfortable as he handed Sam the ticket.

"They just don't make 'em like this anymore," the bewhiskered old man with a red nose said as he packed up his tow truck. "You're good to go. Them brakes will need bleedin' 'cause there's air in the lines. But you got enough brakes to get you into town."

Sam had discovered the problem as soon as he was able to dig out the hood and raise it. Both brake lines for the split hydraulic circuits from the master cylinder, had somehow come loose. Brake fluid was sprayed throughout the engine compartment. He thought it curious, indeed, that the compression fitting could work loose without the aid of a wrench. The old man tightened the fitting and filled the reservoir with brake fluid. "You might wanna dig out that snow packed against your radiator," he said with a wink. "If you'd been a greenie, I'd'a hauled your ass into town and given you a bill to make you think twice about comin' back to Wyoming."

Sam thanked the old man and limped into Laramie. He dropped the Willys off at the GM service center and took their shuttle to campus. Thoughts of Annie had been replaced by anger when he remembered telling her in front of Oscar Roberts where his vehicle was parked. Roberts had ample time to drive to the highway and tamper with the Willys while he and Annie slowly made their way back on snowshoes. Or, maybe Roberts was the skunk that L2 had heard in the night. In any case, it had taken less than thirty miles for the master cylinder to run dry. Others had warned him about Roberts. He would not make the same mistake twice.

CHAPTER THIRTY-NINE

HOFSTADTER

Harrison O'Malley looked over the top of his drugstore readers. "What brings you to my side of the mountain, Sam?"

"I think Oscar Roberts tried to kill me."

"Join the club."

"I'm serious."

"Didn't we tell you to steer clear of that man?"

"Can I get a restraining order or something?" Sam said.

"Not my job. I only enforce them. You'll need a lawyer to petition the court. What else can I help you with?"

"Well, thanks for asking," Sam quipped. "I'm curious about a name and I keep coming up with dead ends."

"I wish you wouldn't use the word 'dead' in our conversations. It triggers some autonomic response that tends to pucker my butt and raise my hackles."

"Sorry," Sam said, "but I've come up short at both the county and state libraries. I could ask Oscar Roberts, but he's trying to kill me."

"That's your story," the sheriff said, swiveling in his squeaky desk chair. His crisp white shirt with a western yoke, snap buttons, and flap pockets had the sheriff's star embroidered in gold thread above his heart.

"Actually, a nice woman from the Wyoming State Historical Society mentioned that you grew up in Laramie County and might know the people I'm looking for."

"Who might that be, Sam?"

"I don't know any given names, but the family name was Hofstadter."

O'Malley leaned forward and removed his glasses. "You've been here long enough to know that most of us in the state are related, and those who aren't at least know each other. I was wondering when you'd bring up that name."

Sam looked puzzled. "I don't follow."

The sheriff ignored him and smoothed his mustache with the web between his thumb and forefinger. "The Hofstadters were squatters that to the best of my recollection came into the county sometime in the fifties. My dad cowboyed for Oscar Roberts' dad on the Rocking R. Oscar's got a few years on me, but if I remember right, he went off to seminary school back east someplace. He was gone for a long time. He didn't show up back in this area until after his dad died, but I digress. Old man Roberts, Oscar's dad, had hired Hofstadter to fix fence and water gaps and other odd jobs, rather than run them off the place. I guess he felt sorry for them since Mrs. Hofstadter was in a family way and they already had a little boy, Billy. We went to school together. He was pretty much a worthless piece of cow dung and was constantly in trouble. He got expelled about once a year and was about to be sent off to reform school, when the family up and moved to a little burg in the Sandhills of Nebraska. Billy never amounted to much. He married a local named June and had a couple of kids. Billy picked up the habit, then got to dealing. He died in the state pen over in Lincoln. That was the last I heard of him until..." His voice trailed off, then his eyes suddenly found Sam, as if surprised he was still there. "What is it that you're not telling me, Sam?"

"Do you know how he died?"

"Don't know exactly. I remember there was a lawsuit and June lived off the judgment—that and welfare. Seems to me it was some medical screwup; he died during surgery. I repeat, what is it that you're not telling me?"

"It's probably nothing," Sam said, squeezing his chin between his thumb and forefinger, lost in thought.

"Let me be the judge of that."

"It appears that Billy Hofstadter might have been Lilly Darnell's grand uncle, since Billy's sister was Lyle's mother."

Harrison O'Malley's face showed no reaction. He grabbed the arms of his squeaky chair and pinned Sam with a piercing gaze. "You've done dug yourself a hole now, Sam."

"How so?"

"You've established a connection between the victim and the potential crime scene. There's only one way you could have linked the old Hofstadter place with Lilly Darnell. You recognized the room in the picture I showed you, the one with Lilly spread-eagle on a mattress."

He paused. "Withholding information in a murder investigation is a criminal offense, Sam."

"Will I get free health care?"

"Yep. Plus free room and board, clothes, and total rehabilitation. Do you have any ideas about motive?"

"Not yet, but I'm working on it. You already knew about the Hofstadter connection, didn't you?" Sam said.

"Not with the Darnell family. That's new."

"It's your turn, Sheriff. What are you not telling me?"

"Well, first off, Sam, I don't need to tell you a damn thing. This is my murder investigation, and I'm still wondering how and why the Hofstadter-Darnell relatedness thing came up. Care to tell me?"

"I think Lilly may have died from a rare, inherited condition called malignant hyperthermia as a result of being injected with succinylcholine, a paralytic drug. It's probably what killed Great-Uncle Billy." Sam paused. "Okay, I've shown you mine, now show me yours."

O'Malley slowly rose from his annoying chair and walked to the window. His view was of downtown Cheyenne and the street below. He hooked his thumbs in the front pockets of his Wranglers. "I was just a rookie, just startin' out. I'd never seen a dead person, except for a couple of wrecks on the interstate where all I did was direct traffic. The undersheriff had sent me out to the Hofstadter place to deliver a notice of eviction, just like the one I gave to your pretty little friend, Annie. Oscar's dad claimed the tenant hadn't paid any rent in a couple of months and he had been unable to contact them." He stared out the window, remembering. Without looking at Sam, O'Malley continued, but his tone was different. "Billy Hofstadter's widow, June, was in the north bedroom. She'd stuck a .357 in her mouth and splattered her alcohol-soaked brains all over the wall. Her daughter, Miranda, was in the barn. She'd been shot in the back of the head with the same gun." He took a deep breath and held it before slowly releasing it. "I threw up all over the crime scene." He paused again. "They'd been dead awhile," he added, as if justifying his reaction. "It was a textbook murder-suicide. No note. The autopsy indicated the daughter had given birth sometime earlier. Case closed."

"Was there any speculation as to why?" Sam asked.

"Depression, maybe. I don't know. June Hofstadter was wilder than a turpentined cat, a barfly, and most likely a prostitute. She frequented a strip joint south of town and had been warned about solicitation. Old man Roberts claimed that she had propositioned him in lieu of rent. She'd given him some hard-luck story in order to get out of paying a deposit. She claimed that her late husband, Billy, had grown up in the house and that she and her daughter were on some sort of pilgrimage to find Miranda's roots. There was something wrong with the daughter. She wasn't quite right," he quickly added and turned to face Sam. "So," he said sharply, "you have established either a connection or a coincidence between the victim and the Hofstadter place."

Sam watched O'Malley's right hand as he ticked off his fingers starting with his thumb. He was counting something. "But there's a whole bunch of years separating these people. That was twenty-two years ago. Lilly Darnell wouldn't even be born for another ten years. I gotta tell you, Sam, I'm leaning more toward coincidence than connection. Without a motive, we're stymied."

"I'm just a curious photographer," Sam mused, "but it seems to me that if we could establish a motive, we just might find the killer."

"Motives are like snowflakes, my friend, there's no two alike. The coroner thinks we might have a homicide. For it to be murder though, we need to show malice. And without strong physical evidence—"

"What about a pattern?" Sam interrupted. "Is there some database somewhere that you can plug in the known variables and it links you to similar cases?"

"Way ahead of you, Sam. We've run 'em all and came up with zip."

"What about DNA on the mother and daughter?"

"The case was an open-and-shut murder-suicide. There was no need to collect DNA samples."

"What about the baby?"

"It was stillborn in Alliance. Look, Sam, you're grasping. This isn't a cold case investigation. The girl got herself in trouble in Dismal River, had a dead baby, and they moved here to start over."

Sam was already halfway across the room.

"Where are you going?" O'Malley asked. "Are we done here? Is this how you end a conversation?"

"Nebraska, yes, and sometimes," Sam said matter-of-factly as he exited the sheriff's office. He walked briskly down the corridor toward the stairs. That was the second time he had heard the name Dismal River.

CHAPTER FORTY

PARSIMONY

Tom Stevens, Annie, and Sidney sat at Sam's kitchen table drowning tea bags. In spite of the soothing aroma of apple and cinnamon, Sam's arrival infused the room with tension. Greetings were polite, but cool. It was Sidney who offered an explanation. "Doctor Stevens dropped by to check on our progress with L2," she said.

Sam smirked at the ridiculous nature of such a pretense. Stevens was there to check on Annie. Sam had to hand it to him. The guy was persistent. "I see," he said thoughtfully.

Annie met Sam's eyes. It was apparent she was uncomfortable and not in control of the situation. She had her hair pulled back in a ponytail and wore one of Sidney's University of Wyoming sweatshirts. For a second, Sam was caught off guard by her beauty. He wanted to take her by the hand and lead her to the far end of the house, tell her that he had been a fool for keeping her at arm's length, and beg her to give him another chance. He longed to kiss her softly and hold her to his chest and ask her to choose him, not Dr. Perfect.

Stevens looked up at Sam and flashed a guileless smile. He was perfectly dressed and perfectly groomed, like a model in the pages of an Orvis catalog. Sam sighed. *I hope the two of you will be happy together,* he thought. He could visualize two perfect children, a boy and a girl; a collie barking in their suburban yard; a European SUV in the driveway; rows of houses, green ones, yellow ones, blue ones all made out of ticky-tacky, and they all looked just the same. Sam was suddenly aware of his own shoddy appearance. He needed a haircut, a shave, and clothes that didn't appear to have been slept in. "Don't let me interrupt. I'm just home to grab a few things, then I'm off to Dismal River in that scenic wonderland, Nebraska. So many cemeteries to photograph, so little time," he said.

"What?" Sidney said. "Is this a new project? What's going on? Does your publisher know about it?"

"I'll pitch the proposal when I get back. It's still pretty conceptual."

"I'm all ears," Annie said. "Should I hold the presses?"

Sam abruptly turned to Stevens. "How's my girl doing, Doc? The smelly one, that is."

"I don't see any progress, Sam. Of course I wouldn't expect to, given the fact that none of you have worked with the dog since I was here last. Has anyone even attempted to implement the therapy I outlined for you?"

"Not me," Sam shot back. "Anybody else?" he said, looking first to Sidney, then to Annie. "I suppose a refund is out of the question," he said, turning back to Stevens.

"And now you've moved the dog again." Stevens shook his head. "Can you imagine the stress? Couple that with all the strange things that Annie was experiencing in that house, and you have a recipe for total regression."

"Hold on," Sam interjected, "she's been telling you her silly ghost stories?" He looked at Annie incredulously. "What happens in the family, stays in the family, Annie."

"There's no need to mock me," Annie said seriously.

Sam saw he had hurt her. *Why can't I communicate with her like an adult rather than some adolescent who tries to mask his true feelings by slamming her at every opportunity?* "You're right, Annie. I apologize." No one spoke for several seconds as it sank in that Sam was sorry for being a jerk.

"Accepted," Annie said softly.

"Are you a believer, Sam?" Stevens said, sitting back, both hands wrapped around his mug of tea.

"Is this a test?" Sam turned toward Stevens.

"Dad doesn't believe any of it," Sidney offered.

"I'm just curious," Stevens said. "People are funny when it comes to the topic of ghosts or other paranormal activities. Most folks don't talk about it, but when pressed they'll tell you that they believe."

"Sort of like God, huh?"

"Oh, don't get him going," Sidney interjected. "Someday a lightning bolt will silence his blasphemous tongue."

Stevens smiled. "You've made a career out of taking photographs of cemeteries and you have never experienced anything the slightest bit out of the ordinary?"

"Can't say as I have, Doc. Unless, of course, you count the time I found identical tombstones for the same guy in different states. Or the time I saw a picture of my dead sister on a tombstone a thousand miles from home. Or the time Annie and I looked for a lost cemetery in Colorado that held the victims of a mass murderer who had buried his victims three-quarters of a century earlier. Oh, oh, I know," Sam said excitedly. "This is most definitely out of the ordinary. Last fall I found a dead guy using divining rods. Does that count?"

Stevens looked to Annie and Sidney for support. They both nodded as if admitting dark secrets. "Uh, I'm not sure," he said. "I guess I was thinking more along the lines of Casper the Friendly Ghost."

"You're a man of science, Doc," Sam said. "Have you ever seen any empirical data to support the kind of things that Annie—and I should add only Annie," he paused, then chose his words carefully, "has experienced?"

"Oh, out of curiosity I've read the usual second-, third-, and fourth-hand case histories of supposed hauntings, all of them unconfirmed. Unlike scientific papers, you'll not find a statistically valid results section. There are entire bookstores dedicated to this sort of thing. Haunted houses, poltergeists, spiritualism, psychokinesis, reincarnation, witchcraft, black magic, and many other unscientific explanations of psychic phenomena that seem to be as popular today as they were a hundred, or a thousand, years ago. The people that write this kind of tripe are usually believers, and they call every inexplicable event a true haunting."

"Or a miracle," Sam inserted.

"Dad," Sidney cautioned.

"There are some common, recurrent themes," Dr. Stevens said thoughtfully. "The noises and the aberrations seem to be a constant. Many people believe that poltergeists are forerunners of demonic infestation."

Sam shook his head. "Somebody call a priest," he mumbled under his breath.

Sidney shot him a look.

"Come on, Doc, you don't really take this stuff seriously, do you?" Sam said.

"I'd like to think I have an open mind, but I tend to look for other explanations. In grad school I was taught to be critical and skeptical and to never let down my intellectual guard. Because when you do, when you get emotionally absorbed into something you want to believe or can't explain, it makes you more susceptible to shaping. I think ghost stories entertain us, perhaps enlighten us, provide validation for something we want to believe, and allow us to gain hope that there is something after death. A French philosopher once said, 'The eye sees only what the mind is prepared to comprehend.' I think there is some truth in that. However, as a scientist, I'm here to tell you that the human brain is a complex chunk of tissue that we don't fully understand. We know little more about abnormal personalities than we do about psychic phenomena."

"What are you saying?" Annie directed a piercing glare at Stevens. "That I'm crazy?"

"No, I'm not saying that at all. I'm saying that I haven't a clue how to explain what has been happening to you.

But I can't help believe that you might be experiencing visual, auditory, and physical hallucinations of some sort. Remember the talk we had about reception versus perception? I do believe that some people may have the ability to perceive things that are beyond the sensory thresholds of other people."

"So now we're back to the Odd Annie from Iowa explanation," she smirked.

"Without hard physical evidence to support your claims—"

"Claims?" Annie said sharply.

"Perhaps," Sam interrupted, "if we put all of this nonsense out of our minds, if we stop talking about it and stop thinking about it, maybe it will go away."

"Oh, that's a great approach, Dad," Sidney said, sliding her chair away from the table. "Ten thousand ostriches can't be wrong. It's moved them right to the top of the evolutionary chart."

"It must work," Sam smiled. "Show me an ostrich that believes in ghosts."

"Do you see what I have to put up with?" Sidney said, gesturing with an upturned palm toward Sam.

"Actually, Sam might be on to something," Stevens said, addressing no one in particular. "For an ostrich, when something goes bump in the night, they probably don't consider the complexities of paranormal stimuli and the frightening aspects of the unknown. Rather, they assume something much simpler, like a predator attempting to sneak up on them." Stevens cleared his throat and looked down at the table. "Zoology and other scientific disciplines are rife with rules, laws, axioms, and postulates. Most such theorems and assumptions are named for the social malcontent who thought them up."

"Like Murphy's Law?" Sidney asked.

"Well, that's more of an adage than an actual law," Stevens corrected. "There is a fourteenth-century principle of logic called Occam's razor that states, if several different explanations for something are possible, the simplest is to be considered the most probable. In other words, the more assumptions you have to make, the higher the probability that your explanations are wrong. In the behavioral sciences, especially animal behavior, there is an application of this principle called Morgan's Canon. It basically states that we should never assume a particular response to be the action of consciousness when a possible explanation avoids that assumption."

The others locked eyes with Stevens in anticipation. It was like a grade school stare contest.

"Let me get this straight," Annie said, leaning forward over the table. "You think I'm crazy."

Sam smiled. "I think he said you were dreaming."

"What I'm saying, Annie, is that we should avoid an explanation that is the result of cognition if we can assign a cause that is more basic, simpler if you will, something innate or reflexive."

The staring contest continued.

"For whatever reason, humans are probably the only species on the planet that can conceptualize ghosts. And that involves cognition. All I'm asking is that we consider an explanation that is involuntary and involves only the simplest possible mental processes."

Annie's eyes narrowed. "Like what?"

"I don't know…anything other than ghosts, which is, by the way, purely anthropomorphic since we can't even describe a ghost without giving it some human attribute."

"Well, that clears it up," Sam said. "Annie is nuts."

"No," Stevens said loudly. "I'm not saying that. All I'm saying is that she has perceived something because she has the physiological ability to do so. To rationalize her perception, she is forced to use her human cognition to conceptualize those eliciting stimuli as something she can explain, something such as ghosts!"

Silence followed as they waited for more—anything they could accept as a conclusion.

"Let me see if I can give you an example," Stevens said, twisting in his chair to look at L2, stretched out on the floor sound asleep. "When you've been away and come home, the dog greets you by approaching with her tail wagging, her ears held back, and the corners of her mouth pulled back and downward. She nuzzles your face, especially the corners of your mouth, and attempts to lick you. Sometimes, she may even vocalize by whining. It would be very easy to interpret her behavior as affection, even love. You'd say that she missed you when you were gone and is happy to see you, and that she wants to kiss you." He paused and looked at each of them. "Can you see how we have anthropomorphized her behavior, how we've assigned human emotional characteristics to what she is doing? Morgan's Canon says, 'Not so fast!' Let's consider the possible unconscious explanations for her behavior. I won't bore you with all the technical stuff about sign stimuli, innate releasing mechanisms, fixed action patterns, or the ontogeny of canine behavior. But I'm here to tell you that her greeting behavior is highly ritualized, with its foundations genetically encoded within her behavioral repertoire."

"Now I understand," Sam said, nodding seriously, then added cheerfully, "I'm going to Nebraska. I'm not going to overthink this. I'm just going to Nebraska."

Undaunted, Stevens continued. "Take those conceptualized human behaviors out of the equation, and what you will see are genetically fixed canine-specific behaviors that have evolved to minimize aggression and maintain social cohesiveness. They have nothing to do with affection or love or happiness. Instead, they have to do with appeasement, recognition of dominant-subordinate relationships, and infantile food begging behavior that have become ritualized in adults as a greeting. All of these behaviors are fixed at birth. There's little or no learning involved. If you wanted, I could tease out the triggering stimuli that release her unconscious pattern of behavior designed to elicit retching and regurgitation of semi-masticated, semi-digested food, which through learning results in adult food preferences."

Sam pulled his chin back and frowned. "All this time I thought she was giving me a little kiss. And now you tell me she wants me to puke up lunch. Let me tell you, Doc, sometimes a little ignorance is bliss."

"Rationalize it anyway you want, Tom," Annie said angrily, "I know what I saw. I know what I heard and what I felt." Her face turned red, and her nostrils flared. "You can talk about dog vomit all day long, but it doesn't change the fact that there is something horribly wrong at that house." She shook her head. "I've got to tell you, Tom, your psychobabble is more than irritating. By the way, I remember a question in my master's defense having to do with the fact that Morgan never intended his canon to be applied to human behavior. Like the scientific principle of parsimony, Morgan simply said we should prefer a simple explanation over a complex explanation of some phenomenon. Did it ever occur to you that some phenomena are inexplicable? Jeez O' Pete, just leave it at that. Not everything can be categorized, compartmentalized, pasteurized, and homogenized into something that we can swallow." She stood up. "Now if you'll please excuse me, I need to go to Nebraska with Sam."

CHAPTER FORTY-ONE

SANDHILLS

The distinctive three-note call of a meadowlark lingered in the morning breeze. The new leaves of the few Chinese elm trees planted in the Dismal River Cemetery east of town, flashed silver in the early morning light. Waves of starlings dove and twisted on unseen currents, then settled single file in long rows on telephone lines. Snow dirty with sand, a remnant of the spring storm, trailed downwind from protected areas. It was chilly, but neither Sam nor Annie seemed to mind. They leaned against the prow of the Willys, the warmth of its radiator seeping through their clothes, the breeze in their face. They held hands.

"I read somewhere that people planted trees in cemeteries in order to soak up the spirits of the dead," Sam said, looking at the silvery display. "I can think of better trees, maybe prettier trees than elm," he added softly.

Sam squeezed Annie's hand as he looked across the rolling hills of grass dotted with black cattle. "I heard my father's voice this morning," he said without warning. "He was listening to a baseball game on his old Zenith AM radio. We were eating black cherry ice cream, his favorite, the spoons ringing against the sides of our bowls. He was imploring the batter to let the pitcher walk him. The count

was three and two." Sam turned and looked at Annie.
"He's been dead for twenty-seven years. I'd forgotten his
voice. Time had stolen it. But this morning, just before I
woke up, there it was, plain as day."

Annie half-smiled at Sam as she attempted to
understand him.

"I could feel the candied black cherry between my
tongue and cheek as I sucked away the ice cream. I could
smell the Brylcreem in his hair. I felt his warmth as he
sat next to me on the couch, the fabric poking my calves
below my Bermuda shorts." Sam looked away. "I never
got a chance to say goodbye to him. He died suddenly
when I was a freshman in college. The loss of my sister
had consumed him, robbed him of his strength. I think
there was so much that he wanted to say to me, lessons he
wanted to give, wisdom to impart, cautions to advise. But
he never got the chance. Perhaps I never took the time."
He took a deep breath. "I don't think life is a single epoch.
It's a continuum of milestones that mark our progress
through time. It's like a book that begins with a hello and
ends with a goodbye, or at least some reflection." He
indicated the graves surrounding them with a sweep of
his arm. "How many times did *their* loved ones promise to
keep in touch? People and things move quickly through
our lives with a wispy grace that barely stirs the air. I think
that as we get older, we realize in advance how transitory
our associations are likely to be. We keep people and things
at arm's length, relationships in perspective. We brace for
the trauma of saying goodbye. I believe goodbyes are

just markers along that continuum. We remember the beginnings and endings clearly; the middles are often a little cloudy."

"I was about to ask if last night changed anything," Annie said, squinting up at Sam, the sun in her eyes. She plucked a strand of hair from the corner of her mouth. "But now I'm wondering if you're breaking up with me?"

He looked down at her. "The level of detail was amazing," he said, ignoring her question. "The dream was so real." He paused. "It made me think of the scary things that have been happening to you. Do you suppose you could have been dreaming?"

"Is this your simple explanation for my inexplicable phenomena? Why on earth would you even bring that up on the morning after we—You are a strange man, Sam Dawson; a complex, driven man who, at times, can be the most frustratingly insensitive person alive. Why can't you answer my question?"

Sam took her in his arms and pulled her tightly against him. He found her lips and kissed her. "I have a hard time expressing myself emotionally. I guess that's why I surround myself with dead people," he said, pulling back and smiling. "I piss off the live ones. But let there be no mistake—I love you, Annie George. I've loved you from the moment you handed me a menu in Oxford, Iowa, nearly nine years ago. And yes, I'm still almost ten years older than you, and yes, I'm still the second cousin once removed you never knew you had. But I'm here to tell you that I love you more than you can possibly imagine.

And last night, I can honestly say I've never experienced anything like that. It wasn't just...," he paused searching for the right words, "sex. It was total emotional immersion in the being of another person. It was making love. I want that feeling for the rest of my life." He paused again. "You asked if last night changed anything. The answer is yes. If nothing else, I think it validated my true feelings for you. It was an affirmation of my total commitment to you for the rest of my life. No matter what stupid things I do or say, I love you and will always love you."

Tears appeared in Annie's eyes and flowed down her cheeks. She made no attempt to wipe them away. Instead, she buried her face in his chest and sobbed her happiness.

CHAPTER FORTY-TWO

YEARBOOK

Nothing," Sam proclaimed, his disappointment evident. It had taken them only a few minutes to check the cemetery for the name Hofstadter. Swiss-German and other northern European names dominated. The Dismal River population was relatively new, as would be expected in the western plains. Few had been buried before the turn of the twentieth century. Sam reached down and stripped the leaves from a fringed sage. He crushed them between his thumb and forefinger and held them to his nose. He inhaled deeply as he surveyed the monotonous, rolling dunes, all devoid of trees.

"Nobody by the name of Hofstadter, but I did find the Darnell family," Annie said. "They're over there." She pointed to the southeast corner of the cemetery.

Sam checked his pocket watch and shoved it back into his cargo pants. "Let's head back to town. I've got an idea."

Annie eyed him suspiciously. "Does this idea involve the Sandhills Motel? Check-out isn't until eleven," she smiled.

Sam looked at her and grinned. "I believe my other idea can wait."

••••

Annie rubbed her leg against Sam's under the table in the high school library. A stack of yearbooks was loosely piled in front of them.

"Mrs. Darnell referred to her husband as Lyle. I'm guessing her age to be around forty. Assuming he was about the same age, he would have been born around 1967. That would have put him in the class of '86." He pulled the thin Warriors yearbook for 1986 from the pile and quickly flipped to the section marked "Seniors." "Small class," he whispered. There were a total of seventy-four students enrolled in grades seven through twelve. Only sixteen of them were seniors. The teacher-student ratio was one teacher to eight very white students. "Bingo," Sam said with a wide grin. Lyle Darnell's smiling face was on the first page of seniors. He wore a light tweed coat and dark necktie and smiled contemptuously out of one side of his mouth. Big hair and big eyeglasses were in fashion for the girls. Like all senior pictures, their smiling faces radiated hope and excitement for a future that was uncertain. Sam could see the optimism in their young eyes.

Only one student, Raymond Hofstadter, lacked a senior photo. A drawing of a mortarboard and tassel appeared above his name. Sam flipped the page forward and then backward hoping to find something more. "Here's our Hofstadter-Darnell connection, and this is all there is?" he said, pounding his finger on the place where Hofstadter's picture should have been. Neither of them was in band, music, Spanish Club, Science Club, National Honor Society, or any of the other typical high

school clubs or organizations. The exception was that
Darnell had been a member of the school rodeo team,
a saddle bronc and bull rider. A photograph of the team
appeared midway through the yearbook. The girls were
in tight jeans and white blouses. Their huge belt buckles
were proudly displayed at their waists. The boys were lined
up in the back, each with a dark cowboy hat and western
shirt. Lyle had the same smirk on his face. Clubs, societies,
councils, and athletics filled the pages of the tiny annual.
Neither Hofstadter nor Darnell had held a class office,
won a scholastic award, or served as a homecoming or
prom king.

"Wait," Annie said excitedly. She pointed at the grainy
black-and-white photograph labeled "Class of 1986
Dismal River High School Commencement Exercises."
Counting under her breath, she tapped her finger across
the somewhat solemn students standing huddled on a
section of bleachers. They wore dark robes and light-
colored mortarboards. Their tassels were all on the right,
indicating they had not received their diplomas at the time
the photo was taken. The girls wore corsages and the
boys wore boutonnieres. "There are only fifteen of them.
There's one missing. But which one? All we have to do
is match fifteen of them to their senior pictures, and the
sixteenth will be the missing student. Let's hope it's not
Raymond Hofstadter."

"You're a genius," Sam gushed and pushed his shoulder
into hers.

They almost broke the binding by flipping back and forth so many times. After twenty minutes, they gave up. Two of the eight boys were unrecognizable in the commencement photo. Partially hidden by the person in front of them and the shadows cast by their mortarboards, they were interchangeable.

"Wait a second," Sam said. He flipped between the rodeo club and commencement photos several times. Lyle Darnell was standing with the same three boys in both photographs. "It's probably nothing, but I'm willing to bet these four were buds. Look, they're standing in the same order in both shots."

The school librarian looked up from behind her desk and smiled as Sam approached. "Find what you were looking for?"

"In part," Sam said, clutching the yearbook to his chest. "Are there any faculty or staff who might have been here twenty-two years ago?"

She thought about his question before responding. She removed her half-glasses from her nose and let them dangle from the gold and pearl chain around her neck. She smelled like lilacs. "I believe most of them have retired or moved on to other schools. Dismal River is one of those places where people start out, but they rarely finish their careers here.... Tell you what, it's almost lunchtime. You might try Harold Wilcox at the tavern. He's retired, a widower, eats there most every day. He taught English here forever."

CHAPTER FORTY-THREE

HORSEMEN

Yes, I remember the lad," Harold Wilcox said, then dabbed the corners of his mouth with his napkin. He wore a coat and tie, both of which had seen better days. He was in need of a haircut and had not bothered to shave that morning. He had eagerly invited Sam and Annie to join him in the booth closest to the tavern door. The sun through the window backlit his mop of gray hair and accentuated the unshaven neck hairs above the soiled collar of his white shirt. "How could I forget?" he added as he rested his fork on the side of his plate. The hot beef sandwich drowned in canned brown gravy was barely touched.

"Why is that?" Sam asked before he poked a French fry into his mouth.

Wilcox shot a nervous glance at Annie, then seemed to gather his thoughts before speaking. "Raymond was a quiet boy, very bright, but a troubled student. He was absent a great deal of the time. He grew up in a single-parent household and seemed to be the primary caregiver to his mentally handicapped sister. He was an introverted loner who was often bullied by his classmates. He stammered a bit."

Annie stopped sipping her Coke and produced the borrowed yearbook from her lap. "What can you tell us about this guy?" she said, pointing to Lyle Darnell's photograph.

"Oh that little prick," Wilcox blurted out. "Excuse my French. He was one of the Four Horsemen." He leaned closer to the album. "Yes, Darnell was his name."

"Four Horsemen?" Sam questioned.

"Of the Apocalypse," Wilcox offered. "That's what the other students called them. It was the rural Sandhills of Nebraska equivalent of a gang. The four of them were inseparable, like a centipede wearing cowboy boots. Harmless pranks and rowdy behavior were their modus operandi. Water tower graffiti, a steer in the principal's office—those sorts of things are etched in my memory. One of them, this guy," he said, tapping a photo, "Frank Zimmerman, provided immunity to the group since his uncle was the sheriff."

"Are these the other Horsemen?" Sam asked, flipping to the photo of the rodeo team, his finger resting on the back row of cowboys.

"That would be them," Wilcox smiled. "Ruffians!" he proclaimed. "They used to bully the Hofstadter boy unmercifully. One of them, I believe Lyle Darnell," he said, placing a finger on the picture, "was even related to Raymond. Cousins, I think."

Sam looked at Annie, but said nothing.

"Especially after Raymond...became the talk of the town," Wilcox inserted.

Both Sam and Annie waited.

Harold Wilcox looked at each of them. Seeing no way out, he sighed. "It was alleged that Raymond took advantage of his sister. Sexually, I mean. The Four Horsemen swore they saw them in the act. Anyway, the girl turned up pregnant."

"And people believed them?" Annie asked.

"It's hard to say what people believed in their heart of hearts. But small-town gossip provided an easy explanation for the handicapped girl's pregnancy. I personally don't believe any of it. Raymond Hofstadter cared for and protected his sister. I saw nothing in his nature that would corroborate such an outlandish accusation."

"Is Raymond still in the Dismal River area?" Sam asked.

"No, he disappeared shortly after his mother and sister left town. The baby was either miscarried or stillborn. I don't remember the details. I do remember that Raymond didn't attend graduation ceremonies and that he had a falling-out with the Lutheran minister, whom he believed had conspired with his mother to separate him from his sister. The mother and daughter, I'm told, met an untimely death somewhere in Wyoming."

"What about the Four Horsemen?"

"Oh, they've all scattered to the four winds, like most young people from the Sandhills. Those boys were ranch kids. The ranches are gone now too. 'Consolidation' they call it. That's where the ranches get bigger and the people become fewer. Ted Turner owns most of the county. Some of the local cowboys work for him, but the original families have died out or moved on. Denver and Omaha, like two giant leeches, have sucked the lifeblood out of the Sandhills. You can't blame the kids, really. They have to go where there's opportunity, and there's none of that here." Harold Wilcox stared pensively out the window at the deserted main street of the town, a town with a future as bleak as its name.

CHAPTER FORTY-FOUR

ABANDONED

Gas stations are rare in the sparsely populated Sandhills. The mostly abandoned towns were evenly spaced at about every ten miles along the BNSF tracks. None of them sold gas. Lost in thought about Raymond Hofstadter and hopelessly infatuated with the way the late afternoon sun illuminated Annie's hair, Sam had left Dismal River without gassing up. The three hundred and thirty horses beneath the Willys's hood were getting thirsty. The gas gauge had stopped shifting to the right on the hills and was bottomed out against the E on the left side of the meter. From past experience, Sam guessed the small gas tank had less than three gallons remaining, not enough to get him to Alliance. He tapped the gauge with his fingernail.

"What's wrong?" Annie asked, suddenly alert.

"We're about out of gas and there are no stations between here and Alliance."

"I've heard that before. Is this some ploy to get me into the backseat, where we'll have to cuddle to stay warm until morning?" Annie smiled coyly.

"As delightful as that sounds, I'm afraid we're really out of gas. When we're done cuddling, we're going to be cold and hungry and still out of gas. Pull the map out of the glove box and see how far it is to the next town."

Annie studied the map, turned it sideways, then back again, like a monkey doing a math problem. "Where are we?"

"The last town, Sheridan, was about five miles back. They didn't have any gas either. None of them do."

"Maybe we can make it to Schoonover? It's about five or six more miles west and another three or four north."

"Never heard of it; I doubt it will have any services, being that far off the beaten path," Sam said, keeping his eyes on the road. "I guess we'll find out when we get there." He reached over and took her hand in his. "It'll be an adventure."

Annie looked ahead too. "Everything with you, Sam Dawson, is an adventure."

••••

An arthritic black-and-white dog, a setter mix with matted fur, limped across the weathered blacktop that stopped short in Schoonover. There was no population, elevation, city limits, or town name sign as they approached the tiny settlement from the south. There was no rail spur or grain elevator or anything else that indicated why the town existed in the first place. It appeared broken, bruised, and abandoned. Elm trees, unruly and stunted, poked out at acute angles from the foundations of dilapidated, single-story houses sitting vacant along the sand streets. A community church with an unusually large steeple, out of proportion with the small building it was attached to, sat forlornly at the end of the block. The only brick building in town had been a school. Its broken windows and rusted swing set were indicators of long-term neglect. It sat in the shadow of the town's water tower. At one time, the tower had been painted silver. The steel lattice of each leg and the cylindrical water tank beneath a tin hat, now appeared orange with streaks of yellow and black. The faint outline of the town's name, too long to be read from any direction, appeared above the precarious catwalk. Now abandoned, there had once been a Schoonover Mercantile that also served as the post office, café, and dry goods store. The clapboard town was a uniform gray from lack of paint.

At the end of the single block, a nondescript building proclaimed with large, faded letters that it was the "Garage." The familiar Standard oval atop a single pedestal loomed above a raised concrete island where gas pumps had once sat. The Red Crown emblem was missing. A smaller, hand-lettered sign across the gable end of the building proclaimed: We Fix Everything… from Daybreak to Heartbreak. The building had been sided with brown asphalt shingles. Large patches were now missing. The exposed tar paper blew restlessly in the wind. Broken panes in the windows had been covered with squares of plywood. But it was the only place in town that appeared to have recent activity, as evidenced by the relatively new machinery parked haphazardly around the building. A New Holland baler, a John Deere tractor, several riding mowers in various stages of disassembly, and a late 1940s or early '50s Ford grain truck with its hood raised were surrounded by rusting implements and other salvage. A giant air conditioner, the kind seen on a warehouse, was partially taken apart. Nailed above the door, a crooked board with "Welcome" handwritten on it seemed deceitful.

"We've traveled to another dimension, not only of sight and sound, but of mind," Annie said as she leaned forward and scanned the scene in front of them. "It is an area which we call the Twilight Zone."

"No kidding," Sam agreed, parking the Willys at the property's edge. "This place is giving me a major case of the heebie-jeebies."

"You don't know what heebie-jeebies are until you've spent the night at Horse Creek Creepy."

Sam ignored her reference to what she considered inexplicable phenomena at her rental house. "Look, if some guy in bibbed overalls comes out of that door wearing a hockey mask and carrying a chainsaw, I'm out of here."

"Sam, I really don't want to spend the night here. I think we should turn around and get back to the highway. We can flag somebody down or call triple A or something."

He placed his hand on her thigh and patted it gently. "Relax," he said. "There might be some gas in those jerricans." He nodded toward the row of flat-sided five-gallon cans lined up against a garage door that had not been opened in many years.

"This is too much like one of those movies where stupid campers go off into the woods and find an abandoned cabin." She turned and looked at him seriously. "If they could grow corn here, I bet we'd find children living in it. Let's go, Sam. I mean it."

Sam turned off the Willys and opened the door. "You smell that? It's woodsmoke. Somebody works here or lives here."

"That somebody is watching you through the window next to the door," Annie said as she leaned across the driver's seat to look up at Sam.

Sam gingerly made his way toward the door of the garage, and a man emerged. He wore grease-stained gray coveralls with black pinstripes. His stringy hair was long and stuck out above his ears, pushed down by the dirty Alaska Airlines ball cap pressed on his head. A few days' growth of dark beard stubble covered his face. He wiped grease from his fingers with a red shop rag as he eyed Sam cautiously, but seemed more interested in the Willys parked in the background. He did not speak.

"Evening," Sam greeted with a tight smile.

Still, the man said nothing.

"I was wondering if you might help us," he said, gesturing over his shoulder with his thumb. "We're out of gas and I was hoping I might be able to buy enough from you to get me to Alliance."

The man leaned slightly to the right and tipped his head to better see the Willys, but was silent.

"I should have gassed up in Dismal River. This thing's only got a ten-gallon tank."

"Fifteen," the man said quietly, without expression.

"Excuse me?"

"Fifteen," he repeated. "The f-fifty-three Willys has a f-fifteen-gallon fuel tank."

"That so?" Sam said, pinching his chin. "I guess I've never let it get so low. When the gauge reads empty, it'll usually take less than ten gallons."

"That's probably because someone bent the f-float arm on the s-sending unit. That way you always have t-two or three gallons left when the gauge reads empty." The man still stared at the Willys wagon parked thirty feet behind Sam.

"How'd you know it was a fifty-three?" Sam smiled.

"The f-five horizontal bars across the V-grille, the split glass windshield, and the f-flat-fender design all said f-fifty-three to me."

Sam studied the man. He thought he might be in his early forties. His dark eyes shone like obsidian from within sockets prematurely creased by weather. "What about the gas?"

"A hundred bucks," he said, turning his attention back to Sam.

"You're joking."

The man's eyes narrowed. "What are your options?"

"Report you to the Better Business Bureau."

The man did not respond. He looked at Sam, his brow wrinkled, and he leaned slightly forward. "Take it or leave it," he said. His lips tightened.

"I just need enough to get to the nearest gas station, maybe five gallons." Sam said.

"Oh, in that case it'd only be n-ninety dollars."

"You serious?"

The man nodded.

"Who do you think you are?" Sam folded his arms across his chest and widened his stance.

"I'm the g-guy with the gas."

"How about I give you fifteen bucks with a promise not to hurt you?"

"Excuse me," Annie said from behind Sam. "Do you have a restroom?"

The man's features suddenly softened as he leaned to his right to see around Sam. He removed his greasy cap and clutched it to his chest as if Queen Elizabeth had just stepped from her royal carriage.

"Hi, I'm Annie," she smiled broadly, showing her teeth as she offered her hand.

"I-I'm...," the man stuttered, "I'm the g-guy with the gas," he said, taking her hand politely in the manner of escorting a debutante into a ballroom.

"Yes, you are," Annie beamed. "So, Guy, have you negotiated a sale yet?"

"Yes, ma'am."

"I'm glad, because I really need to use your restroom."
Annie smiled even more broadly, like a horse taking an
apple.

"Out b-back, ma'am. Just follow the path. It's an
outhouse. S-sorry."

The man stared after her as she gingerly made her
way around the side of the building. Her tight-fitting blue
jeans seemed to entrance him.

"Ever seen a woman before, Guy?" Sam said, tilting
his head slightly.

"Sorry. She reminds me of s-someone from a long
time ago," he said, placing his cap back on his head. There
was a distant look in his eyes as he nervously turned to
face Sam. He walked over to the garage and retrieved a
five gallon gas can and spout. "This should get you to
Alliance."

"How much?" Sam said, with a note of skepticism, as
the man prepared to pour the gas into the Willys.

"F-fifteen," he said without turning around.

Annie made her way back to the Willys through the
accumulated debris in front of the garage, just as the
man finished screwing the gas cap back on the Willys.
"Hey, Guy, do you have anything to eat in there?" she
asked, gesturing over her shoulder with her thumb. "I'm
starving."

The man nervously turned toward her, removed his
cap again, but seemed incapable of making eye contact
with her. "I-I..."

"Maybe some trail mix or jerky?" she said, smiling.

Sam studied the odd man, amused by Annie's ability to intimidate and manipulate him. "Squirrelly" was the one-word description that came to mind as Sam pulled a twenty-dollar bill from his wallet and poked it into the breast pocket of the man's coveralls. "Keep the change," he said.

"Some Ding Dongs or Little Debbie snack cakes?" Annie said as she recited her litany of convenience store goodies.

"I-I was just about to fix dinner. I-I'd be pleased to have you join me. B-both of you," he added, looking nervously at Sam.

"Oh, Guy, we couldn't impose on you like that," Annie cooed.

"It's n-no imposition. I would enjoy your company. I-I don't get many visitors. Please. Do you like f-fish?"

Annie looked at Sam. "Is this the fish dinner you promised me?"

Sam grimaced her way.

"We'd love to, Guy. Thank you," Annie demurred.

CHAPTER FORTY-FIVE

FISHING

Annie did all the talking machine-gun style. Sam loved watching her mouth as she spoke; the words formed perfectly between her lips, then escaped without effort.

A two-barrel carburetor sat on a gas-stained newspaper in the center of the kitchen table. Every surface in the small house behind the storefront was littered with tools and small engine parts. Magazines were piled in the corners of every room. They were an eclectic assortment of periodicals about self-sustainability, mechanics, and fishing and hunting. Sam noticed that the address labels listed various names. A twelve-gauge shotgun leaned against the doorjamb. An assault rifle stood in the corner next to a hutch filled with ammunition, auto parts, and fishing tackle.

Sam spotted Guy watching him suspiciously. "I see you're a fisherman," Sam said. The smell of frying fish had supplanted the odor of engine degreaser.

Guy did not respond. Instead, he pushed aside the carburetor and dealt out three paper plates, forks, and paper towels for napkins. He placed a bowl with a tossed salad on the table, another with fried potatoes and onions, followed by a platter of catfish and assorted panfish fried to a golden brown in a batter of cornmeal and flour. He lit a kerosene lantern before placing it on a sideboard next to the table.

"Crappies?" Sam asked.

"B-bluegills," Guy said. "You f-fish?"

"Whenever I can."

"Why?" Guy asked without looking at him.

Sam stared at him for a long moment as he considered the strange question. "I guess I fish because I love where fish live." He paused. "They live where people don't."

Guy glanced nervously at Sam.

"Maybe it's a form of rebellion," Sam stated as if he had discovered the answer to Guy's complex question. He relaxed, warming to his subject. "Maybe I like interacting with fish better than interacting with people. Maybe I like solitude more than faculty meetings. Maybe I like the sound of water over boulders more than the meaningless chatter at cocktail parties." Sam paused. "I read a quote several years ago from some judge in the Upper Peninsula of Michigan, I think. He said that he fished, not because he regarded fishing as being so terribly important, but because he suspected that so many of the other concerns of men are equally unimportant—and not nearly as much fun."

Guy seemed to ignore Sam's philosophical ramblings as he placed a fourth paper plate on the table and covered it with a paper towel. "Th-that's for bones. Let's eat."

••••

Dinner conversation was light until Annie started to probe about Guy's solitary lifestyle.

"I-I don't have dessert. I wasn't expecting company," Guy said without looking at either of them.

Annie did not take the hint. "Do you have any family in the area, Guy?"

"No," he answered a little too quickly. There was now an edge to his voice and a menacing intensity in his eyes that said he had enough.

"Did you grow up around here?" Annie persisted.

Sam recognized Guy's caged animal look. He was desperately seeking an escape route.

"No!" Guy yelled. "I-I'm not from around here," he said, pushing back from the table.

"Whoa! Hold on, Guy," Sam said, leaning forward and smiling. "You need to dial it back a notch. You'll give yourself a coronary."

"The fish are delicious," Annie said, finally seeing the fear in Guy's face.

Sam noticed her hand was shaking as she attempted to take a drink from her water glass, water sloshing over the brim.

"Are there any coldwater species in these parts?" Sam asked, trying to change the subject, but he was still looking at Annie.

"Some," Guy said reluctantly. "The N-Niobrara to the north and the Snake to the east have trout. This area is more like parts of Minnesota, with hundreds of s-small, shallow lakes. Trout will survive if stocked, but they don't reproduce well here. The p-pike and bass eat them."

"Do you ever come over to Wyoming to fly-fish for trout?" Sam's eyes darted toward the sideboard, where a familiar book titled *Fly Fishing Wyoming* lay atop a Forest Service map of the Pole Mountain unit of the Medicine Bow National Forest. The map would show a tiny black square that represented Sam's inholding.

"N-no," he shot back.

"Guy, could I trouble you for a couple of aspirin?" Annie interrupted. She massaged her temple and had barely touched her food.

Without speaking, he slid his chair back and disappeared into the darkness beyond the kitchen.

"Are you all right?" Sam asked. He studied her contorted face.

"It's just a headache. I think it might have been from the smell of gas and oil on an empty stomach. This place is a Superfund site." She mopped up the spilled water with her paper towel.

Guy brought her two aspirin and handed them to her. "Sorry about this place," he said, obviously having overheard her. "I-I wasn't expecting guests," he repeated.

"What's the population of Schoonover?" Sam asked.

"One," Guy answered.

"It must be lonely here," Annie said.

"It's just right. That's why I live here. I-I see people enough. The ranchers in these parts p-pay me to fix things for them. They all respect my privacy. They p-pay me in cash. No questions asked. They let me f-fish the lakes on their property and k-keep me supplied with beef and venison. I like it here."

They were silent as Guy looked to each of them. Sam nodded his acceptance and Annie reluctantly offered an "Okay."

Sam pulled his flip phone from his pocket, looked at it, then slipped it back in. "No service," he said, glancing at Annie. "Guy, can I use your phone? I need to call my daughter. She'll be worried."

"There's no phone."

No one spoke for a long moment. Looking at Guy, Sam broke the silence. "Electricity?"

"No."

"Gas?"

"No."

"Plumbing?"

"Out back. W-watch for spiders."

"Water?"

"Hand pump."

"Mail?"

"No."

Sam wanted to ask about medical and dental and if he'd filed an income tax return and whose name appeared on his driver's license. "You're really off the grid, aren't you?"

Guy pursed his lips, but said nothing.

"I can't believe how rude we've been, Guy," Sam smiled. "I'm Sam Dawson and this is Annie George."

The strange man who avoided eye contact simply nodded.

"And you are?" Sam coaxed.

"The guy who sold you the gas," he said without looking up.

"I'm sorry," Sam said, shaking his head and smiling. "It's just that you look so much like someone I knew in high school back in Dismal River."

"I-I'm not from there." He looked as if he were about to bolt.

"Thanks for dinner," Sam said pleasantly in an attempt to ease the tension.

"Can we help you clean up?" Annie asked in good Midwestern fashion.

"No," Guy answered immediately.

Both Sam and Annie knew it was time to go.

••••

"He's got to have a driver's license," Sam said, looking into the rearview mirror as the dark town of Schoonover was swallowed by the night. "What does he use for a picture ID? What about a fishing license?"

Annie massaged her temples.

"Doesn't he worry about getting stopped, checked by a game warden, cross-referenced? At some point a state computer is going to flash 'tilt' when Social Security numbers don't match up between licenses. Name, date of birth, place of birth...," Sam paused for a breath.

"He can't help being in a bunch of databases out there. How does he stay under the radar?" he thought out loud. "Any public place has surveillance cameras. The stuff they're doing today with facial recognition is mind boggling. Without surgery or disguises, people can't hide their physical appearance. They can only misrepresent their identity," he said, not talking to Annie directly. "So, all he can really do is muddy the personal identifiers that everybody tries to extract from him: name, date and place of birth, address, Social Security number, and mother's maiden name. That way they can't find him in state or national databases. There's no public record for him." Sam stared into the darkness, but was not seeing anything. "Or," he said suddenly, "you get all those things and establish a false identity. That way everything cross-checks. How would he do that? Where would he start?"

"Baby," Annie whispered.

"What?" Sam said, turning toward Annie, who he suddenly realized looked pale and drawn.

She cleared her throat and massaged her temples again. "Baby," she repeated. "I read about it in a magazine at the doctor's office. You simply research the death records from whatever state you want to be from, to find a baby of the same sex and birth year as you, but who had died in infancy. You order a birth certificate, apply for a Social Security number, get a driver's license, and develop a whole new persona from a child that had not yet entered the system. That way there's no conflict with existing data. Everything cross-checks," she attempted a smile.

Sam glanced at her, surprised. She never ceased to amaze him.

"But, just who is it that he is hiding from, and why?" Annie added with a note of seriousness in her voice. "You don't really think—"

"I don't know what to think," Sam interrupted. "He's hiding from someone or everyone."

••••

Annie slept as the quarter moon rose behind them. Sam believed it had been a lifetime ago, rather than the night before, when they had whispered their pledges of love to one another. He smiled at the thought of her body pressed against him, his hand on the small of her back as she confessed her feelings. He leaned forward and looked through the top of the small, divided windshield. The constellations appeared crystalline in the darkness. The Willys burrowed through the black isolation of the Sandhills, a dim funnel of light moving west. He would call Sidney when they reached Alliance.

Back in Schoonover, Guy hurriedly packed his meager possessions into boxes and slid them into the bed of his rusted Ford pickup. He whistled for the ancient black-and-white dog.

CHAPTER FORTY-SIX

FEELINGS

Sidney usually answered the phone. Sam rarely did. He considered it a nuisance, an invasion of his privacy. Sidney was attempting to place her hearing aids in her ears as Sam poked his head out from his bedroom doorway. He had been in bed for less than an hour, and his eyes felt like they had been glued shut. He squinted at the mantle clock in the living room. It was just after one in the morning. He knew that any call in the middle of the night was bad news. It had to be Marcie, Sidney's mother, Sam's ex. Nocturnal drama was one of Marcie's habitual traits. Sidney's muffled tones and her face cast toward the floor portended such news.

"Who is it?" Annie whispered from just over Sam's bare shoulder. Startled, he turned suddenly and shushed her. "Don't let Sid see you in my room." Sidney had been asleep when he and Annie arrived home from Nebraska.

"You don't think she knows?"

He did not respond immediately. "It's just a little awkward, that's all." Sam reached behind the door and grabbed his bathrobe from the hook. He was sleeping with his publisher, his daughter's best friend, his second cousin once removed, while his daughter talked on the phone with his ex-wife. "Stay here while I find out what's going on."

Sam put the teakettle on the stove and pulled two mugs from the mug tree. "What's up, kiddo?" he said as Sidney walked into the kitchen.

"That was Mom," she said.

"I gathered. Don't tell me, her mother's diverticulitis has flared up again."

"It's much worse than that."

"Hammer toe, varicose veins, incontinence? What's ailing the old hypochondriac now?"

"Grandma's fine. It's Mom," she said, pulling the honey from the cupboard. "She's getting married."

Sam's jaw dropped open and he blinked his surprise.

"She wants me to be her maid of honor, and she wants *you* to give her away."

"Excuse me?"

She thinks it's appropriate since her dad died even before I was born and you are the father of her life's blood, me."

"And if you act now, we'll send you absolutely free this handsome likeness of Elvis painted on velvet. Yes, you heard me correctly. If you call in the next sixty seconds, you will receive both. For only $19.95—"

"Knock it off, Dad. This isn't funny."

"It's hilarious. Anybody we know?"

"Pat Bateson."

"Pat Bateson? *My ex-publisher?*"

Sidney rolled her eyes and plopped down at the kitchen table.

"You've got to be kidding."

"They go to the same synagogue."

"How long has this been going on?" Sam asked, the coffee mugs still in his hands.

"I guess they started getting serious sometime last fall."

The teakettle rattled and popped on the stove. Sam stood motionless, staring at his daughter in disbelief. "That's about when Pat canceled my contract. I wonder if that had anything to do with—"

"You think?" Sidney said sarcastically, looking up at her father.

"Jeez O' Pete, what's all the racket out here?" Annie asked as she padded barefoot into the kitchen, squinting against the light.

"Oh, nothing," Sidney grumbled. "My mom is marrying my dad's old publisher. My dad is sleeping with his new publisher. And me, I'm sleeping with a bloodhound that smells like a bag of dirty socks."

Sam looked at Annie, who raised her eyebrows as if to say, "I told you so." No one spoke.

"Contrary to what Doctor Stevens says, L2 has feelings," Sam finally said. "She can't help how she smells."

Sidney looked up at Sam. She pushed her heavy glasses up on the bridge of her nose. "What about me? I have feelings," she said. "Everyone seems to be finding true love and happiness while I sit at home cleaning my glasses and changing the batteries in my hearing aids. *What about me?*" she pleaded, searching Sam's eyes.

Sam cleared his throat. "It'll happen, Sid. When you least expect it. It'll sneak right up and bite you on the butt. And don't think for a minute that glasses and hearing aids are some sort of chastity belt."

Annie rolled her eyes.

"Look at you," Sam continued. "You're beautiful, you're smart, and not too bad at checkers. Any guy would be lucky to—"

"Lucky to find me up here on Wolverton Mountain with my dad, Clifton Clowers, who's mighty handy with a gun and a knife," she sighed. "When a guy does come sniffing around, you're either condescending, at best, or just plain rude."

"Give me one example." Sam plunked the mugs down on the table.

"Tom Stevens," both Annie and Sidney said in unison.

Sam was caught off guard. "Tom Stevens?" he said, somewhat shocked. "Has he been sniffing around?" The teakettle started to whistle. "I thought he was interested in Annie," he shouted above the noise as he stepped to the stove and turned off the burner. "He's too old for you, Sid. I'll tell that dickhead how the cow eats the cabbage if I ever catch him—"

"The prosecution rests, your honor," Sidney said, staring cynically at her father.

Sam looked desperately to Annie. "Did you know about this?"

"You'd have to be blind with jealousy not to see it," Annie said. "I was in second place all along. He was only interested in me because of your overprotectiveness of Sidney. Truth be known, I think Sidney encouraged me to flirt with him only to make you jealous. And, I believe it worked," she added coyly. "I will have to admit there was a time when I was somewhat attracted to him. I think Sidney held back in an attempt to spur you to action."

"What the hell is going on here?" Sam said, turning away from them and scratching the back of his head. "This whole thing has been concocted? You conspired—"

"No, Sam," Annie interrupted forcefully. "There was never a word spoken between Sidney and me. Women just sort of know these things."

"I'm not buying the woman's intuition thing," Sam said as he brought the teakettle and a third mug to the table.

"Most women don't either," Annie smiled. "However, we do know how to keep our mouths shut and to listen and observe."

"Yeah," Sidney chimed in, "we use our brains rather than our brawn to solve problems."

"If you two are going to jump on me like a couple of bums on a bologna sandwich, I'm going back to bed," Sam announced.

"A bologna sandwich sounds pretty good right now," Annie said, looking at Sidney.

"You get the bread, I'll get the mayo," Sidney ordered, sliding out of her chair. "You in, Pop?"

"Put some mustard on mine," Sam said.

L2 suddenly appeared in the kitchen, a strand of drool hanging from the corner of her mouth.

"L2 says hold the bread, hold the mayo, hold the mustard," Sam laughed. But inside, Sam was not laughing. *Pat Bateson and Tom Stevens invading the family circle*, he thought. *A tangled web indeed.*

CHAPTER FORTY-SEVEN

COINCIDENCE

Y ou are a persistent bastard. Don't you work for a living?" Sheriff Harrison O'Malley said as he twisted the right side of his moustache. "I'm due in court in ten minutes. What can I do for you, Sam?"

"Raymond Hofstadter," Sam said. He paused as he measured the sheriff's reaction. "He's the son of June, brother of Miranda."

"You've got my attention," O'Malley said, leaning back in his annoyingly squeaky chair.

"He was bullied in high school by his cousin, Lyle Darnell, father of Lilly."

"Uh-huh." Sheriff O'Malley looked at Sam blankly. "So what?"

"Motive, that's what. Remember, we established a connection between Darnell and Hofstadter. But without a motive, you said the connection was just coincidence. Raymond Hofstadter was in the same 1986 graduating class of Dismal River High School as Lyle Darnell. Lyle and his buddies claimed that Raymond was the father of Miranda's stillborn baby."

"Uh-huh," O'Malley repeated.

"Re-venge," Sam said slowly, sounding out each syllable. "Do I have to draw you a picture? It's one of the oldest motives there is. You need to find Raymond Hofstadter."

"There you go telling me how to do my job again."

"You're welcome," Sam smiled.

"Really? Don't you have a job or something? You know, vagrancy is a crime in this county."

"I'm on summer vacation from the university. I teach for only nine months, plus I get all the student holidays and breaks off. I figure I actually work only seven months a year, kind of like your job. It's a heck of a deal."

"Get out of my office, Dawson, before I arrest you for first-degree annoying," the sheriff said as he stood up and gathered papers from his desk. "And Sam," he said as Sam was leaving, "thanks for the tip. I'll call you when I have something."

••••

Frank Zimmerman worked at a feedlot in Hereford, Texas. It had taken Sidney less than an hour to find his place of employment, address, and phone number.

"You're a whiz kid," Sam proclaimed, resting against the doorjamb.

"Easy as pie," Sidney mumbled as she applied a pale-pink lipstick to her mouth. She leaned close to the lighted makeup mirror on her dresser. "Unlike Hofstadter, Zimmerman still has tons of relatives in Nebraska. His aunt, the one who was married to the now dead ex-sheriff of Hooker County, still exchanges Christmas cards with

Frank. The old girl was a treasure trove of information and gossip. It was hard to keep her on point." She brushed mascara on her eyelashes.

"Are you going somewhere?" Sam suddenly asked, straightening up.

"Yep! Dinner and a movie."

"Sid, you really shouldn't be driving at night."

"I have a date. He'll drive. He's picking me up in a few minutes. Focus here, Pop. Frank Zimmerman is on wife number three, a barmaid with a bunch of kids from several previous marriages. Wife number two died from uterine cancer a couple years back. No kids involved. Now, are you ready for this?" Sidney turned and looked at her father. "Can you see my hearing aids?"

"No."

"Frank and wife number one divorced after their teenage daughter was kidnapped and murdered seven or eight years ago, when they lived in Amarillo."

"You're sure?" said Sam. "Frank Zimmerman—one of the Four Horsemen, the guys who pinned Miranda's pregnancy on Raymond?"

"The very same," said Sidney.

Sam stared at his daughter for several seconds. "Coincidence?" he asked.

"Odds are way against it."

"Holy crap," he said, squeezing his chin.

Annie pushed Sam out of the doorway and placed a delicate silver necklace around Sidney's neck.

"Holy crap," Sam repeated.

"He'll be like that for several minutes," Annie said. "You look gorgeous. Knock 'em dead, kiddo."

Someone knocked at the door. Both Annie and Sidney brushed past Sam, who was still massaging his chin. He looked up to see Tom Stevens flashing a beaming smile at his daughter.

CHAPTER FORTY-EIGHT

DEVASTATION

The illumination from the Willys's headlights defined the boundaries of their universe as they bounced along the rutted driveway toward Annie's Horse Creek rental. A storm front rushed in from the north. Tufts of grass, large stones, and yucca plants darted at them from the side of the road, leaping into the circle of bobbing light ahead. The landscape became eerie in the darkness; what had been familiar during the day had turned foreboding and sinister at night. Lightning flashed above the unmoving silhouettes of the jagged, red granite foothills to the north, illuminating the remnants of drifted snow and adding to their uneasiness. Rounding the last hillside, the ominous jack-o'-lantern house magically appeared. It sat ominously at the end of the road. Unmoved by the wind, its rigidity contrasted sharply with its frenzied surroundings. The house offered no feelings of warmth or security. The barn crouched in the darkness, just beyond the funnel of light from the Willys.

"You have your car keys?" Sam asked a little too loudly.

Annie shot upright in her seat. "Jeez O'Pete, Sam. Give a girl some warning before you jump out at her yelling."

"Sorry," he said, turning to look at her. She was terrified. "You start the Subaru. Check your brakes," he added with a note of caution. "I'll grab your things from the bedroom."

"No," she said sharply. "I'll come with you. You don't know what I need."

A call late in the afternoon from the Cheyenne Regional Medical Center had prompted a change in their plans. There had been a cancellation, and Dr. Lorenzo could see Annie the following morning. Sam had offered to take her, but she insisted on retrieving her car, some appropriate clothes, and her makeup. When he asked her if she was all right, she said she was fine, it was just women's stuff.

"Okay, start the car and we'll go together to get your things." He parked next to the Subaru and shifted into neutral. He left it running with the lights on as he pushed the door open against the wind. At the back of the Willys wagon, Sam raised the rear window and dropped the tailgate to let L2 out.

The headlights of the Subaru came on when Annie started its engine. The front of the house was illuminated brightly as they both approached, their shadows casting dark outlines against the clapboard siding. L2 squatted next to the frost-proof hydrant in the yard. She arrived at the door first. Her eyeshine shown with a blue glow as she turned toward Sam and Annie. The cardboard that Annie had taped over the broken door window hung from one corner and flapped restlessly in the wind. As Sam reached for the doorknob, he heard L2's low, throaty warning growl. He turned and saw her standing motionless, staring intently at the door to the house. Her tail was held straight out with the end curved slightly upward. The hackles between her shoulder blades were raised, and her ears were laid back fearfully against her head. She lifted her nose and moved her head in a slow rotation, nostrils flaring, as she drank in the odors seeping from the house. Sam trusted dogs and believed they still served man as early warning devices, retaining the sensory acuity that man's evolutionary progress had lost.

"Easy, girl," Sam said as he reached down and stroked L2's back. A gust of wind rushed past his legs into the house when he opened the door. The pages of a dictionary that lay on the floor of the mud porch flipped frantically in the breeze. The noise startled him. He could feel Annie's grip on his upper arm tighten. Sam groped along the wall. "Where's the light switch?"

Annie reached in front of him and flipped the toggle, but nothing happened.

"Great," Sam said with disgust. "That old buzzard Roberts probably had the power turned off."

"There's a flashlight in the kitchen," Annie whispered.

The headlights from both cars provided enough light so they could see the devastation. Plants had been ripped from their pots and thrown on the floor to die. The smell of freshly turned soil still hung in the air. Dry dog meal covered the kitchen floor, along with the contents of drawers and cupboards. The shards of broken dishes that had been swept from their shelves lay scattered among silverware, pots and pans, flour, sugar, macaroni,

and breakfast cereal. The stench of human excrement
was nauseating. Sam turned and looked back toward the
doorway. L2 stood motionless. She had not entered the
house.

CHAPTER FORTY-NINE

APOCALYPSE

You know why L2 scrapes the ground with her hind feet after she poops?" Sidney asked as she plopped down a piece of cinnamon toast on the kitchen table, next to her coffee mug.

"Pray tell," Sam said cautiously.

"Well, I'm glad you asked," she said as she pushed her heavy glasses up the bridge of her nose and sat down. "It's to get the scent up off the substrate and disseminate it over a broader area. Plus—wait for it," she held up her forefinger as if she were silencing a group of children, "it provides a visual mark on the ground that basically says, 'No trespassing, violators will be bitten.' It's a territorial thing."

"How was the movie?"

"We missed the movie because of the maned wolf."

"I'll bite."

"It's a species that lives in the Pampas of South America. Argentina, I think. It has these disproportionately long legs, I guess so it can see where it's going in the tall grass. It marks its territory by building these tall mounds of feces—heaps of wolf poop. They have to back up to the pile in order to deposit their droppings on top—again, a visual territorial marker and a giant room deodorizer. I was thinking of ordering a hot fudge sundae for dessert, but changed my mind."

"Did this go on all night?"

"Oh heavens, no. We talked about normal things like interdigital scent glands, the adaptive significance of a red penis, and the purpose of the copulatory tie. Did you know that ejaculation can take up to five minutes or longer in dogs? If we could patent a drug that caused that in humans, we'd be rich," she mused.

Sam raised his eyebrows.

"He cleaned out half of Applebee's when he presented a dissertation on the function of anal scent glands."

"He's certainly enthusiastic," Sam said. He was trying hard not to mock Tom Stevens. From past experience, he knew it was a bad idea to criticize any of the guys Sidney dated.

Sidney took a big bite of her toast. "I just don't get it. He's intelligent, good-looking, successful—"

"Don't talk with your mouth full," Sam corrected.

"Where's Annie?"

"She has a doctor's appointment in Cheyenne. She said she'd be back by noon."

"Is she all right?"

"I asked her, and she gave me the universally nebulous response of 'women's stuff.'"

Sidney nodded with acceptance. "Was everything hunky-dory at Horse Creek Creepy?"

"Raccoons, I think, had gotten into the house and torn up the place," Sam said. "I wouldn't mention it to Annie. She seemed really upset by it."

"Raccoons," Sidney said slowly and nodded. "I heard about them last night too. Did you know they don't have salivary glands? That's why they often dip their food in water before eating it. I would have preferred to believe that they are just fastidious sanitizers."

"Sometimes ignorance is bliss, kiddo. Maybe that's why there are so many unhappy people at the university. But speaking of seeking the truth, I need your help today. There are two more Horsemen I'd like to locate."

"Do you have their names?"

"Yep, I called the Dismal River High School librarian this morning, while you were dreaming of smelly dog stuff. She looked up the rodeo team picture I had seen in the '86 yearbook." Sam pulled a small, wrinkled piece of paper from his shirt pocket. "In addition to Lyle Darnell and Frank Zimmerman, we have Brandon Kettering and James Carson, the so-called Four Horsemen. Work your magic, Sid. We need to know if it's coincidence or connection. I'll see how the sheriff is doing on Raymond Hofstadter."

••••

Sam flagged down Sheriff Harrison O'Malley in the parking lot for an update on Raymond Hofstadter.

"Hofstadter doesn't exist. He's a ghost," O'Malley said. "Did I mention that you are beginning to annoy me?"

"I'm just getting started. Public officials are my specialty," Sam grinned.

"Again, don't you have a job or something?" The sheriff put the Power Wagon in park. He was only halfway out of his parking space.

"Is this a bad time?" Sam asked facetiously as he rested his forearm on the driver's side mirror.

"Hofstadter doesn't want to be found. That in itself is a little incriminating. I think he's gone well beyond simply hiding his whereabouts. He's assumed a new identity."

Sam remembered the conversation with Annie about Guy.

"Did I ever tell you that there are about as many ways to find someone's Social Security number as there are Social Security numbers?" the sheriff continued. "Raymond Hofstadter doesn't have one. If he's alive, he's now someone else. You don't just fade out of the public record. He's never bought a home, been in the military, registered to vote, been pulled over for speeding, let alone obtained a driver's license. He hasn't applied for credit, owned a business, been sued, had a mailbox, changed his sex, or shown up in any public or private databases. Like I said, Sam, he doesn't exist past May of 1986, when he disappeared from Dismal River." O'Malley smoothed his moustache with the web of his left hand.

"Well," Sam said with some finality, "it's obvious he's changed his identity. The best way to do that, I'm told, is to assume the identity of someone else, like a dead child that has never entered the system."

"As we all know, you can't function in this society without big brother tracking you via a Social Security number. He's most likely applied for a new one, stolen somebody else's, or made one up. Same goes for a birth certificate. He simply needed to research the death indexes of those states that have public files. This guy's no dummy. With a fake birth certificate, a library card, and a bill from the utility company, he'll get a new driver's license. Sam, this guy has obviously gone to a lot of trouble to establish a new identity."

"Speaking of Guy, Annie and I ran into this strange man in an abandoned town, Schoonover, east of Alliance in the Sandhills. He's an odd duck who seems to be hiding from something. You should check him out."

"There you go again, telling me how to do my job."

"No, I'm just saying—"

"If I checked out every oddball in the county, let alone Nebraska, I'd never get anything else done. And by the way, you'd be at the top of the list."

Sam ignored him. "But this guy stammers. Did I mention that we found out that Hofstadter stuttered? And this guy is secretive. Why would he be like that?"

"He might be hiding something from his past or planning something for the future. Maybe he just likes his privacy."

"I really think—"

"What county is Schoonover in?"

"I don't know, Sheridan maybe."

"I'll look it up and give the county sheriff a call. Right now, the only thing we know for sure is who we're not looking for. The original Raymond Hofstadter's gone. If we were sure of his motivation for changing his identity, we might stand a chance of finding him."

"You're not giving up on him, are you?" Sam asked.

"Not yet. We'll establish some identifiers, broaden our public records search, check out some private records sources, do some old-fashioned sleuthing, build a dossier on this guy, cross our fingers, and buy a rabbit's foot. Maybe we'll get lucky," he said with a wry smile as he twisted the right side of his moustache.

"Sidney's working on running down some of his old classmates. She found one in Texas whose daughter had been kidnapped and murdered like Lilly Darnell."

"Same MO?" O'Malley asked, raising his eyebrows.

"We don't know, but it sure looks more like a pattern or a connection than mere coincidence."

"Got a name for me?" the sheriff asked as he pulled a small pad of paper from his shirt pocket.

"Frank Zimmerman. He's in Hereford, Texas, but lived in Amarillo when the murder took place seven years ago. Call Sidney for the details."

O'Malley looked at his watch. "I'm late. I've got to run over to the hospital and check out why the woman we arrested two days ago for bank robbery turned out to be a man, minus a couple of parts. Life's full of surprises."

CHAPTER FIFTY

OBITUARY

The *Amarillo Globe-News* began an online edition in June of 1996 and started archiving stories the following December. The Amarillo Public Library maintained their website and was a member of the "public library underground railroad," that mysterious network of information-sharing professionals who ride their search engines between institutions with anonymity.

Sidney occasionally said something under her breath as she hovered over the screen of her laptop. She adjusted her glasses each time she looked between the screen and keyboard.

"Are you all right, Sid?" Sam asked from the doorway.

"I'm fine, Dad. But I'm thinking it's time you gave up on the silly notion that you can function in today's society without learning to navigate the Web or participate in social media. Being a technophobe is a liability, not an asset."

"I'm not a technophobe," he shot back. "I've come into the digital age. Look at my camera."

"Dad, you can't even download your camera's data chip without my help. More importantly, you don't seem to realize that I have a life beyond servicing your infotech needs. Law school is kicking my butt; my social life is almost nonexistent. I can't see, I can't hear, and worst of all I have a father who thinks he's Sherlock Holmes. Solving crimes doesn't put food on the table, Pop. You don't have a book started, you don't have a contract with the university for next fall, and you don't have any new sources of income. We're living off the royalties from stuff you did years ago. Excuse me if I sound a little worried, but I am."

"Well," Sam said with a huff. "Your job is not to worry. You need to establish priorities and quit succumbing to the temptations of fighting crime and seeking truth, justice, and the American way. But before you do that, if you could just find some of the particulars about the Zimmerman girl's murder, I'd be most grateful."

"Here we go," Sidney announced as if she had just found a missing sock. "Holly Marie Zimmerman, 13, of Amarillo. There's no date of death or location, probably because there was an ongoing investigation." Sidney leaned closer to the computer screen and adjusted her glasses as she read. "'Services will be held at 10:00 a.m. on Saturday in the Eastman Middle School Auditorium. Arrangements are by Kingsberry-Sloan Mortuary.' Let's see…," she said as she scrolled down the page. "She was born April 17, 1988, in Amarillo, Texas, to Franklin Arthur and Dawn Marie Zimmerman. She was an eighth-grade student at Eastman Middle School. Survivors include a brother, Nicholas; grandparents so and so of Plainview, Texas; and so and so of Dismal River, Nebraska. 'The family suggests that memorials be sent to the Eastman Cheerleading Fund or to the Amarillo-Panhandle Humane Society in care of the funeral home.' Cheerleading is a competitive sport in Texas," Sidney added as she looked up at her father, who hovered over her shoulder.

"Okay," Sam said, leaning over his daughter and pointing to the date of the newspaper. "We've got a time frame. Let's go back a week or two and see if we can find out how a thirteen-year-old cheerleader died."

The back door slammed. "Hey, everybody," Annie called as she placed a grocery bag on the kitchen table. "Can a girl get some help around here? I've got food."

"Keep looking," Sam said to Sidney. "I'll get the groceries."

Annie began digging through the sack. "I bought ice cream. We're celebrating."

Sam smiled as he approached her. He loved her in a ponytail. Her blue jeans and a red sweater overwhelmed him with their cuteness. He took her in his arms and kissed her tenderly.

"Please, Sam," Annie complained, "not in front of the children."

"Get a room, you two," Sidney grinned.

"What are we celebrating?" Sam asked as he peeked into the bag. He noted a small, white sack that had Jewell-Osco Pharmacy written in blue letters across its side. "No bun in the oven tricks for me, beautiful. Lest you forget, I've had a vasectomy," he said, pulling the pharmacy sack from the bag.

Annie beamed. "I would never joke about something like that." She gently slapped his hand and took the pharmacy sack from him. "Actually, Sam, I had a wonderful meeting with the director of the Wyoming State Historical Society, who has heard back from the University of Colorado Press," she said. "Sidney," she called, "you're gonna want to hear this."

Sidney looked up from her laptop. "I'm all ears."

Annie redirected at Sam. "Long story short," she said, "they want to contract with you for a book that documents ghost towns, mining, and logging camps of Wyoming."

"That's great," Sidney said, high-fiving Annie.

"You're kidding, right?" Sam said, shifting his gaze from one to the other. "And what do you two know that I don't?"

"No, I'm not kidding at all." Annie looked at Sidney, and they broke out in laughter. "Sidney and I put together a proposal more than a month ago and submitted it to them. We didn't want to jinx it by telling you. You said you were tired of shooting cemeteries. Well, here's something equally dead, but different."

Sam scowled at Sidney. "Why, you little conspirator," he said, then turned back to Annie. "Advance?"

"Modest, but yes. Do you remember Marta Eisenoch with the Colorado Historical Society?"

"Yes," Sam said suspiciously, his eyes narrowing.

"Well, she certainly remembers you. She has been running interference for me and, depending on how well the Wyoming book does, they may want a similar book for Colorado. There are more than a dozen western states,

Sam, all with rich histories of mining and timbering. This could keep you out of trouble for years."

"Not a chance," Sidney scoffed.

"There is one catch," Annie said as she pulled a quart of rocky road from the grocery bag. "They want one of those before-and-after books that show historical photos next to present-day photos of the same site. So, there would be a lot of research involved."

Sidney turned back to her laptop. "Maybe that would satisfy his insatiable need to solve crimes," she said over her shoulder.

"You mean, my work next to that of people like Jackson, Curtis, Adams, O'Sullivan, and Stimson?" Sam seemed apprehensive.

"Yep," Annie smiled proudly.

"Black-and-white?"

"You got it," she said.

"You've sold me to CU?"

"Actually, they weren't in a buying mood. It's more like I gave you to them."

"What's your role? Does this mean the end of Cowboy Press?" Sam said with a note of concern.

"I'll keep my options open," Annie said. "For now, I've given myself the title of Head of Marketing and Chief Concubine. Academic presses are good at hawking scholarly stuff, but they could use a little help selling coffee-table books."

"Concubine?" Sam raised his eyebrows.

"Am I not an unmarried woman cohabitating with a man?"

Sidney swiveled around in her chair to face her father. "Careful how you answer this, Pop. As your attorney, I advise you to structure your response by carefully considering what the next question or statement might be."

Both Annie and Sidney waited, each staring at Sam. He looked from one to the other as a frightened animal would do before bolting.

"They want the book for their fall lineup a year and a half from now," Annie jumped in, seeing the fear in his eyes. "That will coincide with the release of a calendar and a line of greeting cards, neither of which CU is interested in. But I've heard positive things from the folks who handled your alpine imagery stuff several years ago."

"What about narrative?" Sam asked, seeing his escape route.

"These are the most expensive books the press will put out. Page count is critical in keeping the cost down. You have free rein on the text, subject to editorial oversight, of course. But it's got to be tight. And," she said loudly, "you can't use the book as a platform for or against mining, logging, oil and gas development, grazing, or anything else. These are environmentally and economically sensitive topics. Keep it neutral, or the book won't see the light of day."

Sam saluted. "Yes ma'am. I guess you got me." He turned to Sidney, "Excuse me, little one, but I need to kiss my former publisher." With that, he took Annie in his arms. He bent her backward like Eisenstaedt's sailor and nurse in Times Square on V-J Day, planting a big kiss on her lips. "Thank you," he whispered.

"Get a room," Sidney repeated flatly.

CHAPTER FIFTY-ONE

FOUND

The June 12, 2001, headline of the *Amarillo Globe-News* read "Body Found in Junkyard North of Amarillo." An unidentified body found in an auto parts yard would normally not warrant a front-page headline. But the intensive search and news coverage of a missing girl for the previous two weeks demanded a dark banner across page one. Potter County sheriff's deputies had been called to the site at 11:36 a.m. after a salvage crew discovered the body in a school bus. Sheriff's office authorities said the body had been there for some time, and the time of death was undetermined. The Potter-Randall Special Crimes unit was investigating the death due to the suspicious nature of the scene. An autopsy was scheduled for the same day in Lubbock. The special crimes unit was on the scene for a little more than three hours. Law enforcement officials would not provide any early indications of sex or approximate age. However, an unidentified salvage crew member said the body appeared to be that of a young female.

"Check this out," Sidney said soberly. "That was the fourth set of remains found in Amarillo within the previous six months. Texas appears to be a hotbed of unidentified and missing persons. Nearly fifteen hundred cases, and only forty-one percent of them were closed."

"It's a big state," Sam said. "What's your point?"

"With six hundred and seventy-two missing females, our theory of a pattern or establishing a connection gets a little tougher."

"Go to the next day," Sam said.

Holly Marie Zimmerman's remains were identified, and her family notified, the same day her body was discovered. "Holly Found" was the next day's headline. No details were given other than the autopsy yielded inconclusive findings as to the cause of death, and that the coroner had ordered an inquest. When Holly was laid to rest, so was the story. The inquest yielded an undetermined cause of death, and the media lost interest. A dozen years later the case was cold.

"I need to go to Texas," Sam finally said as Sidney closed the lid on her laptop.

"We can't afford it, Pop. We can barely afford a virtual trip. Let Sheriff O'Malley incur the expense of tying the two crimes together."

"What about the other two Horsemen, Brandon Kettering and James Carson?"

"I'm working on it. Kettering has a criminal record. He's ex-military with a dishonorable discharge from the Army after two tours in Iraq. He was arrested in Chapel Hill, North Carolina, for sexual battery. The victim, unfortunately for him, was an off-duty cop. Bad checks and driving under the influence were his other offenses. I haven't found Carson yet, but I'm hot on his trail. If he's who I think he is, he's a Methodist minister in Mobridge, South Dakota."

"Keep it up, kiddo. You know what we're looking for. If you're not using the phone, I want to call Harold Wilcox in Dismal River."

"Why?"

"I'm looking for a school bus driver."

CHAPTER FIFTY-TWO

VOICES

From the driveway, Annie was chilled by the house's ghostly appearance. She believed it looked like a huge skull peering out from a grayish shroud. It leered at her through its window eyes. The vertical doorway looked like an open mouth ready to consume her. She rubbed the goose bumps on her bare arms. *I'm not scared. After what I've been through, how could this scare me? Irritated, yes, but not scared.* She reassured herself as she marched toward the skull's gaping maw, folded packing boxes under her arm. Sam knew she was in violation of the eviction order. But Oscar Roberts had not taken action, so Sam assumed they had plenty of time to retrieve her things. He said he had important phone calls to make and needed to check out the historical collections on mining and logging camps at the American Heritage Center on campus. Sidney claimed to have case work to do at the law library and refused Sam's offer to give her a ride. Her muffled conversation on the telephone led Annie to believe she might be meeting Dr. Stevens again. Annie took a deep breath and walked slowly toward the house—an Eloi marching mindlessly toward the Morlocks' cave as the siren summoned her to slaughter.

••••

The excessive crinkling of newspaper filled the house with a loud sound like water sizzling in a hot frying pan. Annie worked with a purpose that had nothing to do with protecting her dishes from breakage as she packed them tightly into boxes. She immersed herself in the noisy chore to provide relief from the intelligible whispers that began shortly after she had arrived. She might have dismissed them as the creaks and groans of an aged house, as tricks of the wind, but these whispers were discernable—one clearly enunciated word with the accent on the first syllable. "Ba-by," the voice hissed over and over.

She was both confused and frightened. Confused as to whether the whispers were real or the indicators of creeping insanity, and frightened by both possibilities.

Annie wiped a tear from her cheek and checked her watch. She wondered if Sam had returned from Laramie. He would certainly offer her one of his rational arguments as a third elective. In the meantime, she mindlessly swept the spoiled contents of the refrigerator into a plastic bag.

She hastily packed boxes, heavy boxes filled with books. She pushed them across the living room carpet and lined them up in irregular rows. Sam would have to carry them out to Sidney's pickup. She reluctantly entered the north bedroom, leaned the box spring and mattress against the bedroom wall, and dismantled the bed frame. Looking out the window, she was surprised to see that darkness was beginning to descend on the Horse Creek valley. She had to hurry. Without electricity there were no lights, no water, and no toilet. She had already used the remaining water in the toilet tank to flush the bowl in midafternoon. The last of her bottled water had gone to make a mug of cold tea, a mistake that painfully swelled her bladder.

Annie wrestled a large trash bag filled with her remaining clothes out the door, leaving it ajar. She squeezed the bag through the rear hatch of the Subaru. Dancing from foot to foot, she quickly undid the button fly of her jeans and slid them and her panties down below her knees. She squatted next to the car to relieve herself. Looking up, she saw something slowly move across the kitchen floor. The specter was amorphous and ghostly white. She observed it straight on, not as a fleeting glimpse from the corner of her eye, which she had so often done before. She wanted to be mistaken. She craved an explanation—something rational, something logical. Her mind raced, but the possibilities were all rejected. She could feel the intensity and the foreboding sense of urgency that permeated the air. Something was happening that she did not understand. An anticipation of doom seeped into her consciousness.

The hissing, gourd-like rattling of the snake's tail drowned the sound of her urine splashing on gravel. Paralyzed with fear, her urination cut short, she held her breath. The sound, she believed, was coming from under the car.

Daylight had turned to dusk as the sun sank below the western horizon. Beneath the car, darkness prevailed. Annie slowly strained her head down and forward to see under the rocker panel. She had braced herself against the rear door on the driver's side as she squatted. She imagined the dark coils of the snake's body tensed and ready to strike. Beads of perspiration formed on her forehead and threatened to course down her cheeks. She held her breath. Quietly she pushed against the side of the car as she slowly started to stand. She grimaced when her right knee popped loudly and the gravel under her left foot slid noisily. She froze, shifting her eyes left, then right. She had to do something; she had to get away from the car. She felt faint.

The rattler whirred louder, a frenzied buzz that warned an aggravated strike was close at hand. Closing her eyes, she lunged upward and away from the car, forgetting that her pants were down around her ankles. She fell screaming, her arms outstretched, and landed on her palms; her knees and elbows dug into the coarse gravel.

Above her, the foreboding skull-like house loomed stoically.

CHAPTER FIFTY-THREE

VOCALIZATIONS

The lights of Laramie blinked daintily below, along the eastern edge of the Laramie basin. From atop Pole Mountain, Sidney could see the glow of Fort Collins and Denver to the south. To the east, Wyoming's largest city, Cheyenne, with less than fifty-seven thousand people, appeared like a knocked-over Christmas tree. Horse Creek, Lodgepole Creek, Crow Creek, Dale Creek, and a dozen others all had their headwaters in the Laramie range. But at night their drainages blended, their profiles smoothed by darkness into a long tree-covered spine, as the earth rolled into a ball to conserve warmth.

Sidney and Tom Stevens sat shoulder-to-shoulder in the back of his Land Cruiser, the hatch raised, their legs dangling over the rear bumper. Tom had wrapped a blanket around them to ward off the evening chill. They each held a tin mug of hot chocolate in their hands as they gazed upward at the Milky Way.

Without looking at her, Tom said, "Loren Eiseley, the anthropologist, said something to the effect that, 'For the first time in four billion years a living creature had contemplated himself and heard with a sudden, unaccountable loneliness, the whisper in the night reeds.'"

Sidney looked at him, but did not respond.

"I can't help but think of that, especially at night, when I'm in the mountains with the wind drumming through the treetops. The way heaven and earth merge in the darkness always makes me feel small, insignificant—lonely, I guess."

Still looking at him, Sidney furrowed her brow and said, "My dad thinks you're too old for me."

Caught off guard, Tom Stevens snorted as he laughed and shook his head. "Where did that come from?"

"I'm just wondering what your intentions are?"

"How old are you?" Tom said, looking at her.

"I'm twenty-four," Sidney said, sitting up straight, defensively.

"I was twenty-four when I was your age," Tom shot back.

"Very funny. Really, how old are you?" she smiled.

"Does it matter?" He leaned into her shoulder.

Sidney removed her glasses and turned to meet his lips.

They kissed tenderly several times.

"Whew, I guess there's something to be said for maturity," Sidney said, as though speaking to herself.

A coyote called from the dark valley below them. Several others joined in, and the night air was filled with chaotic yips, barks, and howls.

"I'd howl too, but I don't want to give you the wrong idea," Sidney said. "I guess they're happy."

"I don't think happiness has anything to do with their vocalization," Tom said seriously.

"Oh, God, you're not going to tell me about coyote howls, are you?"

"No, not if you don't want to hear my theory," he said, pretending to have hurt feelings.

"Keep it short, buster." She put her glasses on again.

"I promise. First, I think happiness is a unique human emotion and we would be anthropomorphizing if—"

"Yeah, yeah," she interrupted. "Why do they howl?"

"Well, there are several different canine vocalizations, each conveying specific types of information. The one we just heard is called a group yip-howl. When analyzing it using a sound spectrograph, you find the original lone howl, which appears to elicit other members of the social group to vocalize. They all pretty much start with a bark howl then grade into a lone howl, but only until they reach a certain harmonic, at which time they drop out and start over, but now preceded by several yips. The end result is this cacophonous mixture of voices that sounds like a much larger group of coyotes than they actually are. It might only be three or four coyotes, but they sound like eight or ten."

"Uh-huh," Sidney feigned boredom.

"Assuming the howling coyotes are related—most likely an extended family group, the group yip-howl is a selfish genetic strategy that untruthfully conveys misleading information to other coyotes on the periphery of their territory. Basically, they are saying to any would-be trespassers, 'Hey, don't come over here. Do you hear how many of us there are? Don't even think about coming over here. The prey base can't support our numbers now. You'll starve to death, should you still be alive after we rip you to shreds.'"

Sidney jerked her head upright as if she had just dozed off. "I see," she said flatly.

"But here's the real kicker," Tom said excitedly. "I theorize that coyotes use vocalizations to assess population numbers and adjust their fecundity accordingly. Don't you see? The group yip-howl is a lying, cheating strategy to suppress the genetic contribution of unrelated coyotes in nearby populations."

"You've certainly suppressed mine," Sidney said sarcastically.

"Sorry. I guess I blathered on again, didn't I?"

"Going out with you is like dating Bill Nye The Science Guy." She held her wristwatch up to her glasses. "Holy crap! I didn't realize it was so late. My dad will be worried and pissed that I haven't researched the other two Horsemen for him."

"The what?"

"Oh, my dad has a real knack for finding dead people. Do you remember that little girl who was found dead in the forest a while back?"

"No," Tom said, raising his eyebrows.

"Anyway, Dad's the one who found her and now he's been helping the sheriff with the investigation. Sort of," she added as an afterthought. "Mostly, he just gets in the way and makes the sheriff mad."

"Who are the Horsemen?"

"Never mind. Did I mention that my dad thinks you're too old for me?" She reached up and wiped a lipstick smudge from the corner of his mouth.

"Did I ever tell you what Desmond Morris and other sociobiologists say about the adaptive significance of lipstick, cleavage, and high heels?"

"Didn't your mother ever tell you not to talk with your mouth full?" she said, removing her glasses and kissing him passionately.

CHAPTER FIFTY-FOUR

FAMILY

What were you thinking?" Sam scolded Annie as he had the night before. He cleaned and dressed the cuts and scrapes on her knees. She sat on the edge of his bed; her jeans lay next to her. Sam knelt on the floor between her legs. "I told you I would take you over there to get the rest of your things." He tried to sound stern but, as usual, he was easily distracted by her beauty. Annie's legs, like the rest of her, were wonderfully proportioned, her inner thighs sensuously soft. He noticed the tiny, light brown hairs the razor had missed. He dabbed hydrogen peroxide on the gash below her left kneecap.

"When?" she asked softly, rubbing her temple.

"This week sometime. The three of us will have you out of there in a jiffy." Her white panties contrasted against her warm beige skin. He pressed an adhesive bandage over the wound. "Do you want me to kiss it and make it better?"

Annie attempted a smile, but did not respond.

"Dad," Sidney yelled suddenly from the bedroom doorway. "You're not going to believe—" She trailed off as she surveyed the situation. "Why don't you two get a room, for crying out loud?"

"This *is* our room," Sam said, somewhat annoyed by his daughter's intrusion.

"You are not going to freaking believe what I just found," Sidney said excitedly, then pushed up her glasses. "Brandon Kettering's fifteen-year-old son disappeared after football practice back in '02. They found his remains in the woods outside of Chapel Hill in 2004. Horseman number four, James Carson is, in fact, the Methodist minister in Mobridge, South Dakota. He had no children, but his wife's body was found floating in a stock tank just two years ago. All four cases are still open. And get this: Each of them received a nude photo of their missing loved one. I'd say we're talking strong statistical significance here. Four guys from Podunk, Nebraska, each with a family member murdered—what are the odds? You were right, Pop, we got us a serial killer on the loose. Hot damn," she added before turning and disappearing down the hallway.

"Feed the dog," Sam yelled after her. "We're leaving in five minutes." He had promised Sidney lunch before her appointment with the new ophthalmologist at the Cheyenne Eye Clinic.

"I don't get it," Annie said as she slipped on her jeans. "If these are related, what's the killer's motive?"

"Revenge," Sam answered quickly, deep in thought. He paced slowly back and forth across the room. "It's the oldest motive of all."

"I still don't get it. Why not just murder the Horsemen?"

"The killer wanted them to suffer emotionally. He wanted them to go to bed at night and get up in the morning thinking about their loss. Killing the Horsemen was too easy, too quick. He wanted to inflict the maximum amount of pain. That's why he kidnapped his victims, took nude photos of them, and attempted to hide their bodies. There's only one thing worse than finding a loved one dead, and that's not finding them. The murderer has obviously suffered some emotional trauma. This is payback, plain and simple."

"Do you still think Raymond Hofstadter is involved?"

"I think he's our best suspect. He was bullied by the Horsemen, and they set him up for his sister Miranda's pregnancy. Who knows, maybe they raped her. Then he was separated from Miranda, the only person he lived for, and he disappeared before his graduation. The Four Horsemen pretty much wrecked that teen's life. Maybe he held them responsible for the murder-suicide of his mom and sister at your place."

"What?" Annie turned to face Sam. "What are you talking about? What do you mean at my place?"

Sam stared blankly at her for a long moment. "I guess I forgot to tell you," he said, his mind racing for an escape route.

"Tell me what, Sam?" Annie cocked her head and waited.

"Now don't get upset. But in light of your fanciful stories—experiences, rather—at the Horse Creek place, I thought it better that you didn't know."

"Know what?"

"Uh…," he paused, "your place is where Raymond's father grew up."

"I know that, Sam. What is it that you are not telling me?"

Sam scratched behind his ear. "Well, it appears that Raymond's mother killed his sister in the barn, then took her own life in the bedroom of that house."

Annie studied him. Her eyes narrowed, and she placed her hands on her hips. "There's something else, isn't there? What else, Sam? What aren't you telling me?"

"The nude picture of Lilly Darnell that they found in Oscar Roberts' truck was taken in that same bedroom." He paused, then added, "Your bedroom."

"Jeez O' Pete! Isn't that just the icing on the cake! Why didn't you tell me?"

"I didn't want to upset you any more than you already were."

"How long have you known this?"

"Awhile."

"You think my stories are fanciful?"

"I don't know what to think," he said, taking her hand in his. "But I know you haven't been yourself lately."

"How so?"

"You seem preoccupied, distant. I was afraid it was me—again," he added. "I remember how you seemed to withdraw before we broke up the first time."

"Let's not rehash the past, Sam. If I've seemed a little out of sorts lately, it's because I am. A woman's got a right—you know what I mean?"

He had no idea what she meant, but felt compelled to nod as though he did. "Is there something I can do?"

"Stop lying to me."

"I haven't lied to you."

"Don't withhold information or mislead me," she shot back.

"But I'm good at it," he said, smiling. "I've been doing it for a long time. You had no idea how much I've loved you all these years." He pulled her to him and wrapped his arms around her.

Annie wriggled out from his embrace. "You think that solves everything," she said.

"I'm sorry," he said. "I just wanted to protect you. I couldn't stand losing you again."

"Oh, Sam," Annie sighed. "You're not going to lose me."

He took her hands in his and gave her a tender look. He kissed her above each eye, on her nose, then softly on her lips. She yielded.

"Ack," Sidney cried from the doorway. "Not in front of the kids."

Sam turned, grasped the bedroom door by its leading edge, and pushed it closed.

"Some woman, Roberta something-or-other from Dismal River, is on the phone," Sidney yelled through the closed door. "She said she's returning your call."

"Join us for lunch?" Sam asked, turning back to face Annie.

"I can't," she frowned. "I have another appointment. Rain check?"

"You got it."

••••

Roberta Komensky had been a smoker. Her gravelly voice was frequently interrupted by fits of course coughing, and she always seemed to be out of breath. Roberta had driven a school bus for the Hooker County school district for more than thirty years. She remembered Miranda Hofstadter. "Always sat in the same seat, driver's side over the rear wheel," she growled. "Nobody else would sit there 'cause they thought she had cooties." Roberta was quick to tell Sam that Miranda was a special ed student. "She wasn't right in the head, you know. Sweet little thing, but slow." She remembered Raymond too. "The boy doted on her. Combed her hair, packed her lunch, and put her on the bus every morning. He had her trained just like a dog. It's a damn shame what happened to her. The mother was no good, you know—an alky." Roberta coughed and hacked and started giving the family histories of people she assumed Sam knew in Dismal River. He politely let her drone on while he wrote a note to Sidney: "Driver's side over the wheel—Holly Zimmerman???" He waved the note in the air to get Sidney's attention.

L2, with much effort, rose to her feet and padded over to Sam to see if the note he held above his head was edible. Sidney snatched the paper from his hand, yawned, and walked away. Sam watched L2 saunter back to the living room, her rear legs seemingly out of synchrony with her front legs, a dollop of drool hanging from the corner of her mouth. Her nails clicked on the tile floor.

Sam had cut Roberta Komensky off mid-sentence, thanked her, and hung up. Sidney was on her cell phone when he hurriedly passed the door to the study.

"Street," she enunciated slowly into the phone. "S-t-r-e-e-t," she spelled slowly. "Della Street in Mr. Mason's office in Cheyenne, Wyoming. He's a criminal defense attorney working on the Holly Zimmerman case. Yes, yes, that's correct."

Sam shook his head and smiled at his daughter. He dangled his pocket watch in front of her and mouthed, "Let's go."

Sidney nodded, then spoke into the phone: "I have a question concerning where in the school bus the Zimmerman girl's body was found. Yes, I'll hold."

CHAPTER FIFTY-FIVE

WEANING

The Albany Restaurant with its bar and liquor store had been serving Cheyenne lunch since 1942. Near the historic Union Pacific train depot, it was frequented by governors, legislators, lobbyists, and downtown merchants. The straight-backed Philippine mahogany booths were original and provided little privacy in a busy atmosphere.

"Why would you wear mascara when you're going to the eye doctor?" Sam scolded, pushing the remainder of his hot turkey sandwich away from him.

Sidney rolled her eyes and covered her mouth as she chewed her patty melt. She glanced at the booth across from them, where a Mennonite couple sat. The woman made brief eye contact with her.

"I'm sure the doctor will appreciate that you had onions for lunch," he added sarcastically.

"Anything else, Pop?" She stared wide-eyed at him. "What's got your panties in a wad today? Is it the cost? We can cancel, you know. It'll be the same old BS anyway—the same song and dance about retinal degeneration, loss of cones in the macula, and progressive night blindness. None of it is covered, Pop. We've heard the insurance company's arguments a hundred times."

"It's a medical condition, Sid, a genetic disorder. The bastards hide behind their exclusions every time. Eyes and ears aren't covered. Go figure." He shook his head.

"When my ship comes in and I get hired as a junior partner in a prestigious law firm, not only will I be covered under their health insurance policy, I'll sue the insurance company's butt off and make 'em pay."

"Did you ever stop to consider the reason why medical care and insurance are so costly? It's because of you greedy little lawyers and your penchant for suing everybody's butt off. The legal profession is bankrupting and paralyzing this entire country. They're a bunch of bloodsucking social parasites who—"

"Pop, get a grip. Was there something in your gravy? Why are you so angry? You're embarrassing me—and you know how hard that is to do."

"I hope you pass the bar and find a job with benefits, because you'll be twenty-six before you know it, and no longer eligible for coverage under my policy. And that's probably a good thing. It's time you started thinking about your future, Sid." He paused and leaned over the table. "An independent future," he added.

Sidney wiped her mouth with her napkin and slumped back. "So, that's what this is all about. You're weaning me? What's going on? Why are we having this discussion? Am I missing something?"

Sam was suddenly aware of the others around him. He lowered his voice. "I'm not getting any younger," he said, looking down at the table. "I need to make some decisions. I need to consider my own future."

Sidney rested her elbows on the table, a broad smile on her face. "Is this about Annie? Are you two getting married?"

Sam's face flushed red. "I haven't asked her yet, but I'm thinking about it," he muttered and was unable to make eye contact with his daughter.

"Does she know?"

"I think so." Sam was visibly uncomfortable. He straightened his silverware and brushed crumbs from the table with his napkin. "She's been a little off lately. I think she suspects something."

"Do you love her, Pop?"

Sam tossed his napkin onto the table. "I'm going to the restroom. I'll drop you by the eye clinic, then go see O'Malley. I want to share with him what you found out about the other Horsemen, especially where the Zimmerman girl was found in the school bus."

The restrooms were through the bar. The men's room smelled of stale beer, urine, and urinal sanitizer. The old-fashioned cloth-towel dispenser had been used up earlier in the week and was gray with hand grime. With wet hands, Sam emerged from the bar and was momentarily shocked to find Sidney gone, their table wiped clean and set up with new placemats and table settings. He scanned the restaurant as he walked among the tables and booths. He hurried back to the restrooms and knocked on the door labeled "Women" before opening it a few inches and loudly calling her name. There was no response. At the cash register, he quickly paid his bill and asked the heavyset cashier if he had seen his daughter.

"It's a busy place," the man said, his toothpick bobbing between puffy lips.

Sam found his waitress filling water glasses behind a partition at the back of the dining room. He handed her three singles and said, "Did you see where the young woman I was with went?"

"No, sir. I didn't see nothin'."

Sam rudely pushed his way through the line of waiting customers jammed into the entryway and burst onto the sidewalk. He squinted against the sun. Sidney, her back to Sam, stood at the curb talking with Tom Stevens. "Sidney, I thought I had lost you," he said, trying to remain calm.

"I believe that is part of the weaning process," she said with a note of seriousness in her voice, then, "Look who I found." A big smile spread across her face.

"Doctor Stevens," Sam nodded.

"Sam," Stevens acknowledged.

An uncomfortable pause followed as the three of them looked at each other.

"Aren't you a little old for my daughter?" Sam said, his brow furrowed.

"Told you," Sidney said to Stevens.

They stared at Sam for a long moment before bursting out laughing. Sam grinned from ear to ear. "The next time I see you, Doc, I'll ask you what your intentions are. Fair warning, so be prepared," Sam said.

"Told you," Sidney said again. She shook her head, her face red with embarrassment.

Sam pulled out his pocket watch to check the time. "Sid, we don't want to be late for your appointment."

"You go ahead, Pop. Tom said he would drop me by the eye clinic."

"Sounds serious," Sam said. "Maybe I should ask my question now."

"Fire away, Sam," Stevens smiled wide. "I'll give you a dissertation on the biological significance of the prenuptial courtship ritual to include mating strategies and the origins of monogamy and pair bonding."

"On second thought, you two have fun. I'll pick you up in an hour, Sid. I'm going to see the sheriff about Hofstadter."

CHAPTER FIFTY-SIX

CONFIRMATION

Sheriff Harrison O'Malley, wearing his traditional blue jeans and white shirt open at the neck, rocked in his squeaky office chair and listened patiently to Sam.

Sam told of the Kettering and Carson murders and how Holly Zimmerman was found in the same seat position of the school bus that Miranda Hofstadter always sat in. He could not tell if O'Malley understood the significance of the connections. The sheriff repeatedly smoothed his mustache, but did not interrupt Sam. "At some point, each of the families received a photograph in the mail of their missing loved one. They were unconscious or dead, and all of them were nude."

O'Malley raised his eyebrows.

"Well?" Sam finally said, obviously frustrated.

"Are you looking for a job, or what?" O'Malley shot back.

"What?"

"I've got two detectives on this case with all the resources of this office behind them, and I have to rely on some photographer from off the street to bring me evidence and leads. Excuse me, Sam, but I find that incredibly frustrating."

"Raymond Hofstadter—"

"Is a person of interest," O'Malley cut Sam off. "For once I'm ahead of you, Sam. I'm waiting on a photo to be faxed from the current minister of the Dismal River Zion Lutheran Church. Apparently our boy Raymond was confirmed back in about 1980 when he was twelve or thirteen-years old. There's a forensic artist in Denver who can put some age on him. Maybe we can get an idea of what the guy looks like."

A woman in her sixties, overweight and with a permanent scowl on her face, entered the room. She wore an automatic pistol in a pancake holster high on her ample hip. She looked at Sam as if he had just exposed himself to a group of grade school girls. She handed the sheriff a manila folder and shuffled out without speaking.

"Thanks, Bridget," O'Malley said without looking at her.

Bridget, Sam mouthed without speaking, her name contrasting with both her appearance and demeanor. "What did you find out about the squirrely guy in Schoonover?" said Sam.

"The Sheridan County Sheriff said the town's been abandoned for years and he wasn't about to waste the gas to check it out."

O'Malley opened the folder, studied the faxes, then shook his head. He turned the paper over and looked on the back, then tossed the photograph on his desk. "Ain't that a kick in the butt? Who would have thought?" he said.

Sam rose from his chair and leaned over the black-and-white image of six young people, each wearing a long, white robe as they stood in front of a church altar; a crucified Jesus hung sadly behind them. There were three girls and three boys, each holding a certificate of confirmation, their faces beaming with accomplishment as they stood before the camera. The Lutheran minister, his vestment more ornate, loomed above them, a large man with a pocked face, a crooked smile, and greasy hair. Oscar Roberts clutched a Bible to his hip as if it were a six-shooter. Sam stared at the photograph. The room and noisy hallway were suddenly muted. Sam's ears rang from the silence. His head felt like he was at the bottom of the deep end of a swimming pool. Moving was an effort. He could not breathe. His hands shook as he looked up and met O'Malley's gaze.

Sam did not want to hear the vagaries of the Fourth Amendment or probable cause. O'Malley said he needed more, much more in order to convince a judge or magistrate to issue an arrest warrant. "Person of interest" was the less inflammatory euphemism for "suspect." "Everything you've given me so far is hearsay. Just to show up at somebody's house in a nonemergency situation, I'm gonna need a warrant," he yelled as Sam ran out the door.

CHAPTER FIFTY-SEVEN

REMEMBRANCES

Remembrances are illusions of the past. They accentuate the positive and minimize the negative. They form lasting associations with the seemingly irrelevant. One is sometimes left with the overwhelming sense of having experienced the identical event before.

Annie stared blankly at the poisonous house, remembering her life, just as she had when viewing the scans at the oncologist's office. When she felt as though she was about to faint, she would remind herself to breathe. *"Metastasized" is a funny word*, she thought, a word that sticks in your craw. Without looking at her, the oncologist had pointed to each of the spots. The cerebellum—or was it the cerebrum? The medulla oblongata, the hypothalamus, this lobe and that lobe, each name a needle jammed into her eardrum. The tremors had already started. Speech and cognition were next. Treatments without efficacy and with disgusting side effects rolled off his tongue with rote indifference. The success rate was given as brief extensions of time—months perhaps, as opposed to a cure or no cure.

Fear, anger, and depression slowly descended over her shoulders and along the backs of her arms tingling with paralysis, and rolled down her spine. "We need to start immediately," he had said finally, looking at her and thumping his clipboard against his leg. "Any questions, uh, Miss George?" he said as he flipped back to the first page of his notes to find her name. She wanted to scratch his face and scream that it was only a headache.

She did not remember the drive to Horse Creek. Her mind fluttered like a dried leaf dangling from a branch, shaken by the wind. A kaleidoscope of memories twisted with sharp edges in her consciousness, silent snapshots of the things she had held dear as a child. Amber-eyed dogs, a new pair of sneakers with a blue Keds logo on the heel, a jar of paste with an orange applicator, a new box of crayons, the color of a four-cent stamp in her collection, Nana bent from the waist smiling down at her, a picnic— all appeared like pages in a child's flip-book.

At first, she did not know where to go or what to do. *Not Sam, not yet.* She fought back tears. The memory of a cardboard packing box with U-Haul in large green letters, duct tape holding the top flaps closed, came to mind. Unopened since moving to Wyoming, it was stacked with others in the barn. The box held her life in photos— curled black-and-whites from her mother's Brownie, Kodachrome slides in yellow boxes from her father's Minolta, high school and college snapshots all jumbled together, just like her memories. The box had drawn her to Horse Creek.

She wanted to sit on the floor for hours or days and remember. But she would not reminisce here, not in this house, the house that had victimized her. She would take the box somewhere, anywhere. Just not to Sam's house. Her memories were what counted. She needed to get them in order before she could not. Rationality was being strangled by the cancerous cells gnawing through the insulation of her circuitry. Already, she had difficulty separating the real from the unreal. *Funny*, she thought, *how the brain attempts to explain away its own malfunctions.* She could trust the photographs in the U-Haul box. They represented reality. They would ground her. Only then would she go to Sam, whom she loved more than life itself.

Annie walked toward the swaybacked barn, for once unaware of the house and its hideous surroundings. She thought she heard her cell phone ring and pulled it from her pocket. The low-battery message flashed across the screen, then went blank. No bars, no service, no life in the land that time forgot. *No phone, no food, no pets; I ain't got no cigarettes.* She mentally sang the Roger Miller lyrics. Each step was an effort that jolted her hips and sent shock waves through her lower back. She struggled to catch her breath. Tears threatened to explode from her eyes at any moment. *Get the box. Get the box and drive. Get a motel room.* She needed time. She needed to remember.

A layer of crimson sky provided contrast to the uneven undulations of the Laramie range as the sun settled toward the western horizon. A disquieting stillness descended on the Horse Creek valley, a brief respite from the perpetual wind. The hinges on the barn door groaned, then screeched as Annie pulled it open. A shaft of light magically pierced the blackness within, a rectangular beam illuminating the musty interior. Dust particles reflected the light as they floated through the ray, glistening, fluttering like snow in a globe. The smell of dried manure and moldy hay stung her nostrils. She paused to allow her eyes time to adjust. The box she sought was stacked on a pallet beyond the stanchions, near the back of the milking parlor.

She raised the globe on the lantern that hung by the door, fumbled for a farmer's match from the box on the dusty shelf, and struck it down the rough doorframe. The match head exploded with a sulfurous, yellow flame. She brought it to the oily wick of the lantern, adjusted the wick height, released the globe, and held it ahead of her. Annie made her way toward the back of the barn past the molding, stacked bales of hay with a pitchfork leaning against them.

The figure appeared suddenly in the hazy periphery of where the lantern's light met the darkness. It emerged as a woman, a very short woman or girl. Her long, black hair flowed like ink over her shoulders. Her head was bowed slightly, and her arms were held tightly to her sides in a dark, featureless cone rising up from the floor. Annie stood motionless, except for the lantern shaking in her hand. She turned her head sideways, using her peripheral vision to view the apparition, then lowered her chin and stared out the top of her eyes. She leaned forward and extended the lantern toward the unmoving specter. "You don't frighten me," she said, emboldened by her medical death sentence. "I'm dead, too."

The figure slowly raised her tearstained face upward. Her dark hair hung on each side of the gag tied across her open mouth. She was on her knees with her arms bound behind her, her wrists tied to her ankles. Her nostrils flared, and her eyes appeared small without glasses. Sidney squinted upward toward the light.

CHAPTER FIFTY-EIGHT

AFRAID

Sam became frantic when he discovered Sidney had not kept her appointment at the Cheyenne Eye Clinic. He dialed her cell phone nonstop, without success. He had never asked God for anything. Sam did not discuss his agnosticism with anyone, not even himself. It was a topic that he politely kept private, certain of his uncertainty. Yet, today he was hedging his bets by begging out loud. There was no answer. He remembered a quote from Voltaire: *"God is a comedian, playing to an audience too afraid to laugh."* Sam believed laughing and crying were so closely related that, at this point, he could go either way. His blindness to the threat that had been right in front of him was laughable, while his fear brought blinding tears to his eyes.

He never looked at his tachometer. The sound of the engine signaled him when to shift. He double-clutched as he slipped the overdrive gearshift into high. The Willys began to tremble at seventy. At eighty it threatened to explode. The gear ratio was too low. It sounded like stones falling from a sky, blazing with fire. Still, it hurled down the Horse Creek Highway toward Annie and Sidney, straining past its limits. He'd left a vehement message at the sheriff's office. He kept glancing into the rearview mirror, hoping to see the flashing lights of authority, but there were none.

Annie's almost unintelligible call came from Sidney's cell phone. He welcomed it like a life buoy to a drowning man. They were together, and that gave him hope. He flipped open his phone again. There was no service in the land with more antelope than people, no God at the microphone delivering one-liners to a stoic audience. He thought—of all things—of the harsh words, the stinging comebacks in the context of love that they'd never speak again if Sidney died. He called out again to God, but there was still no answer.

CHAPTER FIFTY-NINE

UNSPOKEN

Eyes, the windows to the soul, are more expressive than words. They evolved long before language and are capable of silently speaking volumes. Sidney's eyes told the story. Helplessness, rage, frustration, and betrayal were all conveyed in a split second by minute ocular movements. Annie saw it all. She saw the unspoken bond between the two of them and Sidney's desperation to speak. Then she saw Sidney's warning just before the axe handle crushed the back of her skull with a deafening numbness. She did not hear the killer cursing her as he stepped over her limp body, or Sidney's sobs of anguish at Annie's pain. The ringing in Annie's ears was maddening, but her eyes were open. She watched him kneel over Sidney and pull a syringe from his coat pocket.

Annie spotted the U-Haul box with her life's history inside. In her mind's eye she saw the black-and-white photographs of herself when she was young, a skinny little girl, all knees and elbows, rounding third base, headed for home. She could smell the grass-stain odor of her dog Thumper's feet as he playfully fought to escape her tickling.

Sidney's muffled screams broke into Annie's consciousness. Annie reached out and wrapped her hands around the smoothness of the pitchfork's handle. There was heft in its rusted tines. The lunge was spontaneous. The feel of the kill was exhilarating, the penetrable mass twitching at the end of her weapon. She had taken control. Annie was pleased.

When Sam came to her, Annie felt his touch resonating deep within her. She strained to hear him, but her effort was futile. The world was silent. Sam's eyes told her of the past and the future—of love and anguish. She smiled at him before sleeping.

CHAPTER SIXTY

REFLECTIONS

The rhythmic reflections of the flashing red lights were strangely out of place, bouncing from the abandoned house to the barn. The night had been busy—gaudy with color, lustrous with chrome and glass, raucous with the sounds of police radios and independent conversations. On the eastern horizon, a faint glow above a thin red line bathed the Horse Creek valley in pink. Three sheriff's cars, a state patrol cruiser, three ambulances, two fire trucks, a large emergency services truck, and the coroner's SUV overflowed the driveway. Sam thought it strange that they left their emergency lights flashing in such a remote location.

Two EMTs struggled with the collapsible gurney, the legs refusing to fold back as they pushed it roughly into an ambulance. Something small slid from under the heavy, blue blanket and fell to the ground. Sam stood numbly in the driveway, a deputy at his side. He watched the ambulance sway and bounce through the ruts and then disappear around the side of the hill.

"Flight For Life out of Colorado is standing by if they need it." Sam heard the deputy speaking, but did not acknowledge his comment.

Sam stared at the dark form of the decaying barn—a vacant look of painful understanding. In the cold morning darkness, with revolving lights rhythmically reflecting from his face, sallow with exposure and exhaustion, he looked much older than his years. His shirt was caked in dried blood where he had held her to his chest. His pants were dusty with straw shreds from sitting on the barn floor, cradling her limp body in his lap, rocking and crying. He could feel the mental numbness creeping over his brain like a curtain being slowly drawn between him and the outside world. He was vaguely aware of his retreat from reality, but was helpless to stop its progression. He listened to his lungs filling and flushing, his heart beating calmly in the soft hollowness of his chest. There was a darkness behind his eyes that was forcing him downward into the recesses of his own brain stem. He did not fight the invasion, nor did he especially welcome it. He simply let it happen. It was peaceful.

The sheriff, who had been arguing with Undersheriff Piccard, approached Sam. Piccard followed behind him. O'Malley scratched the back of his head, shifting his Stetson down to his eyebrows. "Damn you, Sam," he said. "From where we stand, this is a mess. We've got a confusing situation here with two dead and a third critically injured. I'm afraid I'm gonna need you to come back to Cheyenne so we can get all this sorted out. Undersheriff Piccard here will drive you." He nodded toward the smug undersheriff. "I'll be along right after the coroner finishes up. We'll get a statement at the hospital as soon as the docs say it's okay."

Piccard took Sam by the arm and attempted to lead him toward one of the flashing patrol cars.

"No," Sam said, shaking his head. "I'm going with the ambulance." He jerked his arm away from the undersheriff.

Piccard grabbed Sam by his wrist and twisted his arm behind him, attempting to push him facedown over the hood of the cruiser.

In a blur, Sam's other elbow caught Piccard hard in the temple. He spun around and kicked the staggering man squarely in the groin. Another deputy rushed toward Sam while fumbling for his nightstick. Sam's punishing right hand sent the man sprawling at the sheriff's feet.

"Jesus, Sam, don't make a bad situation worse," the sheriff yelled, backing up.

From behind, Piccard's nightstick struck Sam without noise between his neck and shoulder. His left shoulder was paralyzed with burning pain. Sam blocked a second swing aimed at his head with his right arm, and with a continuous, fluid movement secured the undersheriff by his throat. His fingers bit deeply as Piccard fought vainly to loosen Sam's grip. From somewhere behind him there was a sharp crack and a searing bolt of pain that shot through the soft layers of tissue that protected his braincase. A bright light flared behind his eyes as he staggered against gravity. He bounced about within himself, protected by the thick, pillow-like cushions of brain tissue as his body crashed to the ground. There were shouts of confusion as deputies ran through the noisy gravel toward Sam, lying facedown in the driveway.

Through the tangle of legs around him, Sam saw what had fallen from the gurney. The ragged and dirty doll with its cracked porcelain face stared accusingly at him. The morning breeze flowed gently through his hair as he attempted to smile in recognition of the whispered word he thought he heard above the din. He repeated it, murmuring, "Baby."

EPILOGUE

Sam had been unable to attend her funeral. He would never forgive the district attorney or O'Malley for that. He had lost an entire season waiting on the vagaries of law. But that was in the past. Yesterday had existed in a different universe, a different dimension. Time had passed without him. Like most people when they were young, she believed she was invincible and would be healthy until the end. How could she know? Sam took a deep breath and held it for a moment before releasing it with an unintended sigh. The deciduous hardwoods of eastern Iowa were giving up their colors, the red oaks brown as cardboard and the hard maples still holding splashes of red as they transitioned to brittle rust. Explosions of leaves fell like rain, twisting and falling among the gravestones. He felt naked being in a cemetery without his camera, but he wanted no photos to remind him. This October was marred with regrets and grief.

Her headstone was common, simple, coarse, and unattractive—everything she was not. Name and dates carved with acute angles were the only reminders of a life cut short. Annie lay next to her beloved Nana, Queen of the 1941 Oxford Harvest Day Parade.

Sam was afraid his memories of Annie would fade and somehow vanish from his heart forever. He looked away, trying to stop his tears. He attempted another deep breath, but this one caught in his chest and sputtered with a slight convulsion as he inhaled. In the distance he saw a green combine crawling up a hill of golden brown corn, rows of cut stalks in its wake. The symmetry of the landscape—like life viewed from the top of a hill—made him weep. He saw his own existence from beginning to end. The fields of harvested grain reminded him that life would not go on forever. Corn the color of the yellow line on a highway was piled tall in the grain cart pulled next to the combine.

He could not speak. He thought of all the things he wished he had said, the feeble attempts to tell her how much he loved her. The words would always be held in the bottom of his stomach to rise up on clear fall days when yellow shone in the distance. Sidney leaned her head against his shoulder. She cried too.

••••

Classic Americana still prevailed at the Tenderloin Grill outside of Oxford. The smell of bacon, eggs, and coffee hung in the grease-smoked air of the café. Farmers, some wearing bibbed overalls, were lined up along the counter and packed into the few booths by the windows. None had removed their caps. The topic of conversation in the booth behind Sam and Sidney was the presidential election, just a few weeks away.

"I'm telling you that Obama is the Manchurian Candidate," said a man with a deep voice, wearing a

DeKalb seed cap and food stains on his pot belly. "He'll deliver us lock, stock, and barrel to the ragheads."

"The hell you say. McCain ain't no better," another man proclaimed, his back to Sam, dozens of organizational pins in his hat. "He's too damn old to be president. He won't make it four years and we'll end up with what's-her-face. Good lookin', but she don't know 'come 'ere' from 'sic 'em' about runnin' this country. Obama's right, you can put lipstick on 'er, but she's still a Duroc."

Sidney stifled a smile as she reached behind her ear and changed the program on her hearing aids. "This is where you met her?"

Sam nodded. "Nine years ago. About this same time of year. She was waiting tables." He turned toward the counter, a faraway look in his eyes. "She was trying to figure out what to do with her life." He sipped his coffee. "Funny how things work out. If I hadn't stopped in—"

"You can't change the past, unless, of course, you're a politician or historian." She paused then pushed her glasses up on the bridge of her nose. "You didn't give her cancer, you know."

Sam swallowed hard and he again fought back tears. He had placed Annie in more jeopardy in their brief time together than most people experience in a lifetime. He had never asked himself why she endured his precarious lifestyle, never comprehended the extent of her love for him.

"If you hadn't met Annie, she wouldn't have saved my life. I would have been just another victim of a deranged serial killer. Annie died a hero, Dad. She knew she was dying and she made her life count for something." Sidney embraced her upper arms and looked vacantly out the window toward the parking lot.

Sam, too, stared out the window. The reversed letters of the Tenderloin Grill—painted in yellow with rough brushstrokes and outlined in red, arched across the plate glass. He reached over the table and took his daughter's hand in his. She had gone through hell and back, and then saved him emotionally. If anyone needed emotional support, it was her. He had put her in harm's way, as he had in Colorado with his manic obsession to find the truth.

It was Sam who had painted the bull's-eye on his daughter's back. Hofstadter did what he always did: He went after a loved one of his primary target to exact the highest amount of emotional pain possible. Annie was collateral damage. While for Sam, the pain was unbearable. In that sense, Hofstadter had won.

Sam's heart ached for Sidney. She had been brutally victimized. Sam knew she was the strong one; she continued to push through the emotional pain, assuming the role of the protectress. But he saw the hidden eye movements, the trembling of her lower lip, and the nervous twitching of her hands. The concussion and post-concussion syndrome he had suffered from the deputy's nightstick was nothing compared to what she had gone through. The combination of ketamine and succinylcholine chloride had pitched her into cardiac arrest. But through Sam's almost hysterical persistence and prolonged CPR efforts, the emergency intubation by the paramedics had secured her airway long enough to buy time. The ER doctors in Cheyenne had been stumped and summoned Flight For Life. It was the coroner who had alerted the emergency room personnel in Colorado to the presence of ketamine and succinylcholine as the helicopter was landing there. Normally, with a sux overdose, routine resuscitative measures are unsuccessful, Sam was told later. His intervention had provided the time necessary for overdose treatment.

Annie had not been so lucky. Autopsy results indicated that the blow she had received to the back of her head, in combination with the dislodged tumor, should have killed her outright. Amazingly, she had found the strength to put a pitchfork through Tom Stevens' midsection as he was delivering the lethal drug to Sidney. The nearly empty syringe was still in Sidney's arm when Sam found her. Stevens' injecting her was the last thing she remembered, but it was enough to exonerate Sam of the more serious charges.

While the paramedics attended to Sidney, Sam had held Annie in his lap. A paramedic had checked her pulse, listened to her chest with a stethoscope, and peeled back her eyelid before simply shaking his head. She was gone. She had been alive when Sam burst into the barn. Her eyes fluttered open several times as she attempted to smile at him. Sam had to choose—a choice no one should have to make. His decision was autonomic, controlled by internal forces that, in effect, gave him no choice. Still, he was tortured by the thought that he could have overridden it, but he did not. He chose his daughter.

Sidney stared at her father's drawn face. She was unaware of the depth of his torment, but suspected that he, in some way, felt responsible for Annie's death. She swallowed the lump in her throat. She did not know how to help him. Her phone chimed with an incoming text message. She picked it up and held it close to her face.

"Can I get you folks anything else?" the waitress asked, coffeepot in hand.

Sam looked up at her as if contemplating a more meaningful question.

"Just the check, please," Sidney interjected with a tight smile.

Sam's gaze followed the waitress as she walked away to deliver more coffee to the other booths.

"Earth to Dad," Sidney said, waving a hand in front of Sam's face. "I just got a text from Helen."

"Who?"

"Helen Jackson, your defense attorney. Pay attention here. The district attorney has dropped the assault charges. Apparently, he thought it would be too costly to fight our temporary insanity plea. Plus, she said Harrison O'Malley was going to testify on your behalf. The worse that could have happened was probably community service. We're home free, Pop. And...the DA dropped the charges against Oscar Roberts. That's good news. And listen to this—Helen said that the house and barn at Horse Creek mysteriously burned to the ground over the weekend, and that Oscar didn't seem surprised. That's good news too."

It was all good news, and he should have said so. Instead, he turned and looked out the window again. In the grease-smeared reflection he saw the black-and-white image of a twelve- or thirteen-year-old boy in a white robe, Jesus on the cross behind him. The boy's perfect smile was unmistakable. Raymond stood next to the Reverend Oscar Roberts, the man he felt had later betrayed him, who had conspired with his mother to take his sister, Miranda, from him. It was "Doctor Stevens" who had planted the incriminating photos in Roberts' glovebox, "Doctor Stevens" who had viciously murdered a loved one of each of the Four Horsemen, "Doctor Stevens" who had sabotaged the Willys's brakes, and "Doctor Stevens" who had targeted Sidney to bring suffering down upon Sam.

Sam saw them all when they were young—Lilly Darnell's distorted face frozen to the ground, Holly Zimmerman slumped over in a school bus, and the other two faceless victims of a killer bent on revenge. They believed they would endure and dreamed only of living.

Morgan's Canon had held. After all, it was the simplest explanation, an eye for an eye. Annie had warned that Morgan never intended his law to apply to human behavior. But Stevens was no longer human. There were no higher psychological processes involved. A powerless teen had grown consumed with revenge, pure and simple.

The rule's human application, Occam's razor, had held for Annie too. Sam rationalized that her experiences at the house on Horse Creek had not been events of consciousness. Rather, they must have been manifestations of an afflicted brain, a tumor pressing against logic. It was a simple explanation that, at the time, no one knew to consider.

On their way to Iowa, Sam had detoured slightly north through the Nebraska Sandhills. Sidney had watched him curiously, but said nothing. At Schoonover, tumbleweeds had piled restlessly against the door of the building that had once been a gas station and garage, but was now abandoned. Like Annie, the guy with the gas had disappeared too. Sam had expected that, somehow, Guy could guarantee the claim printed on the gable end of the building: We Fix Everything…From Daybreak to Heartbreak. That, somehow, the strange man could provide him with hope—perhaps a plan for salvation, and fix the devastating sorrow he felt deep within his chest.

Sam gazed through the grease-stained window of the café. He watched another combine in the distance—this one red, cutting a large swath through a field of golden corn. The combine slowly descended below the horizon as it slipped silently over the hill. It left in its wake a cemetery of cornstalks. A straight line of demarcation between those cut down and those left standing disappeared without a hint of the emptiness he felt in his broken heart.

The End

ACKNOWLEDGMENTS

For me, writing is a very personal and often lonesome process. I do not share my musings until they have gone through the torturous process of self-editing, numerous rewrites, sufficient self-doubt and loathing, ample whining, and the fierce battles between love and hate of the writing life. Writers may not be the easiest people to live with. Through it all, my partner and loving wife and first reader, Margaret, has endured. Her patient understanding and encouragement have made my novels possible.

As always I am thankful to my daughters, Tiffany, Melissa, and Amanda, for their inspiration and support. They, better than most, understand how fact and fiction become inextricably intertwined in the writing process. They have heard all the ghost stories and appreciate how scientific credibility and objectivity are often sacrificed when faced with inexplicable phenomena.

Tonya Talbert, as usual, contributed so much more than an early read. Her gentle persuasions are a comfort to a bruised ego. Peter Decker, Rachel Girt, and David Worthman all offered valuable suggestions. Thank you for your time, amazing energy, and honest evaluations. Laramie County Coroner Ron Sargent gave freely of both his time and knowledge. Melissa Kepler, CRNA, not only provided an astute review of the manuscript, but attempted to keep me in the shallow end of the anesthesia pool. Sharon Field was most helpful in clarifying the relationships of descendants from common progenitors. Tina Worthman, graphic designer extraordinaire, sees what needs to be conveyed and makes it a visual reality. Saying Kate Deubert is an editor is like saying Leonardo da Vinci is just a painter. Her talents are boundless. Thanks for all you do, Kate.

Finally, I must thank the members of the many book clubs that I've had the pleasure of speaking with over the years. Their probing questions and frank discussions help me immensely when crafting the next Sam Dawson Mystery.

ABOUT THE AUTHOR

Steven W. Horn is the author of the award-winning Sam Dawson Mystery novels. The first Sam Dawson Mystery, *The Pumpkin Eater*, won the 2014 Benjamin Franklin Gold Award in the Mystery/Suspense Category. Both Sam Dawson mysteries, *The Pumpkin Eater* and *When Good Men Die*, were 2014 and 2016 Eric Hoffer Category Finalists, respectively. Horn's debut stand-alone novel was the highly acclaimed *Another Man's Life*. *When They Were Young: A Sam Dawson Mystery* is Horn's third book in the Sam Dawson mysteries. He lives in Wyoming.

CPSIA information can be obtained
at www.ICGtesting.com
Printed in the USA
LVHW03s2338110618
580423LV00001B/168/P